SEDITION

Sedition

How America's Constitutional Order
Emerged from Violent Crisis

Marcus Alexander Gadson

NEW YORK UNIVERSITY PRESS
New York

NEW YORK UNIVERSITY PRESS
New York
www.nyupress.org

Library of Congress Cataloging-in-Publication Data
Names: Gadson, Marcus Alexander, author.
Title: Sedition : how America's constitutional order emerged from violent crisis /
Marcus Alexander Gadson.
Description: New York : New York University Press, 2025. |
Includes bibliographical references and index.
Identifiers: LCCN 2024039852 (print) | LCCN 2024039853 (ebook) |
ISBN 9781479828883 (hardback) | ISBN 9781479828890 (ebook) |
ISBN 9781479828906 (ebook other)
Subjects: LCSH: Sedition—Law and legislation—United States—History. |
Subversive activities—Law and legislation—United States—History. |
Treason—Law and legislation—United States—History. |
Constitutional history—United States.
Classification: LCC KF9397 .G33 2025 (print) | LCC KF9397 (ebook) |
DDC 345.73/0231—dc23/eng/20240828
LC record available at https://lccn.loc.gov/2024039852
LC ebook record available at https://lccn.loc.gov/2024039853

The manufacturer's authorized representative in the EU for product safety is Mare Nostrum Group B.V., Mauritskade 21D, 1091 GC Amsterdam, The Netherlands.
Email: gpsr@mare-nostrum.co.uk.

Manufactured in the United States of America

10 9 8 7 6 5 4 3 2 1

Also available as an ebook

CONTENTS

Introduction

Americans who hate their constitution will do anything to change it. No one demonstrated that better than South Carolina's white supremacists after the Civil War. Though they were a minority of the state, they were used to being told in every way possible that their skin color entitled them to rule. So they were enraged when their former slaves made a constitution guaranteeing racial equality and encouraging Black participation in the political process for the first time. As soon as that constitution was written, white supremacists pledged their lives, fortunes, and honor in support of a decades-long effort to rewrite it. They formed two terrorist organizations and used them to wage a war against the government that included murdering public officials in broad daylight. To win an election that would eventually allow them to call a new constitutional convention, some of them voted twenty times in one day and threatened Black voters at gunpoint. When that yielded an election dispute instead of a clear victory, they formed their own legislature, took over the state house, inaugurated their preferred candidate governor, and convinced the federal government to let their coup d'état stand. And when white supremacists finally called their constitutional convention in 1895, they hurled the word "nigger" at the handful of Black delegates during official proceedings before disenfranchising Black voters across the state.

This is not how we usually picture constitution making. Instead, we picture our founding fathers gathering in Philadelphia during the summer of 1787 to turn their high-minded ideals into the US Constitution. We imagine George Washington presiding silently while intellectual giants debated how best to select the president of the United States. Or we envision Benjamin Franklin urging delegates to sign the final document even if they had doubts and then emerging from the convention to tell concerned citizens that they now had a republic if only they could keep it. And because the US Constitution has endured for over two hundred years, we can literally go see it at the National Archives in Washington, DC, and revel in the fact that it is still in force. This is an inspiring part of our nation's constitutional story and an important one. But there is another dispiriting constitutional story that is just as important. One that involves failure and violent crisis instead of success and calm deliberation. One where constitution drafting has torn us apart instead of brought us together. Our constitutional order today owes as much to places like South Carolina in 1895 as it does to Philadelphia in 1787.

To tell that constitutional story, I will focus primarily on our state constitutions. Although we generally pay less attention to state constitutions than the US Constitution, they are an equally important part of the American constitutional system. Every American lives under two constitutions, one for their state, and one for the entire nation. State constitutions affect you in profound ways. They protect rights that the US Constitution does not, like the right to an education. They determine who can be a member of your state legislature and how it can tax you. They define who is eligible to be governor and whether that person can veto the maps the legislature drew to elect your state's representatives to Congress. If you are one of the millions of Americans who has business in a state court every year, state constitutions regulate how the judge presiding over your case is chosen. And they informed discussions about whether your state's government could close schools or require you to receive a vaccine when the COVID-19 pandemic raged. More than that, state constitutions powerfully influenced the US Constitution. Most of what you value about the US Constitution, such as its right to free expression and separation of powers, started in state constitutions. In short, state constitutions can teach you things about American constitutional law that you wouldn't know just by learning about the US Constitution.

In our polarized era, the term "constitutional crisis" is overused. I use the term to refer to specific moments when our constitutional order threatens to break down. I mean things like contested elections producing two governments and successful military-style campaigns to overthrow the government. The book proceeds in two parts. The first is about state constitutional crises prior to the Civil War. During the American Revolution, states drafted the first constitutions. These early state constitutions played a crucial role in defining America and informed how the founders wrote the US Constitution in 1787. I examine the difficult and divisive questions drafters of the first state constitutions had to resolve. These include what "popular sovereignty" and "liberty" would mean in a new republic. I then demonstrate how these same issues caused state constitutions to break down in dramatic fashion. Such incidents both foreshadowed and helped cause the country's worst constitutional crisis: the Civil War.

The second part considers state constitutional crises during Reconstruction and the rise of Jim Crow. The Civil War and Reconstruction have cast a long shadow over our history. That is unsurprising for a war that produced more dead than all of America's other wars combined. For many Americans worried about constitutional crisis, the Civil War serves as an example of how constitutional crisis can produce devastating consequences. We are still fighting about the war's legacy in debates over what we should teach students about slavery and whether we should remove confederate memorials. At one time or another, every student learns about amendments to the US Constitution abolishing slavery, guaranteeing equal protection under the law, and prohibiting racial discrimination in voting. Yet, we have failed to appreciate another important legacy from the Reconstruction era: a steady stream of state constitutional crises. Aside from the founding era, Reconstruction saw the greatest burst of constitution writing at the state level in American history. In this part, I document how a conflict between a new constitutional vision of racial equality and an older one of white supremacy culminated in almost every southern state experiencing a civil war of its own—just a few years after the one at the national level.

In total, I provide six examples of constitutional crisis. Think of them as six episodes telling one constitutional story. Along the way, you will meet founding fathers you learned about in school. You will get to know heroes committed to building a more just country, villains fighting tooth and nail to defend an unjust constitutional order, and people who were both. You will know the terror that vulnerable Americans who most needed constitutional protection felt as they came up to the edge of the constitutional abyss, the trauma they experienced when they were shoved in, and the heartbreak they lived with while they wondered if anyone would ever pull them out.

In the conclusion, I explain how revisiting forgotten state constitutional crises can help us remember important lessons about American history and confront an underappreciated threat to our constitutional system's health. The past several years have seen more Americans than ever worry about constitutional crisis at the national level. On January 6, 2021, then President Donald Trump told supporters that the recent presidential election had been stolen from him. He warned, "If you don't fight like hell, you're not going to have a country anymore."[1] His supporters, many carrying weapons, breached security at the capitol building, caused officials to fear for their lives, and temporarily prevented Congress from certifying electoral votes. The aftermath saw a passionate national argument about whether President Trump was criminally liable for his conduct and whether the US Constitution disqualified him from the 2024 election. With the nation's politics already on knife's edge, Americans then witnessed President Trump narrowly survive an assassin's bullet and considered whether concerns over President Joseph Biden's mental capacity justified using the Twenty-Fifth Amendment to remove him.[2] In trying to navigate these constitutional dangers, Americans have also debated a variety of fixes to ensure the stability of our constitutional system. In the conclusion, I ask us to channel some of that attention to our state constitutions, which may be even more likely to fail under pressure than the US Constitution.

I believe this book will benefit legal scholars, historians, judges, and lawyers. But if you are none of those things, this book is just as much for you. Our state constitutions, like the US Constitution, belong to all of us, regardless of background. Whatever your educational level or occupation, you need to understand our full constitutional history to truly appreciate the constitutional dangers facing us. And you have just as important a role to play in maintaining our constitutional order.

PART 1

Part 1 Overview

Before we can meaningfully engage with our history of constitutional crisis, we must first ask what a constitution is. Although the question seems easy, previous generations have found agreeing on an answer hard. So, I propose thinking of "constitution" in the most basic sense possible: "constitution" is a noun that describes how something is "set up" or "established."[1] Every organization you have ever been a part of has a constitution whether it is written down or not. Your family has a constitution. To think through how your family is "set up," you would pose several questions. Who is in charge? How are day-to-day decisions made? How do you all share a space? What responsibilities and rights does each member have? What are your family's dreams and fears? And what happens when the family disagrees on these questions? The answers to these questions form your family's constitution. But even more importantly, they define its identity. As with individuals, families can suffer an identity crisis. Perhaps two spouses have fundamentally different ideas of what marriage is supposed to be. Perhaps children have rejected their parents' religious convictions. Or perhaps the family disagrees on how to care for an aging relative. Such issues can tear families apart.

Constitutions are just as likely as families to go through an identity crisis. In the 1760s and 1770s, British Americans and their rulers living in Britain experienced a constitutional identity crisis so severe that they separated into two different nations. Both sides believed they shared a constitution and that it deserved reverence. But with ever increasing intensity, they disputed what their constitution meant. To help retire debt incurred fighting a war with France, Britain's Parliament—without any members from America—raised taxes on sugar, stamps, and tea. Just as bad from a colonial perspective, Britain took cases involving tax issues from local juries, which they saw as too sympathetic to tax evaders. In an era when citizens frequently try their hardest to avoid jury duty, it may be surprising that British Americans valued the right to trial by jury as much as many of us value the right to own a gun or vote. Because America's British rulers saw the constitution—which was and still is unwritten in Great Britain—as an evolving set of customs and laws over which Parliament had ultimate control, they never questioned their authority over the colonies. William Blackstone, a celebrated British judge at the time, maintained that "if the parliament will positively enact a thing to be done which is unreasonable, I know of no power that can control it."[2] British Americans rejected this constitutional vision. They were coming to view the constitution as a separate body of law with a fixed meaning. Since it was a higher law that limited Parliament's power and protected basic rights, Parliament could not change it. One of the constitution's principles was that only a lawmaking body which gave British Americans a voice could constitutionally tax them. And they were questioning whether, even if they could send a few representatives to London, it was constitutionally appropriate for a legislature three thousand miles away to tax them when assemblies closer to home were more familiar with local conditions.[3]

To accomplish their constitutional vision, British Americans tried petitioning the King and Parliament. They boycotted British goods. They rioted. They organized into groups like the Sons of Liberty and bullied, threatened, and tarred and feathered people who cooperated with Britain's tax regime. Britain passed ever more laws asserting its authority and sent soldiers to intimidate the colonists—and made colonists pay the cost. Communication and goodwill continued to break down until the two sides were shooting at each other. British Americans stopped thinking of themselves as British. America as we know it was conceived in a constitutional crisis.

That left Americans with a constitutional void. States rushed to fill it. In 1776, the same year Americans declared independence, states wrote the first American constitutions. Intellectuals everywhere recognized what a momentous development this was in world history. They translated the constitutions into several languages, endlessly reprinted them, and debated their merits.[4] The Declaration of Independence shares important features with the early state constitutions. It was shaped by them. It then shaped the state and national constitutions for the next two hundred years. Virginian Thomas Jefferson wrote a first draft in a Philadelphia boardinghouse attacking the British in bitter personal terms.

He drew heavily on George Mason's proposed Declaration of Rights to the Virginia Constitution. Benjamin Franklin of Pennsylvania and John Adams of Massachusetts made edits.[5] The Continental Congress made more changes, including removing a denunciation of the King's participation in the slave trade, to arrive at the final version we know today. The Declaration of Independence would remind a criminal defendant of an indictment. The Declaration charged Great Britain with constitutional crimes, provided evidence against it, and sought a punishment of permanent separation. In the twenty-first century, the beginning continues to resonate. It reads:

> We hold these truths to be self-evident, that all men are created equal, that they are endowed by their Creator with certain unalienable Rights, that among these are Life, Liberty and the pursuit of Happiness.—That to secure these rights, Governments are instituted among Men, deriving their just powers from the consent of the governed,—That whenever any Form of Government becomes destructive of these ends, it is the Right of the People to alter or to abolish it, and to institute new Government, laying its foundation on such principles and organizing its powers in such form, as to them shall seem most likely to effect their Safety and Happiness.[6]

The Declaration has inspired Americans for more than two centuries and raised difficult questions that go to the core of what America means for just as long. Who are "the people" who hold political power? How would "the people" go about altering and amending their government? What does "liberty" mean? How should the claim that "all men are created equal" affect how we think about those questions? And perhaps hardest of all, what do we do when we disagree on the answers? In taking these questions on in the 1770s and 1780s, states wrote the first draft of America's constitutional story. Like any good story, it has had more than its share of tension, drama, and crisis moments.

The First Draft of American Constitutions

Although you may not have read our first state constitutions, you have heard of at least some of the men who wrote them. Among others, John Adams, Benjamin Franklin, and Thomas Jefferson played roles in drafting early state constitutions. If you think back to something you're proud of writing, whether for work or school, you probably had to revise it several times. Yet, as any storyteller can attest, first drafts are essential. They begin the process of making a final product. They give the writer a chance to receive feedback about what they need to improve. And they give us valuable insight into the writer's thinking—insight we cannot gain solely by looking at the final draft. The same was true of our state constitutions. Our first state constitutions tell us the hopes and fears our founders had as they created a new nation. They tell us things about our constitutional heritage that we would not understand just by reading the later US Constitution. Just as those who had abusive parents sometimes make every choice with an eye to avoid living like those parents, the founders in 1776 wanted to get as far as possible from the British constitutional and political system. And like any youth becoming independent for the first time, they struggled to figure out their identity. In this section, I explore how Americans wrestled with the basic constitutional questions the Declaration of Independence posed.

The first state constitutions announced that the sovereign in America was no longer the King of England, but "the people." Before they could confront the difficult question of what popular sovereignty meant, states had to confront even more divisive ones. Who are "the people"? Which people get to decide who "the people" are?[7]

The Declaration of Independence and state constitutions may have said that "all men are created equal," but voting rights were decidedly unequal at the founding. No colony had permitted women to vote. Many founders believed that men without property lacked the independence to make good voters. As a result, early state constitutions generally followed Virginia's lead in insisting that voters have "sufficient evidence of permanent common interest with, and attachment to, the community" demonstrated by property ownership.[8] States were divided about permitting racial minorities to vote. Some followed Georgia's lead in limiting voting rights to "male white inhabitants."[9] But Massachusetts residents refused to ratify a constitution in 1778 that would have disenfranchised racial minorities. Several other states used race neutral language in describing eligible voters and held out the possibility that racial minorities who met property requirements could participate in the political process.[10] The contest over who was part of "the people" was nothing less than a battle for the emerging nation's soul at the same time it was fighting a war. It would establish how Americans understood the phrase "all men are created equal." Was it simply an assertion that white male property owners in the colonies had the same rights as white male property owners in England? Or was it a statement of universal human rights that extended to everyone? The legitimacy of the new constitutions in the eyes of many state residents hinged on the answers to these questions.

While Americans navigated disagreements about who "the people" were, they also disagreed over exactly what it meant to say they were sovereign. Perhaps the most important act the people could undertake was making new constitutions. States had to settle on the proper procedure for writing constitutions and decide whether, once in place, constitutions should be easy or difficult to change. States had to decide which powers to give officials and how to keep them in check. And finally, once a constitution and government structure were in place, states needed to hold elections to fill positions and ensure that they accurately reflected the will of the people. All these issues proved difficult.

Surprisingly, eight states wrote constitutions during the American Revolution making the people sovereign without the people giving them express permission to do so. And voters never ratified those documents. But New Hampshire and Massachusetts residents insisted on a different course. When New Hampshire's legislature wrote a constitution, citizens objected that only a separately elected convention should draft the constitution. The legislature gave in and called a convention. Similarly, Massachusetts voters rejected the legislature's attempt to write a constitution. Only when the legislature relented and called a convention did voters ratify a constitution in 1780.[11] In the coming years, a widespread—though not unanimous—custom of using special conventions to write constitutions and submitting them to a popular ratification vote emerged.[12] As the Declaration of Independence had, early state constitutions insisted that the people had a right "to reform, alter, or abolish" the government.[13] After a revolution where Americans raised an army to change their rulers, these guarantees presented a dilemma. Did the people have to work through existing government institutions at all to make or change constitutions, or could they act on their own? What if they regarded the current government as tyrannical or the current government refused to call a convention?

How to change state constitutions once in force presented another thorny problem. Six of the constitutions written in 1776–77 contained no method of amendment. Perhaps this was because state residents viewed these initial constitutions as emergency documents to be replaced after the Revolutionary War ended.[14] As time went on, state constitution drafters specified how constitutional change would happen. In doing so, they had to decide whether to adopt a posture of openness or suspicion to constitutional change. That meant choosing between the constitutional visions of two close friends and political allies: James Madison and Thomas Jefferson. Madison worried that "frequent appeals" for constitutional change "would, in a great measure, deprive the government of that veneration which time bestows on every thing, and without which perhaps the wisest and freest governments would not possess the requisite stability." In a letter to Madison, Jefferson responded that "no society can make a perpetual constitution, or even a perpetual law" and that the current generation had a right to "manage [the constitution] then, & what proceeds from it, as they please." He also didn't trust government to be the gatekeeper of constitutional change. In Jefferson's view, legislatures were "unequal & vicious" and "bribery corrupt[ed]" public officials.[15]

States quickly took sides. Delaware, Maryland, and South Carolina gave their legislatures sole authority to amend their constitutions. Delaware made its Bill of Rights and certain other provisions unamendable. By contrast, Pennsylvania and Vermont both elected a separate group of citizens called a council of censors who could call a constitutional convention without the legislature's approval. In Pennsylvania, citizens could instruct their delegates on what to do at the convention. Georgia and Massachusetts pioneered methods allowing the people to call conventions on their own without getting any institution's approval. Georgia required the legislature to call a constitutional convention when a majority of counties petitioned for a convention. The 1780 Massachusetts Constitution required holding a vote in 1795 about whether to call a new constitutional convention and, if two-thirds of voters agreed, holding a convention.[16] While debates about the proper method of constitutional amendment might seem theoretical, they had practical consequences for early Americans. This is because whatever method applied affected their ability to put strongly held views into a constitution. That was especially true for suffrage restrictions and slavery. With stakes this high, disagreements about how to change state constitutions were so bitter that they sometimes became bloody.

Since "the people" were now in charge, states agonized over how to keep governments in check. Revolutionary zeal colored their decision-making. Virginia's 1776 constitution provided that the governor "shall not, under any pretence, exercise any power or prerogative by virtue of any Law, statute, or Custom, of England." Consistent with this thinking, early state constitutions made governors weak. They could not appoint judges. They generally could not veto legislation. They were usually selected by the legislature instead of having an independent power base. They typically had to share executive power with councils, making them more like a committee chair than a modern governor or president. Judges did not have what we would recognize as judicial independence. In many states, they served for a set number of years instead of having life tenure, and the legislature could change their salaries at will. Procedures for removing them were relatively easy. This all meant that the legislature was the most powerful branch of state governments.[17]

With a basic structure in place, states had to ensure elections reflected the people's will. Most early state constitutions insisted that elections be "free." At a minimum, "free" election guarantees implicated concerns about coercion and voter intimidation. Pennsylvania's 1776 constitution fought bribery by punishing voters who "receive[d] any gift or reward for his vote, in meat, drink, monies, or otherwise." Delaware's 1776 constitution forbade residents from bringing weapons to the polls to "prevent any violence or force being used at the said elections." Eighteenth century Americans often had to vote orally while their boss, parent, or pastor watched. Vermont, North Carolina, Georgia, and Pennsylvania charted a different course by implementing ballot voting. State constitutions also often required that elections be "frequent." The most radical provided for annual elections while others permitted longer terms.[18] Behind the decision of how long terms should be were the difficult questions of how responsive officials should be to the people, how much faith we should have in the wisdom of the people, and how much trust politicians deserve.

* * *

During the Revolution, Americans agreed that "liberty" referred to some things like the right to a jury trial or freedom from being forced to have soldiers stay in their homes. But they disagreed on what the term meant in other contexts. This was inevitable. British settlers had brought different understandings of "liberty" to America. The Puritans who settled New England understood "liberty" to refer to community rights and not just individual rights. It encompassed a community's ability to build a Christian paradise. It was therefore perfectly consistent with "liberty" for courts to punish picking strawberries on the Sabbath. The Cavaliers who settled Virginia and other southern colonies interpreted "liberty" as the right to impose their will on those below them in society's hierarchy. As Edmund Burke said, "Freedom is to them not only an enjoyment, but a kind of rank and privilege." The Quakers believed in reciprocal liberty and extended the same rights they sought to members of other Christian denominations, a progressive approach for the time. British settlers from backcountry regions thought of "liberty" as freedom from government intrusion.[19] Members of these different groups sometimes settled in the same state. When they did, they disagreed on how a state constitution should define "liberty."

The contradictory attitudes toward "liberty" were most evident in the nation's argument over slavery. During the Civil War, Abraham Lincoln acknowledged that "we all declare for liberty; but in using the same *word* we do not all mean the same *thing*." For some, "the word liberty may mean for each man to do as he pleases with himself, and the product of his labor." For others, it meant some men could "do as they please with other men, and the product of other men's labor."[20] When it came to slavery, there were three definitions of "liberty." Slaveholder liberty, slave liberty, and liberty *from* slaves and Black people. Virginia's 1776 constitution best demonstrated the intellectual legerdemain slaveholders performed to define "liberty" in a way that was consistent with bondage. George Mason's first draft of Virginia's Declaration of Rights had said "[t]hat all Men are born equally free and independant [*sic*], and have certain inherent natural Rights, of which they can not by any Compact, deprive or divest their Posterity; among which are the Enjoyment of Life and Liberty, with the Means of acquiring and possessing Property, and pursueing [*sic*] and obtaining Happiness and Safety." The men revising Mason's draft readily understood that it put slavery in jeopardy. To assure slaveholders that the new constitution wasn't hostile to slavery, they changed the provision to read "[t]hat all men are by nature equally free and independent, and have certain inherent rights, of which, when they enter into a state of society, they cannot, by any compact, deprive or divest their posterity; namely, the enjoyment of life and liberty, with the means of acquiring and possessing property, and pursuing and obtaining happiness and safety." By limiting the natural right of "liberty" to those who had "enter[ed] a state of society," the drafters meant to exclude slaves. Slavery so informed the worldview of some southerners that they saw the Revolutionary War as a conflict between masters and slaves. That's why North Carolina's 1776 constitution complained that "George the Third has also sent fleets and armies to prosecute a cruel war against them, for the purposed reducing the inhabitants of the said Colonies to a state of abject slavery."[21] After the Revolution, it colored their views of other constitutional guarantees such as the right to free speech and how "the people" could pursue constitutional change.

By contrast, Vermont committed to slave liberty in its 1777 constitution. Like other states, Vermont declared that "all men are born equally free and independent, and have certain natural, inherent, and unalienable rights, amongst which are the enjoying and defending [*sic*] life and liberty; acquiring, possessing, and protecting property, and pursuing and obtaining happiness and safety." But Vermont parted from Virginia in understanding that idea to be incompatible with slavery.[22]

At the founding, some Americans wanted liberty *from* slaves and Black people. By 1776, America had a large slave population and some free Black people. Like many Americans at the time, Thomas Jefferson owned slaves. Like many slaveholders, he recognized that "there must doubtless be an unhappy influence on the manners of our people produced by the existence of slavery among us" because the "whole commerce between master and slave is a perpetual exercise of the most boisterous passions, the most unremitting despotism on the one part, and degrading submissions on the other." Like many whites, he did not believe a multiracial republic was possible. Jefferson feared that "deep rooted prejudices entertained by the whites; ten thousand recollections, by the blacks, of the injuries they have sustained [during slavery]; new provocations; the real distinctions which nature has made; and many other circumstances, will divide us into parties, and produce convulsions, which will probably never end but in the extermination of the one or the other race." To avoid this catastrophe, Jefferson suggested freeing the slaves and making them leave the United States.[23]

Americans believed those who defined "liberty" differently in the slavery context were not just misguided, but immoral and dangerous. State constitutions had to take a side in the controversy. In some cases, there was a consensus in support of one definition or another. But in others, conflict ensued when different groups fought to incorporate their definition into a state constitution.

* * *

Early constitution drafters contended with a difficult irony. They were only in a position to write constitutions seeking to ensure that we would peacefully resolve disagreements because they were violently resisting England. After America's armed revolution against Britain had succeeded, citizens of the new republic continued to ask an important question. Could Americans ever be justified in taking up arms against their new governments? During the economic and constitutional instability in the 1780s, many Americans said "Yes." Shays's Rebellion has received the most attention from historians. To retire its Revolutionary War debt, Massachusetts imposed new taxes and made vigorous attempts to collect them. Residents, especially in central and western Massachusetts, fought back. They withdrew representatives from the legislature. They forced courts to close at gunpoint. The legislature failed to fully meet their demands and instead passed a Riot Act and permitted the governor to suspend the writ of habeas corpus. This failed to intimidate the rebels into submission. Under the leadership of Revolutionary War veteran Daniel Shays, they marched on a federal armory in Springfield. Though the attack was repulsed, Massachusetts's government was unable to crush the rebellion. Private citizens themselves had to raise the money to equip and pay a militia. Eventually thousands of troops did prevail in a confrontation with Shays's men.[24]

The incident attracted attention from prominent founders like George Washington and James Madison. Madison spoke for many when he wrote, "Our latest information renders it not improbable that civil blood may be shed, and leaves it somewhat uncertain whether the Govt. or its adversaries will be victorious." He added, "These events are distressing beyond measure to the zealous friends of the Revolution, and furnish new proofs of the necessity of such a vigour in [a central government] as will be able to restore health to any diseased part of the federal body."[25] As they were writing the first state constitutions, Americans had collaborated to make our first attempt at a national charter, the Articles of Confederation. Shays's Rebellion and similar incidents helped illustrate their inadequacy. Within a few months, the founders met in Philadelphia to build the stronger federal government Madison called for. State constitutional crisis therefore helped inspire a major revision of our constitutions.

Revising America's Constitutions

The US Constitution was a product of an extended conversation about how well America's first constitutions had served it. Delegates to the Philadelphia convention in 1787 abandoned the Articles of Confederation. They borrowed many features from state constitutions, repudiated others, and left some of the Declaration of Independence's biggest questions unresolved. Delegates created a more powerful executive. As Massachusetts and New York had done with their governors, the new president would not be selected by the legislature and would therefore have an independent base of power.[26] Unlike earlier state constitutions, the president would not be forced to share power with an executive council. Judges would have fixed salaries that Congress could not change and life tenure. Both the president and judges would be very difficult to remove. Overall, the US Constitution enhanced the powers of the executive and judicial branches at the expense of the legislative branch. In this light, it can be seen as a counterrevolution. At the same time, because it gave the federal government limited and defined powers, the US Constitution left an important role for state constitutions. Exactly what role the state and federal governments should play in our lives and how to decide what those roles are is a question that still bedevils us.

The US Constitution either refused or failed to address important questions around who "the people" were and what "liberty" was. This should be unsurprising now that we understand how much state constitutions differed on the subjects. It never attempted to define who was an eligible voter and, in fact, assigned states the responsibility. Racial minorities and women might be "the people" of some states and not others.[27] Delegates passionately argued for slaveholder liberty, slave liberty, and liberty from slaves and Black people. Gouverneur Morris called slavery a "nefarious institution" and a "curse of heaven on the States where it prevailed." As slaveholding southerners insisted on counting slaves toward representation, Morris responded, "Are they men? Then make them Citizens and let them vote." In demanding that the federal government have the power to end the slave trade, George Mason, a slaveholder himself, claimed "every master of slaves is born a petty tyrant. They bring the judgment of heaven on a Country. As nations can not be rewarded or punished in the next world they must be in this. By an inevitable chain of causes & effects, providence punishes national sins, by national calamities." He worried that slavery taught poor whites to look down on work and "prevent[ed] the immigration of Whites, who really enrich & strengthen a Country." On the other hand, Charles Pinckney of South Carolina argued that "S. Carolina & Georgia cannot do without slaves," and that slavery was morally acceptable. He warned that "an attempt to take away the right [to import slaves] will produce serious objections to the Constitution which he wished to see adopted."[28] The final document tried to split the difference. It allowed, but did not require, Congress to end the slave trade in 1808. It obligated states to return fugitive slaves to their masters. It counted slaves as three-fifths of a white person when calculating the population off which representation was based. But the founding fathers couldn't bring themselves to use the word "slave" in the US Constitution, suggesting discomfort about recognizing slavery's existence. Abolitionists and slaveholders would spend the next eighty years arguing over whether the US Constitution was proslavery or antislavery.[29]

In the meantime, the US Constitution still had to be ratified. Foreshadowing later constitutional developments, the ratification process was highly democratic by the era's standards. Most states eliminated or lowered the usual property ownership requirements for voting on delegates to special ratifying conventions. Likewise, free Black men could vote for delegates in most states.[30] Over and over again, the lack of a bill of rights was raised as an objection, and supporters of the US Constitution felt compelled to promise one to secure ratification. Since 1776, voters had become accustomed to seeing rights guarantees in state constitutions, so omitting one in the US Constitution struck them as odd. That was one part of our first draft of constitutions they did not want edited out.

As the US Constitution went into effect, another wave of constitution drafting swept the states. Delaware, Georgia, Pennsylvania, South Carolina, and Vermont wrote new constitutions in the late 1780s and 1790s adopting certain features from the US Constitution such as life tenure for judges and expanding executive authority.[31] The many new states entering the country during the 1790s and 1800s wrote their first constitutions. Although they now had guidance from the first batch of state constitutions and the US Constitution, they continued to struggle with the same basic questions. And they carried a heavy psychological burden while they did so. The term "founding father" suggests a familial relationship between the men who wrote our constitutions and Americans who came afterward. In the 1790s and early 1800s, state constitution drafters were the literal children of the founding generation. Many Americans saw writing new constitutions the same way a talented athlete sees following in the footsteps of a parent who was a legend in the same game. Whatever they accomplished, could they ever hope to measure up? Many others experienced writing constitutions as the profound conflict of a person who admires their parents but nonetheless feels compelled to question important choices their parents made as they start their own families. Could they repudiate things their parents believed and did and honor them at the same time? And finally, white men without property, racial minorities, and, later, women viewed writing new constitutions the way a child who has never had a real relationship with an absent parent views striving to get that parent to finally recognize them. If they demonstrated their worth, could they finally join the family? Constitution making after the founding was thus an intensely personal endeavor where Americans tried to prove to themselves and others that they deserved their beloved parents' approval.

One thing early Americans hoped the country would no longer struggle with was constitutional instability. By 1815, the federal government had successfully put down the Whiskey Rebellion and Fries's Rebellion. It had endured the development of political parties. Americans had seen the peaceful transfer of power from John Adams to Thomas Jefferson after a hard-fought presidential campaign and a prolonged election dispute in 1800–1801. And the country had survived the War of 1812 with Great Britain. But any expectation of permanent constitutional calm was soon dashed.

The Constitutional Crises Before the Civil War

Now that we have seen how America's constitutional story began, we are ready to appreciate the dramatic moments when that story unraveled. As the nineteenth century progressed, the big changes to America's constitutional order happened largely at the state level. And so, unsurprisingly, did the biggest constitutional crises. In the next chapters, I describe three of them.

The first is the Buckshot War, which took place in Pennsylvania in 1838. A bitter campaign in an era of heightened partisanship took place after a divisive constitutional convention. It produced a contested election for governor with both candidates claiming victory. Instead of providing clarity, the legislature became paralyzed by uncertainty as both the Whigs and the Democrats claimed control. Meanwhile, riots raged in the streets. The situation so deteriorated that the governor called out the militia and begged the federal government for help. This chapter introduces in more detail themes I will continually revisit, such as how revising a state constitution can affect politics, how state constitutions have often been inadequate to resolve political disagreements, and what the relationship is between states and the federal government in addressing state constitutional crises.

The second is Dorr's rebellion. While most states abandoned property qualifications on the right to vote as the nineteenth century unfolded, Rhode Island clung as tightly to them as it did to its seventeenth century charter from King Charles II. After years of fruitlessly attempting reform, Thomas Dorr and his supporters held a constitutional convention in 1841 in defiance of state authorities and then raised a militia to implement that constitution by force. Dorr's rebellion illustrates the profound disputes over who "the people" are and how they can change their constitutions that Americans experienced before the Civil War.

The third is Kansas just before the Civil War. In the 1850s, Americans went there in droves once Congress allowed the new territory to decide for itself whether to permit slavery. Kansas subsequently experienced the contested elections and partisanship of the Buckshot War, the disagreement over who "the people" are and who gets to make constitutions of Dorr's rebellion, and the armed militias of both. Add disputes about the meaning of "liberty," as well as other states and the federal government attempting to influence affairs in Kansas to preserve a fragile balance of slave states and free states, and you have a recipe for the most explosive constitutional crisis of all.

1

The Buckshot War

Most ambitious politicians are happy to see crowds gathered around them in the legislature. On the evening of December 4, 1838, Thaddeus Stevens was not one of them. The people moving ever closer believed he had stolen an election and were there to kill him. If he did not find a window to jump out of quickly enough, he would become the first casualty of Pennsylvania's Buckshot War.

Stevens's crusade against freemasons was the reason he first achieved a position of political power and, hence, part of the reason he was running for his life. Paranoia around freemasons was not America's first moral panic. But it created one of America's first third parties. Although George Washington and Benjamin Franklin were freemasons, many Americans viewed freemasonry with suspicion. That suspicion grew to a fever pitch in 1826. That year, William Morgan finished writing about the group's secret rituals. But soon after, he disappeared near his home in New York and was never found. Widespread speculation ensued that the freemasons had murdered him. The Anti-Masonic Party formed to suppress the group.[1]

As Joseph Ritner could attest, Anti-Masons struggled initially in Pennsylvania. Born to German immigrants, Ritner was a farmer before becoming a state legislator. As the Anti-Masonic Party's nominee for governor, he lost races in 1829 and 1832. Both campaigns were uphill struggles because of the Democratic Party's dominant position in the state. But in 1835, the Democrats split into two factions. Each fielded a candidate for governor. After forming an alliance with the Whigs, Ritner successfully exploited the situation to win the election. The Anti-Masons and Whigs won control of the legislature as well, giving Anti-Masons the most power they would ever hold in American politics.[2]

The coalition attempted to placate Anti-Masons by formally investigating freemasonry in 1836. Stevens led the effort. Born in poverty and abandoned by his father at a young age, Stevens nonetheless graduated from Dartmouth College and became an accomplished lawyer. Clean-shaven with a thin nose and piercing eyes, he was renowned for his "scathing sarcasm and terrible invective" in the courtroom. Stevens had participated in the 1831 Anti-Masonic convention that nominated William Wirt for president before he entered Pennsylvania's legislature in 1833.[3] During his investigation, Stevens subpoenaed prominent freemasons including a former governor, but most refused to testify. During hearings, his temper repeatedly flared, and one hostile newspaper disparaged him as an "inquisitor."[4] Although the legislature took no action against freemasons, Stevens remained prominent in Pennsylvania politics. His enemies portrayed him as the power behind Ritner's throne.

The Whigs funded construction of railroads and canals that employed many workers, but these projects became politically contentious. One worker was warned that Stevens "made it his business to inquire into the political sentiments of all persons employed on the public works" and that he would have to promise to support Ritner's reelection campaign for governor to remain employed. He alleged that he was later fired after refusing to support the Whigs.[5]

Critics even accused the Whigs of trying to steal the 1836 presidential election. The United States uses an electoral college rather than a direct popular vote to choose presidents. As a result, Americans technically vote for electors who then cast votes on their state's behalf in the electoral college to select the president. States can decide how to choose electors. Today, Americans expect electors to support whichever presidential candidate received the most votes in their state's election. But early in the nineteenth century, legislatures sometimes picked electors. Other times, states were divided into districts, with voters in those districts picking an elector. Still other states used a statewide vote to pick electors. Although Pennsylvania traditionally used a statewide vote, the *American Sentinel* reported a scheme where the Whigs would instead use district-wide votes to select electors, and then "gerrymander the state . . . in such a manner as to take as many votes as possible from the democratic candidates, Van Buren and Johnson." This plan never came to fruition, but it may have predisposed Democrats to believe allegations of fraud in the 1838 elections.[6]

In any event, Democrats retook control of the legislature by 1837. Pennsylvania had divided government: a Whig executive and a Demo-

cratic legislature. The two experienced constant conflict. Political controversy gave way to economic calamity when the Panic of 1837 hit. Though
the economy suffered nationwide, Pennsylvania had a particularly hard
time. The price of basic goods like wheat rose over 70 percent in just
one year. Businesses across the state went bankrupt and thousands of
workers lost employment.[7] The Panic of 1837 would influence delegates
as they wrote a new constitution and play a role in the 1838 elections.

A Major Constitutional Revision

By 1837, Pennsylvania had already had two constitutions. Its first came
in 1776 and its second in 1790. The 1790 constitution still did not provide a way to amend it. That issue, along with concerns about suffrage,
the scope of the governor's authority, and the regulation of corporations, produced pressure to hold a new constitutional convention. The
legislature finally agreed in 1836. Delegates were popularly elected. Any
amendments would take effect once a simple majority of voters ratified them. Pennsylvania's legislature—like states generally throughout
American history—had departed from the federal model of making
the US Constitution very difficult to amend. The only ways to propose amendments at the federal level are for either two-thirds of both
houses of Congress to do so or for two-thirds of state legislatures to
call a convention for that purpose. Then, three-quarters of the states
must ratify.[8]

In May 1837, 133 delegates assembled. Little did they know that their
work would take almost a year. Persistent polarization was partly to
blame. One newspaper observed that "the two parties are so equally balanced in numbers [that] compromise is necessary to effect the steady
progress of business." Another claimed that just one swing delegate had
the power to decide important questions.[9]

A divided convention took on constitutional questions that have
been divisive since the founding. The biggest dispute was about who
"the people" were. The 1790 constitution had required individuals to live
in the state for two years and pay a state or county tax to vote. Delegates
quickly agreed to shorten the residency requirement to a year. But they
rejected one delegate's argument that linking suffrage to tax payment
"cannot be sustained on any principle of justice or equity."[10]

The major innovation, and the one that spurred the most debate, was to restrict voting to white men. The 1776 and 1790 constitutions permitted free Black men to vote.[11] Disenfranchising Black men drew fierce criticism at the convention and in the press.[12] But several arguments against Black voting won the day.

First, some delegates wanted to preserve liberty from Black people. Pennsylvanians may have disapproved of slavery, but part of the reason was to avoid having to live near lots of Black people. One delegate worried that if Pennsylvania continued to let Black men vote, word would "spread . . . far and wide, that this State is a depot for free negroes, slaves and runaways." Philadelphia was a cautionary tale. There, Black people "came together . . . from all the southern States, and have so corrupted each other, that they are now in a situation far worse than the bondage from which they have escaped." Disenfranchising Black Pennsylvanians would send a helpful message to other Black people considering moving to the state: don't come here.

Second, some Pennsylvanians wanted to protect slaveholder liberty to preserve the Union. As a result, one delegate argued that withholding the vote from Black men "would be better for them, and for the peace and safety of the State, and the Union." In explaining his vote for Black disenfranchisement, another delegate explained that "he had not forgotten the south." Instead, he had "looked to the south [and] regarded her feelings" because "their interests are dear to us." The idea that permitting Black men to vote in Pennsylvania would undermine slavery in Mississippi is hard to take seriously, but outside observers agreed that the possibility genuinely worried delegates. In a protest, Pennsylvania's Black community argued "that they [the delegates] have laid our rights a sacrifice on the altar of slavery." It was not the first time "that northern statesmen [had] 'bowed the knee to the dark spirit of slavery,' but it [was] the first time that they [had] bowed so low!" A commitment to slaveholder liberty had distorted southern constitutions. It also distorted constitutions in northern states that had abolished slavery.

Third, some delegates believed they needed to disenfranchise Black men to avoid race war. Race war was a persistent fear at the founding. One man argued that it "must be apparent to every well judged person, that *the elevation of the black, is the degradation of the white man*; and by endeavoring to alter the order of nature, we would, in all probability, bring about the war between the races—a state of things that every lover of his country must regret." Another delegate cited the same curse of Ham slaveholders had used to justify slavery to register his agreement with this sentiment. He claimed that "God had made them [Black people] a base race, and nothing could be put into our Constitution or laws, that would reverse the decrees of PROVIDENCE."

Finally, some delegates believed nonwhite people lacked the intelligence to make good voters. A delegate who had spent considerable time defending Black disenfranchisement argued that it was "altogether futile and useless to pursue the experiment of making the African and Indian equal to the white citizen." He became convinced of this when he discovered some Native Americans had attended college and then made "no other use of their education than to beg from door to door, and ask for whiskey, in Hebrew, Greek, and Latin." Apparently, he couldn't recall any white people ever failing to fully use their educations. Thaddeus Stevens eloquently replied to these claims. In response to the argument that God's will was to prevent Black people from voting, he expressed shock to "hear it contended here, that God did not, out of one clay, create all mankind; nor to hear the Holy Scriptures cited as apology and license for oppression." In response to the worry that allowing Black men to vote would make the South anxious, Stevens declared, "I would rather be the degraded subject of a southern master, than to be a northern freeman without the power and the courage freely to speak my sentiments on every subject."[13] His efforts to preserve Black voting rights failed—for the time being.

It would be difficult for Black people to ever change the new constitution. Amendments would require the legislature to pass them twice—a common method in many state constitutions at the time—before voters could ratify them. But since Black people couldn't vote for legislators, the legislature had no incentive to prioritize the issue even if most Pennsylvanians agreed with ending disenfranchisement. The only way for Black people to regain the vote was to hope enough white voters felt so strongly about the issue that they pressured the legislature into proposing an amendment.[14]

A second topic that caused passionate debate was how to structure the government. In the end, delegates made important decisions. First, they limited the governor's appointment powers. The 1790 constitution allowed him to appoint almost every executive branch official on his own. But now, he could only appoint the secretary of the common-wealth on his own and needed senate confirmation for anyone else. In this, Pennsylvania delegates mirrored the US Constitution, which also requires confirmation of most presidential appointments. At the same time, unlike the US Constitution then with regard to the president, they continued to impose term limits on the governor.[15]

Second, delegates broke with the US Constitution and Pennsylvania's 1790 constitution and rejected life tenure for judges. Several delegates argued unsuccessfully that life tenure was necessary to ensure able, impartial judges. One contended that life tenure was the only way to convince a lawyer with a lucrative practice—the kind he assumed would make a good judge—to take the bench. Since a government salary wouldn't match what the lawyer made in private practice, there had to be some other incentive. Life tenure would theoretically provide that. In trying to convince a lawyer to leave private practice for a judgeship, the governor could offer him the prospect of being forever financially secure. In addition, another delegate feared what would happen if judges had to worry about reappointment and presided over a case powerful politicians cared about. Wasn't it possible, he asked, that the judge in that situation would "turn his eyes from the cause and its merits to himself, his home, and his dependent family"? In the end, delegates found concerns about unaccountable judges more persuasive. As one delegate put it, "Power long continued in the hands of any man, however pure and upright when he first succeeds to it, makes him despotic, tyrannical, overbearing and disgusting to the republican sense of the people."[16] Pennsylvania's decision not to imitate the US Constitution in granting life tenure to judges might be surprising at first glance given the esteem with which we hold the men who drafted it. But it has been a common decision. In time, most states would also permit voters to directly elect judges instead of having the executive appoint and the legislature confirm them. Many others would also impose mandatory retirement ages.

Finally, delegates considered what "liberty" should mean going forward. They retained traditional liberties like the right to a jury trial and free expression. But they confronted the difficult question of how the new constitution should regulate corporations. Corporations were rare when the US Constitution was written in 1787 and, three years later, when the 1790 Pennsylvania Constitution was written. But they were increasingly prominent by 1838. One delegate went so far as to claim that "modern banking" was "a device of Satan." To make his point, he drew on the discussions about slavery that had taken so much of the convention's time. Corporations, he said, "make slaves of the laborers, and tyrants of the managers of such corporations." To the obvious response that new corporations could create wealth, he replied that "it is a fallacy to say that corporations create wealth" because "labor [alone] is the source of all wealth."[17] The Panic of 1837 made these arguments resonate with the many Pennsylvanians who had lost jobs. In the end, the new constitution made meaningful albeit modest changes. It required at least six months of public notice before the legislature could grant a public charter and gave the legislature authority to revoke any corporate charter it granted.[18]

Delegates scheduled a ratification vote to take place at the same time as the October general election. In doing so, they placed a time bomb in Pennsylvania politics that threatened to detonate at exactly the wrong time. The election results for the legislature and governor might hinge on which constitution defined eligible voters. Both the 1790 and 1838 constitutions gave the legislature authority to determine contested elections. But the 1790 constitution permitted Black men to vote, and the 1838 constitution didn't. In advocating disenfranchising Black men, one delegate complained that "the election had this year been influenced by negro votes, in the county of Bucks, and that they had come within twelve votes, last year, of electing their member of Congress."[19] If Black voters were decisive before, they could be again. If an election contest continued until January 1839, when the new constitution officially went into effect, whichever side benefited from Black votes would argue for counting them. Whichever side found Black votes a barrier to overcome would argue against counting them. Chaos would reign. Conflicting vote counts could lead to uncertainty about which legislators had won seats. A legislature uncertain about who was truly a member would then have to decide who was really the governor. How could such an election contest be settled if neither side agreed on who was an eligible voter? Adding to the difficulty, it was likely that the ratification vote would be very close given how divided the convention was. What would happen if there was disagreement on whether the new constitution had passed or not? How would the state resolve an election dispute if residents couldn't even agree on which constitution applied?

The 1838 Campaign

As the constitutional convention ended in 1838, campaign season began. Democrats nominated David Rittenhouse Porter. Porter had distinguished-looking gray hair and a ruddy complexion. He was the son of a respected Revolutionary War soldier. One brother became governor of Michigan, and another became secretary of war for John Tyler. Yet, despite his privileged background, Porter went bankrupt as a young man. Porter eventually recovered and entered politics. He was the rare politician who gave brief speeches.[20]

The campaign quickly degenerated into mudslinging. The process was accelerated by media outlets that made no pretense of objectivity. Instead, newspapers were often explicitly partisan and dedicated as much space to editorializing as they did to reporting the news. The Pro-Whig *Telegraph* dubbed Porter "David the Dodger" for allegedly missing so many votes in the legislature. The nickname stuck. In addition, the paper claimed Porter frequently blasphemed God and was "PROVERBIALLY, NOTORIOUSLY PROFANE."[21]

Three attacks were more serious. First, the *Telegraph* reported that Porter had committed perjury and defrauded his creditors when declaring bankruptcy. It printed an affidavit alleging that Porter transferred bonds to another individual that he could have used to pay his debt, then petitioned for bankruptcy while claiming to have no assets. After being declared bankrupt, Porter then retrieved his bonds and sold them for $4,500. A pro-Porter newspaper disputed this account. Second, Porter's enemies insinuated that Porter was a masonic leader who had played a role in William Morgan's murder. Third, they accused him of supporting interracial marriage, something that would be taboo for well over another century, and of being sexually immoral. The *Telegraph* alleged that Porter had fathered two children out of wedlock and then advised his mistress to marry a Black man.[22]

Ritner's opponents tried linking him to abolitionism. Ritner's supporters understood the charge was dangerous. The *Telegraph* explained abolitionism, properly defined, meant that a person was "in favor of turning the slaves of the South into Pennsylvania, to drive our Farmers from their homes and take possession of their estates; of amalgamating the white and black races by intermarriage, social intercourse, etc; of electing them to office." To demonstrate confidence that Ritner didn't hold such beliefs, the *Telegraph* offered a $500 reward for anyone who could provide hard evidence that he did hold those beliefs.[23]

Partly because of the patronage distributed from public works projects, Ritner's supporters were confident of victory. The *Telegraph* believed that Ritner would win by at least 14,250 votes. Democrats were just as confident. After "convers[ing] with a number of gentlemen from different parts of the State, some of whom are the supporters of General Porter, and others the friends of Mr. Ritner," the *Mifflintown Spirit of the Times* reported that "not a single doubt exists in the democratic ranks—all concur in the opinion that David Rittenhouse Porter will receive one of the most overwhelming majorities ever known in Pennsylvania."[24]

Instead, the October elections produced uncertainty. Initially, Pennsylvanians disagreed on whether the new constitution had been ratified. Over a week after the vote, the *Philadelphia Inquirer* wrote that "the result is still doubtful" and that "the majority either way will be very small."[25] Similarly, there was disagreement over whether Ritner or Porter had been elected governor and over which party had a majority in the state house of representatives; there was widespread agreement that Whigs would control the state senate. By mid-October, a Whig newspaper acknowledged that Porter was ahead in the official count by around five thousand votes, but it claimed that "no one can read the majorities without being convinced of the fact, that great and extensive frauds upon the elective franchise have been committed." The *Telegraph* even argued that Porter had benefited from twenty thousand illegal votes.[26] The consequences of such a polarized media environment were becoming evident. Pennsylvanians who had been told for months that their preferred candidate would win a commanding victory experienced the close election as a shock and were receptive to conspiracy theories about what really happened. In a healthy political climate, citizens treat the election's victor as legitimate and try to keep an open mind as that person governs. They expect elected officials in their party to accept the election results. But Pennsylvania in 1838 was not a healthy political climate. And the media was partly responsible.

Unhealthy political climates can provide a fertile ground for constitutional crisis.

The Northern Liberties District in Philadelphia was at the center of the controversy over the election. The Whigs would control the state senate, but whether they controlled the house of representatives depended on votes from the district. Both the 1790 and the 1838 constitutions required both houses of the legislature to determine contested gubernatorial elections.[27] If Whigs captured the house of representatives, they could allow Ritner to contest Porter's election and choose him to serve another term. Both sides therefore had a huge stake in the results in the district. The situation called for election officials to count votes fairly and honestly—and, just as importantly, to be perceived as doing so. Yet, the election judges in charge of counting votes were affiliated with political parties. A majority of the judges were Democrats, though several were Whigs. These judges had an incentive to manipulate results to favor their political party. In addition to preferring to see their party in power, politicians who benefited from their decisions might reward them by, say, appointing them to government offices. Even if Democratic judges behaved with integrity, Pennsylvania Whigs would perceive their decisions as political and might refuse to accept them, and vice versa. As it happened, the judges did not behave with integrity. The *Telegraph* reported that the Democratic judges had met without their Whig counterparts and schemed to fiddle with the vote tally. They cited alleged irregularities to eliminate votes from wards that supported Whig candidates. Regardless of whether there was such a conspiracy, the Democrats voted to exclude the disputed votes over the Whigs' dissent. Undaunted, the Whig judges met separately and decided to exclude votes from areas that favored the Democrats, allegedly "on the grounds of fraud, or because they could not obtain the accurate vote." They crafted a vote total from the Northern Liberties District that would lead to the Whigs controlling the house of representatives and took the extraordinary step of giving their returns to the sheriff to send to the secretary of the commonwealth. The Democratic judges soon submitted their own returns as well.[28] Pennsylvanians couldn't agree on who won the election when they couldn't even agree on which vote count to believe.

The difficulty was compounded because a partisan official decided whether to accept the Democratic or Whig returns as the official tally from the district. Thomas Burrowes, secretary of the commonwealth, made that call. He was a prominent Whig. After concluding that "the General Election has resulted in a manner contrary to all our reasonable calculations and just expectations," Burrowes demanded an investigation. Until that investigation was complete, Burrowes encouraged Whigs to "treat the election of the 9th inst. as if we had not been defeated."[29]

Thaddeus Stevens shared that perspective. In November 1838, the *Gettysburgh Compiler* warned that Stevens was scheming to prevent Philadelphia Democrats from taking their seats and admit Whigs in their place. Then, the legislature could elect a Whig to the US Senate and a Whig state treasurer and pass an appropriations bill to complete all the public work projects started during the Ritner administration. The paper suggested that Stevens wanted to "contest the Governor's election long enough to secure the approval of the above acts by Joseph Ritner."[30]

Pennsylvania found itself barreling toward a constitutional crisis. And it was unclear which constitution would resolve it. Eventually, it emerged that voters had ratified the 1838 constitution by a margin of just 1,212 out of over 226,000 cast.[31] But even this clarity came with a caveat. Pennsylvanians shared a new constitution, but not a consensus that it was legitimate. Speaking for many, certainly in the Black community, the *Philadelphia Inquirer* argued that "voting rights away does not destroy them" because "their foundation is broader, and a more solid one, than the voice of majorities or a clause in a constitution." Instead, rights were God-given, which meant that any manmade document violating them was entitled to no respect. As a result, reformers should "begin the work of alteration immediately, by preparing the people for it, and so changing their views and feelings that their representatives will vote to" end Black disenfranchisement.[32] As the close vote demonstrates, many Pennsylvanians disliked the constitution for other reasons.

Pennsylvania Descends into Constitutional Crisis

On December 4, 1838, Burrowes announced the returns from the Whig judges in the house of representatives as the official results. Undeterred, Philadelphians claiming that they had been elected tried to introduce returns from the Democratic judges. Thaddeus Stevens moved that the members who had won according to the Whig returns elect a speaker. Whigs promptly voted for Thomas Cunningham. Democrats retaliated and elected William Hopkins speaker. Pennsylvania now had two houses of representatives.[33] This was to become a common phenomenon in the nineteenth century.

Both men went to a raised platform at the front and began trying to hold proceedings. Amid the confusion of two sessions going on at the same time, the crowd in the galleries made itself heard. They would "[applaud] their own speakers and [hiss at] those of opposite politics." At least they remained peaceful. Until they went to the senate, that is. Late in the afternoon, hundreds of men "scaled the bars of the Senate and threatened personal violence to the Senators." Three of the men who did so were federal officials. Another was "Balty" Sowers, a "terror and rowdy" known nationally for leading Philadelphia's "Butcher Boy" gang. They refused to let senators leave, all while crying "Kill Stevens! Kill Penrose! Kill Burrowes!" Prominent Whigs including senate president Charles Penrose and Thaddeus Stevens escaped by jumping out of the windows. As soon as Penrose left, "the window was surrounded by some seven or eight men, uttering the most atrocious threats of vengeance." He escaped because he "was fortunately sheltered by the darkness of the night and the shadow of one of the public buildings." Penrose later alleged that "[the mob's] transportation had been paid for in masses to the owners of the rail road lines." He claimed the men were "of desperate fortunes and of atrocious characters—men who had signalized themselves in many a broil, and were distinguished for their personal prowess and open disregard of the laws."[34]

Rumors of more violence swirled. The *Telegraph* reported on a meeting of about three hundred men "hired" by Democrats that took place at Harrisburg's courthouse later on December 4, 1838. There, some speakers "went so far as to recommend & Urge the Assassination of Messrs. Stevens, Penrose & Burrowes while they heaped the most demoniac threats upon our own head." Some in the crowd apparently offered a $2,000 reward for murdering Burrowes and Stevens. If someone followed through on the threat, Pennsylvania could find itself in a vicious cycle. An angry Whig would conceivably have murdered a prominent Democrat in retaliation, leading to reprisal after reprisal. With such great danger in the air, the *National Gazette and Literary Register* reported that the state arsenal "has been surrounded and that the rioters are proceeding to the worst excesses of brutal violence." Days after that, the *Telegraph* reported that Porter had reviewed a company of volunteers prior to using them in "the Harrisburg war." As the paper was going to print, Porter had set off for Harrisburg. His plan was to "[be] inaugurated on next Tuesday, and then . . . to issue his Proclamation [if he was not permitted to take his seat peacefully] calling upon the Military of the Commonwealth to march to Harrisburg, to put down who may oppose him." With Pennsylvania threatening to erupt in civil war any day, both bodies claiming to be the house of representatives continued to meet. Before legislatures can govern, they generally need a quorum (a majority of members) to be present. Neither body had a quorum. Ritner tried to boost the Cunningham House by recognizing it as the legal house of representatives, but the body was still reduced to meeting at a nearby hotel.[35]

* * *

On December 4, 1838, Ritner wrote to Edwin Vose Sumner, commander of a federal military post in Pennsylvania. Ritner explained that the state was in the midst of insurrection. He therefore asked Sumner "to march the troops at your command to Harrisburg, for the protection of the constituted authorities of the Commonwealth, for the suppression of the insurrection, and for the preservation of our republican form of government, agreeably with the Constitution of the United States."[36] His invocation of Article IV, Section 4, in the US Constitution deserves special mention. The section provides that the "United States shall guarantee to every State in this Union a Republican Form of Government, and shall protect each of them against Invasion; and on Application of the Legislature, or of the Executive (when the Legislature cannot be convened) against domestic Violence." The mobs blanketing Harrisburg had unwittingly unearthed difficult substantive and procedural questions buried in the Guarantee Clause's text. Substantively, who in the federal government was responsible for enforcing it? On many occasions, the US Constitution explicitly assigns a task to one branch or specifies how branches are supposed to cooperate to complete a task. It gives Congress authority to regulate commerce, makes the president commander in chief of the military, and permits courts to decide cases involving citizens of different states. It instructs the president and Congress to collaborate in filling judgeships—the president appoints, and the US Senate confirms. But maddeningly, Article IV, Section 4, simply gives the "United States" and not a particular branch of government the responsibility to execute the Guarantee Clause.[37] The US Constitution had thus sown uncertainty into a situation that desperately needed clarity. What would happen if Congress and the president disagreed over who had the power to enforce the Guarantee Clause? What if Congress and the president declared different men governor? And was there a role for federal courts? Could they decide whether a government was sufficiently "Republican" or what constituted "domestic Violence"?

Even after a consensus formed about which branch had primary responsibility over the Guarantee Clause, procedural questions awaited. Specifically, who decided whether the legislature could or could not meet? Did the federal government have to take the governor's word, or should it carry out its own investigation? What if the legislature maintained that it could meet and did not want federal involvement, but the governor insisted that the legislature could not meet and that he did want federal involvement? Pennsylvania—like every state today except Nebraska—had a bicameral legislature. What if one house believed that it couldn't convene, and the other house believed that it could? Would the Buckshot War set a clear national standard for future state constitutional crises, or would those be resolved on a case-by-case basis? Oh, and the federal officials mulling these questions over had better think fast. Bullets might fly at any moment.

On December 5, 1838, Sumner rejected the request, claiming that "as the disturbance at the capital of this state appears to proceed from political differences alone, I do not feel that it would be proper for me to interpose my command between the parties." Ritner appealed directly to President Martin Van Buren. He submitted a statement of facts signed by senate Whigs about what happened on December 4, 1838, and asserted that neither branch of the legislature could meet at the time due to the violence and intimidation. Ritner's letter put Van Buren in a difficult position. Van Buren was a Democrat and would have been hesitant to use the military to undermine the Democratic Party in Pennsylvania. But, in refusing to act when lawless mobs made credible threats to murder prominent Whigs, he risked a perception that he was playing politics in a life-or-death situation. Perhaps seeking cover, Van Buren had Secretary of War Joel Poinsett respond. On December 11, 1838, Poinsett again denied Ritner military aid. He gave three reasons. First, he worried about setting a dangerous precedent by involving federal troops in a mere "political" contest. Second, he argued that the request was inappropriate because Ritner had made it instead of the legislature. In his previous letter, Ritner claimed that the legislature couldn't assemble. But Poinsett had received intelligence "which, although not official, comes in a form sufficiently authentic to entitle it to credit, [that] it appears that both branches of the legislature were in session in the Capitol of the State on the 8th inst. and transacted business there." Since Poinsett believed the legislature *could* meet, the US Constitution's text required *it* to request federal help. Finally, Poinsett argued that the Pennsylvania militia was capable of handling the situation by itself. Poinsett's letter ended the immediate possibility of federal intervention, but not the controversy. Ritner wrote another letter protesting Van Buren's decision and the US House of Representatives investigated, suggesting that Congress believed it also had a role in enforcing the Guarantee Clause.[38]

Ritner had one last card to play: calling out the state militia. Accordingly, General Robert Patterson ordered volunteers to "assemble in winter uniform, with knapsacks, provided with thirteen rounds of buckshot cartridge, and seven rounds of ball cartridge."[39] The ammunition distributed later gave the "Buckshot War" its name. But it was unclear how far Patterson would go to support Ritner. The two—along with cabinet members—held a meeting on December 8, 1838. When a cabinet member asked whether Patterson would obey Ritner's orders, Patterson said he would have to consider whether he felt a particular order was appropriate. When pressed, Patterson said he would refuse to forcibly install a Whig as speaker of the house of representatives, and that he would not permit the militia to fire on the crowds Ritner believed to be in insurrection unless attacked first.[40]

The standoff ended when three Whigs left the Cunningham House and joined the Hopkins House. That gave the Hopkins House a quorum, which led even the Whig-controlled senate to recognize it as the lawful house of representatives. The Whigs also stopped contesting the governorship and Porter was inaugurated. The Buckshot War was over without any casualties.[41]

The Buckshot War's Aftermath

David Rittenhouse Porter won a resounding reelection as governor in 1841. Thomas Burrowes became the superintendent of the school system and, later, president of the Agricultural College of Pennsylvania. Ritner retired to his farm, though at one point he did seek a position in the US Treasury Department. An obituary hailed him as "a man of considerable intellect and force of character."[42] Stevens eventually won a seat in the US House of Representatives. There, he played an important role in crafting the Thirteenth, Fourteenth, and Fifteenth Amendments to the US Constitution. The Thirteenth Amendment abolished slavery. The Fourteenth Amendment established that former slaves were citizens and promised them equal protection of the laws. The Fifteenth Amendment prohibited racial discrimination in voting. Stevens remained controversial notwithstanding his achievements. Upon his death in 1868, one newspaper wrote, "Fifty years of his life had been spent in public positions of various kinds, and throughout them all it can scarcely be said that he done [*sic*] one act for which his memory deserves to be revered by his countrymen, now that death has removed him from time to eternity." As a final insult, it added, "May his ashes find in the grave what he refused to his country while living—Peace." Speaking of graves, Stevens used his as a parting shot in his war for racial equality. His epitaph read: "I repose in this quiet and secluded spot, not from any natural preference for solitude, but finding other cemeteries limited as to race, by charter rules, I have chosen this that I might illustrate in my death the principles which I advocated through a long life, equality of man before his creator."[43]

The Buckshot War saw enraged mobs that brought the government to a standstill, a fervent belief that one political party was planning targeted assassinations of its opponents, and the state militia called out to preserve order. It was a best-case scenario for a constitutional crisis. Posing a few questions helps us see just how much worse things could have been. What if the disagreement in December 1838 had not been over who had won an election with normal stakes, but over the more fundamental question of whether Black men and white men who did not pay taxes deserved to vote? What if confusion persisted about which constitution was in force? How would Whigs across the state have reacted if one of their leaders *had* been murdered? What if the Whigs had maintained their position that Ritner had really won when accounting for fraud and tried to inaugurate him for another term? What if the militia had not remained neutral and had used force in support of one of the candidates? For Pennsylvania, these questions turned out to be scary hypotheticals. For other states, such questions became a frightening reality.

2

How a Traitor to His Class Brought Rhode Island to the Brink of Civil War

For most Americans, pursuing constitutional reform looks like advocating on behalf of amendments or arguing why a court should interpret a constitutional provision in a new way. For Thomas Dorr, it looked like leading an unsanctioned constitutional convention and raising a militia to implement the constitution it produced by force. The resulting struggle pitted him against Rhode Island authorities, the federal government, and his parents.

Given Thomas Dorr's background, you would expect him to be a pillar of Rhode Island's political establishment instead of working to destroy it. In 1805, Dorr was born to wealthy parents who could trace their ancestry back to Rhode Island's founding. As a child, Dorr attended the famous Phillips Exeter Academy before entering Harvard at thirteen. After graduation, Dorr studied law under New York Chancellor James Kent, an opportunity aspiring nineteenth century lawyers sought out as eagerly as twenty-first century law students seek out clerkships with US Supreme Court justices. The experience launched him into a successful legal practice. Dorr's good fortune did not extend to his physical health. Short and round in the middle, he suffered from respiratory and stomach problems. By twenty-three, he needed a cane to walk. Luckily, family money made working under these circumstances optional. He took a vacation for several months to tour the South in search of a cure for his ailments and then lived in New York and Philadelphia off an allowance from his father. Health challenges aside, Dorr accomplished everything his family expected out of a young man with his talents—except finding a wife.[1]

Dorr entered politics when he returned to Rhode Island. He began as a Whig, but later became a Democrat. His early career demonstrates a concern for the common man. As a legislator, Dorr investigated the state's banks and wrote a forty-page report accusing them of charging excessive interest rates. That same year, he authored legislation requiring Rhode Island to invest its surplus from the Federal Deposit Act into public education.[2] Dorr also held racially progressive views for the time. Invoking the Bible to condemn racial segregation, he once wrote that "in the 'house' of 'many mansions' there will be no negro gallery!" Hostile to slavery, Dorr personally presented a petition from abolitionists for use of the state house to meet. He attended a meeting of the American Anti-Slavery Society where he introduced a resolution praising abolitionists for fighting "the slave interest in this country" by resisting the annexation of Texas and exhorted abolitionists that their work "can be terminated only by the downfall of the entire system of Republican Slavery."[3]

Most importantly, Dorr advocated constitutional reform. Rhode Island was one of two states that hadn't written a new constitution during or after the American Revolution. It continued to use its 1663 charter from King Charles II. The charter established a legislature with six representatives from Newport; four each from Providence, Warwick, and Portsmouth; and two from other towns. This proportion was fair in the seventeenth century but unfair in the nineteenth century when Providence became the state's major population center. In order to vote, the legislature required men to possess substantial wealth. By 1798, prospective voters had to own $134 in property, have an annual rent income of $7, or be the eldest son of someone who did. In the 1830s and 1840s, these requirements disproportionately disenfranchised factory workers at the same time the Industrial Revolution brought so many to the state. As a result, about 60 percent of Rhode Island's white men couldn't vote, to say nothing of Black men or women.[4] At the same time, allowing the eldest son of an eligible voter to vote established a hereditary elite who controlled Rhode Island's affairs. The charter made no provision for changing it.

Reformers tried to change the suffrage requirements and adopt a written constitution for years. The most recent effort had been in 1834, when Rhode Island held a failed constitutional convention. Dorr was a delegate to that convention and founded the Constitution Party while the delegates were meeting. In an address advocating for a new constitution, Dorr began by asking "whether it be consistent with the spirit of the Declaration of American Independence, and becoming the character of Rhode-Island Republicans, any longer to acknowledge the charter of a British King as a Constitution of civil government." He then criticized the charter primarily for keeping so many men from voting and giving certain areas of the state dramatically more representation in the legislature than others.[5] His arguments didn't carry the day in 1834, but they planted the seeds of the constitutional rebellion that sprouted a decade later.

Dorr tried as hard to win high political office as he did to achieve his political and constitutional vision. He ran for Congress on the Constitution Party's ticket in 1837 but lost. He ran again in 1839 on the Democratic Party's ticket. Despite an enthusiastic endorsement describing him as "endowed with the highest order of intellect, possessed of talent, integrity, and independence," he lost again.[6] His political opponents may eventually have regretted his losses. If he had been in Congress, he might have been unable to lead the movement against them.

Rhode Island's Constitutional Contest

The failures over the years to modernize Rhode Island's suffrage requirements did not quiet complaints. To illustrate the injustice of property requirements to vote, one newspaper claimed that "we have known a tory, who fled his country in the revolutionary war, and joined her enemies, subsequently return, enjoy the right of franchise, and be elected to responsible offices, because he was rich. We have seen the man who faced the cannon's mouth in his country's defence, return from the field of battle, bearing honorable scars, driven by law from the ballot box, because he was poor!"[7] In 1840, a politically diverse group of citizens interested in extending the franchise formed the Rhode Island Suffrage Association. As the group made inroads in public opinion, the legislature decided to call a new constitutional convention in February 1841. However, they guaranteed widespread skepticism of what became known as the Landholders' Convention when they permitted only property owners to select delegates.[8]

The Suffrage Association also called a convention and permitted all adult males to elect delegates. Rhode Island authorities condemned what became known as the People's Convention as illegitimate and illegal. Nonetheless, the convention went forward. It met at almost the exact same time as the Landholders' Convention. The dueling constitutional conventions presented Rhode Islanders with two dramatically different constitutional visions.

With Dorr playing a prominent role, the People's Convention made significant changes to the status quo. Delegates redefined "the people" who were sovereign. They included a variation of language from the Declaration of Independence and insisted that "[a]ll men are created free and equal and are endowed by their Creator with certain natural, inherent and inalienable Rights." Such language was and is common in state constitutions but was an innovation in Rhode Island. King Charles II's charter never recognized such a principle. Consistent with this language, delegates abolished property restrictions on the right to vote. Instead, every white man over twenty-one who had resided in the state for a year could generally vote. Ordinary Rhode Islanders—including thousands of Irish immigrants—would have a much greater voice in government.

While the People's Convention expanded the definition of "the people," it took several steps to accurately determine their will and enhance their power. First, it gave more seats in the legislature to growing areas like Providence and fewer to rural areas which had previously held a stranglehold on power. When combined with liberalized voting requirements, this change meant the legislature more accurately represented Rhode Island as a whole. It also shifted political power from the property-holding elites who had dominated state politics to laborers and nonelites.

Second, it combatted electoral fraud by establishing secret ballot elections and imposing strict registration requirements. In past elections, employers and landlords often threatened to fire workers and remove tenants if they didn't vote as directed. Because there was no secret ballot, those employers and landlords could monitor how their workers and tenants voted. To further game the system, employers would give property to their workers temporarily so those workers could vote, then force those workers to vote how the employers wanted. Though we take secret ballots for granted today, in 1841, they marked a major advance for election integrity.

Third, the People's Convention conferred on Rhode Islanders "a right to give instructions to their Senators and Representatives." In the eighteenth century, communities often gave their representatives to colonial legislatures binding instructions about how to vote on particular matters. Legislators who received such instructions could no longer make an independent judgment about how to vote on those issues. The practice was controversial but endorsed in several early state constitutions. Rhode Islanders could now expect to exert more direct control over their legislators.

While the People's Constitution commenced a revolution in the fortunes of formerly disenfranchised white men, it confirmed the subordinate place of formerly enslaved Black men. Earlier in the nineteenth century, Black men could vote if they possessed the required property, but they were disenfranchised in 1822. Black men working to restore their voting rights hoped Dorr would aid their cause. Dorr obliged and introduced a petition to enfranchise Black men. One delegate who spoke in favor of the petition called the rejection of Black voting "a libel upon the Great Eternal." He argued that the Golden Rule—do unto others as you would have them do unto you—required the convention to accept Black voting. Many other delegates saw the justice of allowing Black men to vote, but believed political reality prevented them from doing so. After hearing testimony that many white voters wouldn't support the People's Constitution if it permitted Black suffrage, one delegate contended that "it was the duty of the Convention not to sacrifice some 16,000 men because they could not include some two or three hundred . . . they were bound to act 'for the greatest good of the greatest number.'"[9] Their decision was lamentable, but unfortunately, understandable. As we saw in chapter 1, racism in the North ran as deep as it did in the South. Although most northerners were antislavery, that didn't mean they saw Black people as equals. By 1841, many northern states joined the South in refusing to let Black men vote. Northern cities had seen frequent race riots where white mobs victimized innocent Black people. Just a few years later, the principle of "separate but equal" originated in a Massachusetts Supreme Judicial Court decision finding that segregated schools didn't violate the Massachusetts Constitution. In this context, the fear that enfranchising Black people would hurt the People's Constitution's chances of ratification was a logical one.[10] Acting on that fear would have fateful consequences.

Despite Dorr and some other men with similar ideological commitments participating in the Landholders' Convention, the final constitution reflected little of their worldview. It refused to declare that "all men are free and equal." Like the People's Constitution, it restricted the franchise to white men. But instead of abolishing property requirements outright, the Landholders' Convention applied them to some Rhode Islanders but not others. Native-born American citizens who had resided in Rhode Island for two years could vote without owning property. However, native-born American citizens who had only resided in the state for one year had to own $134 of property. Rhode Islanders who had immigrated to the United States and become naturalized American citizens could only vote if they owned at least $134 in property. The move deliberately excluded thousands of Dorr's Irish supporters and guaranteed that they would continue to support the People's Constitution. The Landholders' Constitution didn't require secret ballots in elections. It left in place a senate that gave rural areas and small towns disproportionate representation and rejected giving the people the right to instruct representatives.[11]

No compromise was possible between these two constitutional visions because they reflected irreconcilable answers to the fundamental questions of how to define "the people," how the people should pursue constitutional change, what the greatest threat of tyranny was, and what "liberty" meant. They also reflected conflicting interests. If these stakes weren't high enough, both sides appealed to the founding fathers for support, making the contest about the meaning and legacy of the American Revolution as well.

The Landholders' Convention narrowly defined "the people." Before the American Revolution, all colonies except one required voters to own property. Several of the founding fathers believed that men without property could not make good voters. Propertyless men were dependents like women and children who rightfully—in their view—held no political power.[12] The Landholders' Convention grudgingly permitted native-born Americans who had resided in the state for two years to vote without owning property, but insisted on property qualifications for everyone else. Expanding the franchise even more threatened the political dominance of the economic elites accustomed to governing Rhode Island.

The People's Convention and the Landholders' Convention disagreed on whether state residents could lawfully draft a constitution without permission from the government in power. There had been unsanctioned constitutional conventions before 1841. Americans disagreed about whether those conventions were legitimate.[13] In a document written to demonstrate that the People's Constitution was lawful, Dorr argued that the people had an inherent right to change their constitution even outside of formal lawmaking channels. In his view, the people were the boss and the legislature the employee. Just as a company boss would not have to get an employee's approval to change company rules, Dorr believed that the people did not have to get the legislature's approval to change the constitution. As support for his argument, Dorr appealed to the Declaration of Independence, federalist papers, US Supreme Court opinions, and George Washington's farewell address.[14] James Wilson—whom George Washington appointed to the Supreme Court—confirms that Dorr offered a plausible reading of founding-era history. In Pennsylvania's debates over whether to ratify the US Constitution, Wilson argued that "in our governments, the supreme, absolute, and uncontrollable power *remains* in the people. As our constitutions are superior to our legislatures, so the people are superior to our constitutions. Indeed, the superiority, in this last instance, is much greater; for the people possess over our constitutions control in *act*, as well as right." Wilson agreed with Dorr that this meant "the people may change the constitutions whenever and however they please."[15]

In important ways, the People's Convention was a logical successor to the American Revolution. Before the Revolution, colonists organized into groups such as the Sons of Liberty to resist English policy and then used those groups to govern society outside the formal English political structure. They ultimately rejected the King's and Parliament's authority. It was in this context that Americans wrote the first state constitutions. Consistent with this history, the People's Constitution—like most other state constitutions and the Declaration of Independence—recognized that "[t]he PEOPLE have therefore an inalienable and indefeasible right, in their original, sovereign and unlimited capacity, to ordain and institute government, and, in the same capacity, to alter, reform, or totally change the same, whenever their safety or happiness requires."[16] For Dorr and many delegates, this commitment was ideological. But for many others who didn't own property, it was practical. The legislature was dominated by property owners actively hostile to their interests. The legislature controlled the political process. The only way they could enter the political process was to move the legislature out of the way.

The Landholders' Constitution never embraced popular sovereignty. Nowhere did it assert something like "all political power is vested in and derived from the people only." Nor did it say in its Declaration of Rights that the people had a right to "alter or amend" government.[17] To be sure, most delegates to the Landholders' Convention would have said they believed in popular sovereignty if asked. Still, it is telling that their constitution refused to explicitly endorse the concept. To the extent they did accept popular sovereignty, they believed that existing institutions had a right to channel it. In this, they could cite none other than Samuel Adams, famously associated with the Boston Tea Party in 1773, where angry colonists dumped British tea into the ocean to protest Parliament imposing taxes on them without their consent. In a letter to Noah Webster, Samuel Adams began by acknowledging "County Conventions & popular Committees servd [sic] an excellent Purpose when they were first in Practice." But then he cautioned that "it is my Opinion, with Deferrence [sic] to the Opinions of other Men, that as we now have constitutional & regular Governments and all our Men in Authority depend upon the annual & free Elections of the People, we are safe without them."[18] In other words, it was no longer appropriate for the people, however defined, to pursue change outside the prescribed political process. That meant the People's Convention was illegitimate from the beginning. This position just so happened to give the wealthy who controlled the political process a veto over disfavored constitutional changes.

Third, and on a related note, the two constitutions illustrate that Rhode Islanders worried about different kinds of tyranny. The People's Convention worried about tyranny of the minority. Restrictive suffrage and a malapportioned legislature had kept a tiny clique in power and allowed it to prevent changes most Rhode Islanders wanted. In urging Rhode Islanders to ratify the People's Constitution, the Rhode Island Suffrage Association asked them whether they wanted to continue to "place in the hands of an ARISTOCRATIC MINORITY, THE SOLE POWERS OF GOVERNMENT [and] give to the MAJORITY, THE RIGHTS OF THE SLAVE—to BOW AT THE FOOT OF TYRANNY, and to OBEY?" In celebrating majority rule, People's Constitution supporters could cite Jefferson. In his first inaugural address, he had called "absolute acquiescence in the decisions of the majority" the "vital principle of republics."[19]

By contrast, opponents of the People's Constitution worried about tyranny of the majority. Brown University President John Wayland warned if the people could change the constitution without working through existing institutions, "all that would be necessary, in order to establish unlimited power over us, would be, without forms of law, to lay claim to a majority, and assemble a sufficient number of armed men to carry its decisions into effect." Then, "the only law that would be known, would soon be the law of force." One People's Constitution opponent observed for comedic effect that if a majority could draft a constitution as they saw fit, Rhode Island's women could draft a constitution. Rhode Islanders concerned about majority rule could plausibly cite Federalist Paper #51. "If a majority be united by a common interest," James Madison worried, "the rights of the minority will be insecure." The founding fathers designed the US Constitution to limit popular influence in several ways. These include using an electoral college to select the president, giving state legislatures the decision of whom to appoint to the US Senate for six-year terms, and awarding federal judges life tenure. Some of the founders had wanted to go even further. Alexander Hamilton, for example, supported giving life tenure to the president and members of the US Senate.[20]

Finally, the two conventions disagreed about the meaning of "liberty." Today, most Americans think of voting as a right. But at the founding and early in the nineteenth century, many Americans maintained that voting was a privilege. A delegate to Virginia's 1830 constitutional convention argued that voting was a matter of "expediency and policy, and . . . we ought to so regulate it, as will best promote the happiness and prosperity of society." Many Landholders' Convention delegates shared this view. It allowed them to craft an electorate that held similar interests and policy preferences. By the 1840s, however, many other Americans had come to see voting as a key aspect of "liberty." Dorr had once argued that *a participation in the choice of those who make and administer laws is a Natural Right; which cannot be abridged nor suspended any farther than the greatest good of the greatest number imperatively requires.*[21] If voting were a natural right just like the right to protection of property or the right to self-defense, then a property qualification on suffrage contradicted the Declaration of Independence. A government imposing that property qualification was oppressive like England before the American Revolution and therefore not entitled to obedience.

Both the People's Constitution and the Landholders' Constitution faced serious opposition. Two of the nation's most prominent abolitionists, Frederick Douglass and William Lloyd Garrison, criticized the People's Constitution for disenfranchising Black men. Born into slavery, Frederick Douglass taught himself to read and write, beat up an abusive master, and escaped to freedom. He became famous for traveling around the country to deliver eloquent speeches about his experience as a slave.[22] William Lloyd Garrison founded *The Liberator* to demand an immediate end to slavery. He would eventually become infamous for burning a copy of the US Constitution on July 4, 1854, and calling it "a covenant with death, and an agreement with Hell."[23] In a speech, Douglass said that he "was bound by the laws of God" to raise his voice in protest. Garrison went a step further and compared Dorr to Pontius Pilate, a grave insult in a time when intimate knowledge of the Bible was assumed. According to the Bible, some Jews were so angered by Jesus Christ's message that they conspired to murder him. They turned him over to the Roman governor of their province, Pontius Pilate, to accomplish their goal. The Bible indicates that Pilate knew Jesus had done nothing to deserve death and offered Jerusalem's Jews a choice of having Jesus or a petty criminal named Barrabas released. When the crowd demanded Barrabas, Pilate ordered Jesus crucified. After noting that Dorr had opposed restricting the franchise to whites, Garrison observed that Pilate, "being willing to release Jesus, urged the infuriated Jews to let him go; but as they were unwilling to do so, he gave sentence that it should be as they required."[24] Meanwhile, the Landholders' Constitution was unacceptable to many Rhode Islanders because of its continued restrictions on suffrage and its refusal to fairly apportion the legislature.

The Suffrage Association held an election, again unsanctioned by Rhode Island's government, to ratify the People's Constitution on December 27, 1841. When the results were in, 13,944 voted in favor of the new constitution and only 52 voted against, though many people loyal to the charter authorities refused to participate in the election. The final tally meant that a majority of Rhode Islanders eligible to vote under the charter supported the People's Constitution. This fact allowed People's Constitution supporters to use the US Constitution's origins and journey towards ratification as support for their movement's legality. By the mid-1780s, many Americans had soured on the Articles of Confederation—the first document attempting to unify the various states—because of the central government's inability to levy taxes, regulate commerce, or enforce treaties and fears that the central government was too weak to combat constitutional instability at the state level. In 1787, Congress therefore called a convention "for the sole and express purpose of revising the Articles of Confederation." Delegates proceeded to disregard these instructions and draft a completely new constitution. While there is a lively scholarly debate today about whether the founding fathers acted illegally, Americans ultimately sanctioned their conduct by ratifying the US Constitution. Similarly, there was now a plausible argument that any objection to the People's Convention became irrelevant when Rhode Islanders accepted its constitution. This claim took on even more force when Rhode Islanders voted down the Landholders' Constitution, 8,689 to 8,013, a couple of months later.[25] Rhode Islanders clearly preferred the People's Constitution.

Rather than submit to the People's Constitution, opponents insisted that the 1663 charter was still in force. As part of that effort, prominent judges reiterated the argument that the People's Constitution was illegal, ratification vote notwithstanding. John Pittman, who presided over Rhode Island's federal trial court, distributed "printed effusions" against the People's Constitution at government expense. The Rhode Island Supreme Court, whose justices were chosen by the charter legislature, declared in an advisory opinion that "the Convention, which formed the 'People's Constitution,' assembled without law; that in forming it they proceeded without law; that the votes, given in favor of it, were given without law."[26] The judges' conduct raised a troubling question. What if they had to decide a case involving Dorr or one of his supporters?

People's Constitution supporters pressed on and scheduled elections for governor and the legislature. To maintain control, politicians calling themselves the Law and Order Party made it a "high crime and misdemeanor" for Rhode Islanders to "signify that he or they will accept any executive, legislative, judicial or ministerial office or offices" in upcoming elections under the People's Constitution. The punishment was a fine of two thousand dollars and a year's imprisonment. They then made exercising powers of office under the People's Constitution a treasonable offense punishable by life imprisonment.[27] Critics called this an "Algerine" law, purposefully invoking the North African pirates based in Algiers whom the United States had fought decades earlier.

Rhode Island Descends into Civil War

If the Law and Order Party thought they could intimidate Dorr and his supporters, they were mistaken. Dorr himself was apparently reluctant to run for governor in the upcoming election under the People's Constitution, but allowed his name to be put forward when other candidates declined to do so. The election under the People's Constitution proceeded in April 1842, and Dorr won easily, though fewer voters participated in the election than had participated in the referendum on the People's Constitution. After winning, Dorr was determined to take office and implement the People's Constitution. Not even his parents could dissuade him. In a letter on April 8, 1842, they wrote, "It grieves us to the heart to know that a son of ours arrived at so mature an age and so well versed in the laws of his Country should be a participant in acts calculated to bring the state into destruction, arouse passions which you cannot allay and which God forbid produce civil strife attended with bloodshed and murder." They asked him to stop "before [he passes] the Rubicon and become engulfed in political criminal degradation, where our feeble prayers will not avail to save you from disgrace and ruin." The Rubicon was a reference to when Julius Caesar marched on Rome at the head of an army in defiance of the Roman Senate and began a civil war which ended with him becoming a dictator.[28] Caesar was not the last Roman revolutionary Dorr would be compared to, and Dorr would cross Rhode Island's Rubicon. The letter is not just revealing because it unveiled Dorr's family drama. It also underscored the extent to which Dorr was a traitor to his class. Harvard-educated, wealthy, successful, and a member of Rhode Island's elite, Dorr wasn't whom you would normally expect to wager his political future fighting for the poor and dispossessed.

Samuel Ward King, governor under the charter, responded to Dorr's resolve by asking the federal government to send troops to Rhode Island. Like Joseph Ritner during the Buckshot War, King cited the US Constitution's guarantee to the states of a "Republican" form of government and assistance in cases of "domestic violence."[29] King's invocation of the Guarantee Clause raised an important question: could a state where 60 percent of white men were disenfranchised because of onerous property requirements and where the legislature was unfairly apportioned credibly claim that it was "Republican"? Answering this question requires raising still another: what is the proper way to interpret a constitutional provision? One way would be to focus on what the founding generation understood "Republican" to mean in the 1780s when the US Constitution was drafted and ratified. In that case, two things stand out. First, property qualifications on suffrage were almost universal then. Second, James Madison promised in Federalist Paper #43 shortly after the US Constitution had been drafted that "as long, therefore, as the existing republican forms are continued by the States, they are guaranteed by the federal Constitution." That included Rhode Island's charter government. Another way to think about these questions is to ask what Americans in 1842 understood the term "Republican" to mean. By then, most states had abandoned property requirements, and most Americans would likely have agreed that, at the very least, "Republican" governments allowed white men to vote without owning property. Recognizing this reality, the *New Age and Constitutional Advocate* described the People's Constitution as "having the features of a Republican constitution" and condemned the failed Landholders' Constitution as "anti Republican."[30]

The ball was in President John Tyler's court. It wasn't supposed to be. Tyler had been elected vice president in the 1840 election and was only poring over King's request in the White House because his running mate William Henry Harrison died shortly after being inaugurated. To make taking on presidential duties in a nation where there was no precedent for a president dying during his term and prominent citizens questioned his legitimacy even more difficult, Tyler lacked a sure base of political support. He was a Democrat for decades but had allied with the Whigs in recent years, leading members of both parties to distrust him. While some Americans once called George Washington "His Excellency," Tyler's critics mocked him as "His Accidency." With such uncertain political footing, Tyler must initially have been unsure of how to proceed. Indeed, after admitting that he had heard about "the unhappy condition of things in Rhode Island," Tyler declared, "I shall not adventure the expression of an opinion upon those questions of domestic policy which seem to have given rise to the unfortunate controversy between a portion of the citizens and the existing government of the State." He maintained that he could only intervene in cases of violence and that as Dorr had committed none, he must stay on the sidelines.[31] But violence was coming.

In early May of 1842, Dorr held an inaugural procession. A newspaper account described how "at 10 o'clock, a procession, civil and military, was formed of great length, to escort the Governor and members of the legislature elect, to a building prepared for the meeting [to swear them in]." Ominously, the article noted that "dignitaries were guarded on both sides by soldiers with bristling bayonets." It marveled that no actual bloodshed occurred. If the war between the Dorrites and the charter authorities was still cold, so was Dorr's relationship with his parents. Dorr wrote a letter to his mother when he received some clothes from her. "You are the only person related to me, so far as I know," he wrote, "who entertains toward me any feelings of kindness, and I was much affected by the expression of them."[32]

Dorr left the state after his inauguration and competed with King for support from the federal government and other states. Dorr's time in Washington, DC, convinced him that "We have the moral & intellectual weight of Congress on our side, and perhaps the numerical weight, after a full and fair discussion; but this I will not positively assert." He lamented that some southerners "are with the People of Rhode Island, but not with all People in asserting a principle, which might be construed to take in the southern blacks and to aid the abolitionists." Dorr was right that white southerners were leery of him. If they accepted that a majority of inhabitants could abolish an old government and create a new one, they were in trouble. Many southern slaveholders lived in predominantly Black areas, and South Carolina was majority Black. Just eleven years previously, Nat Turner put white people across the South on edge when he led a rebellion killing fifty-seven men, women, and children. Ever since, they had lived in constant fear of the next uprising. What if Dorr's example inspired more Nat Turners? On the other hand, if Tyler set a precedent of using the Guarantee Clause to intervene in a free northern state's affairs, what would stop an abolitionist president from using that precedent to justify intervening in a slave state's affairs? As a Virginia slaveholder, Tyler was surely troubled by these questions.[33]

Dorr did receive some congressional support, but not enough to make a difference. Ohio's US Senator William Allen proposed resolutions, which were ultimately rejected, declaring that "it is the right of the People of Rhode Island to establish for themselves a constitutional form of State Government . . . provided its form be left republican," that "it is not the right of the Federal Government to interfere in any manner with the people to prevent or discourage them from" making a constitution, and that, "on the contrary, it is the duty of the Federal Government to guaranty to them, as a State, such Republican form of State Government that, when so established, can be altered or modified."[34] Dorr tried to woo the Tyler administration in a meeting at the White House. Tyler struck Dorr as "a very good natured weak man, unequal to his situation, and having his mind made up for him by others." He called Tyler and his secretary of state, Daniel Webster, "Tories of the rankest sort." During the American Revolution, patriots frequently referred to Americans who remained loyal to Great Britain and in some cases took up arms against their neighbors fighting for liberty as "Tories."[35]

In the end, Tyler decided to support the Law and Order Party. Instead of genuinely weighing whether King or Dorr was Rhode Island's true governor, Tyler advised King on how to deescalate the crisis. He told King, "I deprecate the use of force except in the last resort, and I am persuaded that measures of conciliation will at once operate to produce quiet." He further claimed "*I am well advised*, if the general assembly would authorize you to announce a general amnesty and pardon for the past, without making any exception, upon the condition of a return to allegiance, and follow it up by a call for a new convention upon somewhat liberal principles, that all difficulty would at once cease." Somehow, Dorr must have gotten wind of this or similar communications because he wrote a supporter that "the President will support the old Charter government by his own forces upon a failure of the civil posse to enforce the laws upon us. This is what he is committed to by his letters." Still, Dorr left Washington feeling confident, telling one supporter that he expected one thousand volunteers from New York to support his efforts to implement the People's Constitution.[36]

Tyler continued to work for a peaceful end to the conflict. One newspaper indicated "that a report has gained currency, that the President had instituted a commission, to consist of an equal number from the government and from the conspirators, with two members of the cabinet as umpires, to settle, by compromise, the difficulties in this State." Dorr later confirmed that two allies had participated in negotiations but denied authorizing them to do so. Instead, he promised followers, "I have neither made nor attempted to make a compromise of your Constitution, or of your rights."[37]

What became known as the Rhode Island Question received national media attention as Americans debated the underlying constitutional issues and waited eagerly to learn what would happen next. Newspapers as far away as Florida and Illinois covered the events on their front pages. The conflict within Dorr's family proved particularly captivating. A Georgia newspaper calling Dorr "the arch-demagogue of Rhode Island" even passed along a rumor that Dorr had threatened his father, saying that "I should not hesitate to march over your dead body, provided I could carry my point in no other way." Dorr apparently did not actually make such a threat, for another out-of-state paper hostile to him observed that "it is denied on good authority that the pseudo-governor Dorr, ever threatened to annihilate his own father, even if that achievement should be indispensably necessary to the success of the suffrage party."[38]

Dorr ventured to New York, where he received an outpouring of support from Democrats. The *Evening Post* reported that "a large number of citizens called upon Governor Dorr, of Rhode Island, on Saturday at Tammany Hall." Dorr addressed the crowd there "in an impressive manner, in the midst of frequent applauses." He left Tammany Hall for a steamboat heading to Rhode Island amid a procession with hundreds of onlookers. Hearing such enthusiastic cheering and being addressed as "Governor" must have boosted the ego of a man who had twice failed to win a seat in Congress. And the promise of military aid from two New York labor leaders surely increased his confidence that he could prevail in a showdown with charter authorities.[39]

Dorr returned to Rhode Island in a militant mood. The *Newport Mercury* reported that he gave an "inflammatory speech" where he "drew the sword he had on from its scabbard, and added that it had belonged to an officer who had fallen in Florida, that it had been presented to him by a brother of the fallen man while he was in New York." That sword, he said, "had been already dyed in blood, and if necessary, would again be dyed in blood, should the suffrage cause demand it." In a proclamation, Dorr threatened federal authorities that as "soon as a soldier of the United States shall be set in motion by whatever direction, to act against the People of this State, in aid of the charter government, I shall call for that aid, to oppose all such force, which, I am fully authorized to say will immediately and most cheerfully be tendered to the service of the People of Rhode Island from the city of New York and from other places. The contest will then become national, and our State the battle ground of American freedom."[40]

Statements like these led Dorr's enemies to portray him as a would-be tyrant. Charles Coffin Jewett called him "a Catiline, talented, reck-less, *mad*, [who] was attempting to subvert the liberties of the State, and was threatening with the torch and the dagger all who dared to oppose him." Jewett acknowledged that Dorr was "at first sincere in his convic-tions respecting the political changes which he proposed in this State." But thwarted ambition had led to him urging followers to take up arms. That stemmed, Jewett claimed, from "his love of power, which amounted to a monomania [which] suggested to him what he considered a more speedy way, and he pursued that with all the determination of his char-acter, disregarding to the last, the most tender and earnest entreaties of all of his relatives, and heeding not the awful consequences which must have attended the execution of his Robespierre-like plans."[41]

In the eighteenth and nineteenth centuries, calling someone a "Ca-tiline" or a "Robespierre" was like comparing them to Adolf Hitler in our time. Catiline was a politician who failed in his efforts to become one of the two chief executives of the Roman Republic. Determined to take power, he had allegedly conspired to murder Cicero—Rome's most important leader—and burn Rome to the ground. Denounced by Cicero in the Roman Senate's chamber, Catiline fled the city and then fought the Roman army with his supporters. He was said to have died in battle. Robespierre was a central figure in the French Revolution. He played a leading role in the reign of terror that executed thousands of political opponents during the 1790s. To horrified observers worldwide, his name called to mind the image of the guillotine used to chop the heads off vic-tims. The founding fathers commonly invoked Catiline and Robespierre when they wanted to portray political opponents as dangerous.[42]

Dorr was no Catiline, and certainly no Robespierre, but he was de-termined to take power. On the early morning of May 18, 1842, Dorr led an attack on the state armory in Providence with his own relatives inside. What happened before and during the attack is disputed. Jewett described the attack in unflattering terms. According to Jewett, Dorr led a force of about six hundred men, half of them armed, to demand surrender of the arsenal around 2:00 a.m. When the colonel in charge refused, "Dorr then ordered the cannon—two six pounders, to be brought within musket shot. They were heavily charged with ball and slugs. He gave the order to fire." But the cannons didn't shoot, and he repeated the order. When the cannons again failed to fire, Dorr "suspect[ed] his men of treachery . . . [and] brandished his sword, and with bitter imprecations seized a match and applied it himself." Still, "the powder flashed harmlessly upon the piece." Jewett speculated that, at that moment, Dorr "probably saw the truth, that his own followers would not sustain him in his desperate career." He further claimed that it was "said that some of his own party, after having done all they could to dissuade him from his mad course, and shrinking from a participation in the horrors which they saw he would bring upon the community if permitted to carry out his plans, had removed the priming, and crowded the chamber of each piece with wet paper." When charter troops poured into the city, Dorr ordered his men to defend him to the last, but then fled the battle. At that point, the proceedings degenerated into farce. Jewett described Dorr's soldiers as "ferocious by nature, desperate in circumstances and infuriated by liquor." They kept trying to fire the cannons, but "several times [were] prevented from firing only by some one of them less drunk, who struck off the match with a sword just as it was descending upon the powder."[43]

Dorr later described the attack himself. He claimed his advisors had asked him to remain at the headquarters for his safety, "but [he] deemed it [his] duty to direct the operations in person, and accompanied [the] men on foot to the field." Although it is questionable whether Dorr's men really needed him at the frontlines given his lack of military training, I suspect Dorr personally needed to be there. If you knew Dorr and saw him—short, portly, and limping along at the front of a group of men—you would assume he was leading them into a university lecture hall to deliver a talk about the intellectual history of the American Revolution. But here he was, despite all his physical limitations, leading soldiers into battle to fight for the ideals of the American Revolution. On a psychological level, this must have been thrilling. On a practical level, it was a recipe for disaster. Dorr knew nothing about military tactics. He lacked the command presence that makes soldiers instinctively respect a general. He lacked the record of military success that inspires a general's soldiers to believe in victory. And so, it should have been unsurprising that Dorr's 250—by his count—soldiers became "separated and partly disorganized" and that one of his most important lieutenants was missing. Dorr admitted that "an ineffectual attempt was made to fire the pieces of artillery," but claimed "they were properly loaded, and served for the occasion by men of undoubted bravery and competency." The problem was that the cannons were plugged with wood and iron. Dorr called off the attack with the understanding that it "would be renewed under more favorable circumstances." Dorr ordered his men to prepare fortifications. However, many of them became disheartened after learning that members of the People's legislature had resigned and quit the battle. Dorr insisted that "those who remained would have sacrificed their lives to a man for my protection" and that "their subsequent conduct fully confirmed their sincerity."[44]

Dorr never said whether he personally tried to fire the cannons. A witness at the scene, Charles Carter, claimed that Dorr "did not have a torch in his hand that night, or apply a portfire or torch to either of the pieces." Carter disputed that anyone had sabotaged the cannons and said that they were "entirely unserviceable" and that "the powder was old and poor, and, becoming damp, had hardened, so that the priming wire would not go down through it." We will never know for sure whether Dorr actually tried to light the cannon that could have killed relatives in the armory, but his zeal in support of his cause makes it plausible.[45]

Whatever the truth about the attack, it caused alarm both in Rhode Island and in the nation at large. President Tyler, who had previously downplayed the threat Dorr posed, complained that "Mr. Dorr's recent proceedings have been of so extravagant a character as almost to extinguish the last hope of a peaceable result, and yet I can not but believe that much is meant for effect for purposes of intimidation merely."[46]

Dorr fled to New York where he managed to evade capture despite a $1,000 bounty on his head. Meanwhile, charter authorities persecuted Dorr's supporters. Rhode Island's US Senator William Sprague observed that at "present there is a very bad feeling on the part of the workmen against those they work for but this will change as they will soon understand that it is not for their interest to indulge this malicious feeling." His solution was to fire them all and replace them with immigrant laborers. On June 3, 1842, a letter informed Dorr that two supporters had been indicted for treason and that another one had just been imprisoned. Dorr lamented that "suffrage men are thrown out of tenements, out of employment" and "liable to be stopped in the streets by an armed patrol, and insulted & roughly treated." Banks refused to lend People's Constitution supporters money or insure their houses.[47]

But Dorr remained determined to return to Rhode Island and make a stand. He intended to do so at the sleepy village of Chepachet. Though the failed attack on the armory had cost him political capital, by mid-June, a supporter could write that "[their] friends have nearly recovered from our late defeat and are organizing with renewed vigor." Men continued to enlist in Dorr's militia. King worried about an invasion. In a letter to Tyler, King described how Dorr's men had stolen 1,200 pounds of gunpowder from a Providence merchant and effectively put Chepachet under martial law. Daniel Webster visited Rhode Island on Tyler's behalf and wrote that authorities "fear an irruption upon them of an armed force to be collected in other States, and this is the only difficulty of which they now have any apprehension." Though Webster was skeptical that such an invasion would take place, others were more concerned. Tyler's Secretary of War, J. C. Spencer, received reports that Dorr's men had collected muskets and cannons and "that a number of men, not citizens of the State, with arms, were in and about Woonsocket and Chepachet . . ." These incidents provided "strong [indications] that Mr. Dorr and his party are determined to enter the State in force, and that in a few days serious difficulties will arise." Whatever the actual threat Dorr's men posed, the charter legislature was sufficiently worried that it placed the state under martial law on June 25, 1842, and recruited militia units to fight Dorr.[48]

The charter government also attempted to take the wind out of Dorr's political sails by calling a new constitutional convention to expand suffrage. All adult men who had resided in Rhode Island for three years were eligible to vote for delegates. The *Providence Journal* carried a message to King congratulating him on calling a new constitutional convention and espousing the hope that a new constitution's "liberal provisions will satisfy the great body of people" such that "we hereby earnestly recommend a like acquiescence on the part of all our friends." The *Herald of the Times* published an appeal from prominent citizens who had voted for the People's Constitution to "acquiesce in the act of the General Assembly, authorizing a call for a new convention to frame a constitution."[49]

Yet, Dorr felt confident enough to call the People's legislature into session on July 4, 1842. His forces were entrenched on a hill a few hundred yards from Chepachet. A newspaper estimated that he had seven hundred troops at his disposal and reported that there was "an abundance of live stock for the marauding parties" and that "they have from ten to twenty pieces of artillery," though some of the cannons were in better shape than others and not all of Dorr's men were armed. Months later, Dorr claimed his men had behaved honorably. He explained that he had "cautioned our partisan officers at Chepachet to abstain from the seizure of private property, and the more carefully, because it was the design of the enemy to represent our movement as that of mere marauders, caring nothing for the Constitution, and bent solely on rapine."[50]

By all appearances, Dorr welcomed a climactic final battle. In Chepachet, "He made a furious speech to his men, and avowed his determination upon victory or death." In a proclamation, Dorr directed "the military of this State, who are in favor of the People's Constitution, to repair forthwith to head quarters [*sic*], there to await further orders" and requested "all volunteers and volunteer companies so disposed, to do the same." Dorr asserted that "the only alternative is an abject submission to a despotism, in its various practical effects, without a parallel in the American states." But Dorr soon got cold feet. On June 27, 1842, after he "received such information as induces me to believe that a majority of the friends of the People's Constitution disapprove of any further forcible measures for its support," he dismissed the troops. The *Herald of the Times*, which was hostile to Dorr, claimed that he had fled "with fifty men, in the direction of Connecticut.—His own men were ignorant of his flight, and many of them declared that they would shoot him, could they find him."[51]

What dampened Dorr's militancy in such a short time? The reality that he couldn't win probably sank in. Dorr's forces consisted of volunteers whom he admitted "came and went freely" to such an extent that he "had to regret the little discipline which prevailed." He must have wondered how men with such careless attitudes would hold up under fire. Months later, Dorr would also downplay the forces he had available. He claimed that he had only 250 men who were up against 3,000, and so decided to disperse. A year after that, he downgraded the number of troops to between 180 and 190. Whatever the actual number, Dorr didn't have the necessary men to win a battle. In an ironic twist of fate, Dorr's refusal to insist on Black suffrage came back to haunt him as Black men provided crucial support for the charter authorities. The *Herald of the Times* noted that "*the Colored Population* of our city, have come forward in the most honorable manner, and taken upon themselves the charge of the fire-engines. They have pledged themselves to assist in protection of property from fire and plunder, while the other inhabitants are engaged in the defence of the State." Dorr's own men apparently feared Black soldiers. In a portion of his memoir reflecting on the period, William J. Brown remembered that Dorrites "were not overburdened with love for the colored people, for they held them responsible for their defeat in great measure." Years later, Dorrites who had been at Chepachet insisted that "if it were not for the colored people, they would have whipped the Algerines, for their fortifications were so strong that they never could have been taken by them." When Brown asked why they surrendered if they were in such a strong position, a Dorr supporter responded, "Who do you suppose was going to stay there when the Algerines were coming up with four hundred bull niggers?"[52] Black men hoped that their service would be rewarded with voting rights.

Changing political tides surely played a role. As he read the newspapers and talked to his supporters, the realization that "the people" no longer backed his aggressive course became inescapable. That probably accounts for why Dorr didn't have the number of troops he planned on. Dorr firmly believed that 1,300 men had pledged to serve in his militia, not the 700 the *Herald of the Times* reported showed up, or the 180–90 he eventually claimed were at Chepachet.

After dismissing his soldiers, Dorr fled first to Connecticut, then to Vermont, and ultimately New Hampshire. He insisted, "My spirit is not broken by the burden of defeat & obloquy that has been cast upon me," though he added, "My health is impaired by the trials & excitements of the last four months." He hoped that People's Constitution supporters could elect enough Democrats to Congress in the next election to ensure that the federal government would intervene on his side. New Hampshire's Democrats welcomed Dorr with open arms. The June 1842 New Hampshire Democratic Party platform accused Tyler of "a flagrant act of usurpation" when he supported the charter government. New Hampshire's governor, Henry Hubbard, even refused King's extradition request. Instead, he rebuked King, writing that any "pretended Government in any one State not derived from this source [the people] is no government at all."[53]

Dorr's greatest threat shifted from kidnapping to irrelevance. While Dorr was gone, Rhode Islanders ratified a new constitution by a margin of 7,024 to 51. In many respects, it was similar to the Landholders' Constitution that had previously failed. Native-born American citizens who had lived in Rhode Island for two years and paid a $1 poll tax could vote. As late as 1872, an Ohio newspaper reported that even this $1 poll tax was "so onerous that thousands of poor men never cast a ballot unless their taxes are paid for them by some rich candidate for office who wants their votes." Foreign-born Rhode Islanders—who were primarily Irish—could only vote if they had $134 of property. Given that many had only recently come to the United States and were working in low wage jobs, the restriction effectively disenfranchised them. The one saving grace was that Black men regained the franchise in a separate referendum, enabling opponents of the People's Constitution to claim they were on the right side of history. The new constitution rejected Dorr's vision in three other important ways. First, it made no provision for a secret ballot, ensuring that wealthy Rhode Islanders could continue to manipulate the political process. Second, it continued to give rural areas and small towns disproportionate representation in the senate. Finally, and most unforgivably for Dorr, it dismissed his expansive view of popular sovereignty by borrowing language from George Washington's farewell address to insist that the constitution was "sacredly obligatory on all" until the people had gone through the proper channels to change it.[54]

Dorr on Trial

Dorr now had only one option left to retake center stage: go on trial for treason. He returned to Providence, Rhode Island, in October 1844 and was soon arrested. He hoped his case would receive widespread publicity and allow him to argue for his constitutional vision. If the People's Constitution was lawfully adopted, then he couldn't have committed treason in 1842 by attacking the armory. Instead, he was simply claiming state property over which he had lawful authority. Conversely, the decision of charter authorities to engage in armed resistance against Dorr would have been treasonous. In fact, Dorr was so eager to force this debate at trial that he never denied allegations that he had tried to forcefully seize power. When one witness was protective of him, Dorr said, "I release you from all the honorary obligation which you regard yourself as being under, that you may relate all you know." At best, Dorr could hope for a groundswell of support that might sweep him into power. At worst, however, he could expect to hang. Adding to the drama, Dorr acted as his own counsel alongside another lawyer, George Turner.[55]

The deck was stacked against Dorr. The Rhode Island Supreme Court conducted the trial, which was highly unusual, since criminal cases generally take place before a trial court and state supreme courts generally only review lower court actions. Presiding over his trial was Job Durfee, who along with other justices had condemned the People's Constitution in 1842. He had gone so far as to "[characterize] their acts as *treason against the United States!*" Durfee was as biased as his record suggested he would be. He prevented Dorr from arguing that the People's Constitution was in force and from bringing in records to show that a majority of citizens had adopted the People's Constitution. Dorr wouldn't get a real opportunity to argue that the jury should acquit him because he had acted lawfully in implementing a constitution that a majority of citizens had the right to make without government approval. Even if he had, authorities had ensured a jury hostile to Dorr by holding the trial in Newport, a city of prosperous merchants. In short order, the jury convicted him. Facing the death penalty, Dorr remained unrepentant. "The sentence which you will pronounce, to the extent of the power and influence which this court can exert," he said, "is a condemnation of the doctrines of '76, and a reversal of the great principles, which sustain and give vitality to our democratic Republic; and which are regarded by the great body of our fellow-citizens, as a portion of the birthright of a free People." Dorr received a life sentence.[56] His conviction qualified him for the history books in a way he didn't intend: he became the first American convicted of treason against a state. Years later, he would be joined in that exclusive club by John Brown, whom we will meet next chapter.

Prison is rarely a pleasant place, but it must have been a uniquely difficult one for a man like Dorr who was accustomed to both luxury and health challenges. The prison regime was so restrictive that he resorted to writing in Latin to get around limitations on his ability to write letters or keep a diary. Despite his deteriorating health, prison authorities didn't respond to his request for a doctor for six months. Yet he insisted that he would never admit that he had behaved criminally, even if that were the only way to get out. Dorr's most frequent correspondent in prison was his mother, and her love for him shines through in their letters. She frequently asked about his health and sent care packages to him. But their political differences lingered. In one letter, he wrote that "being in prison for the good cause of freedom and justice, & with spirits unbroken, it seems to be a part of my duty to administer consolation to desponding friends on the outside. But, alas! You and my father are of the opposite school of politics, and cannot rejoice in my devotion to what I deem sound principles." He added, "There is one thing however that you can rejoice in, that I have not sacrificed my honest convictions of truth & duty for the sake of getting out of this half way house between the living and the dead." Indeed, his parents must have felt conflicting emotions. On one hand, they disapproved of their son's cause and the means he had used to advance it. On the other, there was something admirable about a son who had the courage of his convictions and who had exhibited more bravery than most others would in similar circumstances. At the end of the day, it can only have been heart-wrenching to watch him waste away in a prison cell.[57]

Fortunately for Dorr and his parents, a movement to free him was afoot. Northern Democrats used Dorr as a campaign issue in 1844. In New York, twelve thousand people marched through the street carrying banners reading "Polk, Dallas, and the Liberation of Dorr" right before election day. James K. Polk went on to win the election and one of Dorr's correspondents believed that Polk benefited from being associated with Dorr. Charles Jackson, a Democrat, was elected governor with support from Dorr's followers.[58] Polk would go on to wage and then win the Mexican War which added vast territory to the United States. All that new land sparked a vigorous national argument about whether it should be open to slavery. It was in this context that tensions between the North and South simmered before they boiled over in the Civil War.

In 1845, the legislature pardoned Dorr. Though he remained disbarred and unable to practice law any longer, he got his freedom. His health was broken by his time in prison, so he moved home where his mother could care for him. His interest in politics, however, was unbroken. Followers nominated him for the US Senate and the US House of Representatives. As a critical newspaper lamented, "The Dorrites of Rhode Island . . . have ventured once more to strive for the resuscitation of their party, and to place its head [Dorr] in honorable and influential office."[59] Dorr lost both times, but his nomination showed his staying power in Rhode Island politics.

The Dorr Rebellion's Consequences

Though calm now prevailed in Rhode Island, the federal government wasn't finished with the Dorr Rebellion's implications. During the chaos in 1842, charter authorities broke into Martin Luther's house to arrest him for supporting Dorr and instead found his mother. Eventually, both Luthers brought a trespass claim against Luther M. Borden, the official who had searched the home. The most important issue in the case was who was in power when Borden acted. If the People's Constitution was in effect and Dorr was governor, then Borden wouldn't have had any legal authority to enter Luther's home. He would have been a trespasser like any other private party who had broken into someone's dwelling. If, on the other hand, the charter authorities remained in power, the court had another important issue to consider: was Rhode Island's charter government—dating from 1663—"Republican" as promised by the Guarantee Clause? In finding for Borden, the lower court ducked the issues and refused to admit evidence that the People's Constitution had been ratified. That was unsurprising given the judges who presided. One was John Pittman, who condemned the People's Constitution in 1842. The other was Joseph Story, who had found Pittman's critique of the People's Constitution persuasive.

This set up an appeal for the US Supreme Court, which had an opportunity to establish an important precedent on when state residents can abolish an existing government. The Supreme Court first held that whether the charter government had been replaced by the people's government was a political question that judges shouldn't try to answer. Instead, Congress and the president got to make that call. The court briefly suggested that whether the charter government was "Republican" was also a political question. It worried about the effect of declaring that the charter government had not lawfully been in power in 1842; that would mean "the laws passed by its legislature during that time were nullities; its taxes wrongfully collected; its salaries and compensation to its officers illegally paid; its public accounts improperly settled; and the judgments and sentences of its courts in civil and criminal cases null and void, and the officers who carried their decisions into operation answerable as trespassers, if not in some cases as criminals." Second, the court tacitly admitted the legitimacy of Dorr's constitutional argument. In a part of the opinion that receives less attention, the court declared that "no one, we believe, has ever doubted the proposition, that, according to the institutions of this country, the sovereignty in every State resides in the people of the State, and that they may alter and change their form of government at their own pleasure."[60] The next Dorr has a plausible argument that they can form a new constitution without following the process outlined in an existing constitution and without getting the approval of state authorities. But they had better win any armed conflict with the government they seek to displace.

Dorr died in December 1854 unmarried and with no children. He was as controversial in death as he had been in life. A critical obituary admitted that "he was a man of fine natural powers and first-rate education, a good lawyer, and an accomplished politician." It then claimed that Dorr "very faithfully remembered real or supposed injuries; and disappointed ambition drove him into acts of folly which forever ruined his worldly prospects." A favorable obituary treated him as a secular saint. "All his endowments, all his zeal and energy, he nobly consecrated to the public welfare . . . [a]spiring after something better than personal advancement, he sacrificed his position, his brilliant prospects, his liberty, even, for the sake of principle, for the rights of the citizen."[61]

Dorr is an obscure figure today, but he remained prominent well after his death. For decades, newspapers outside of Rhode Island retold Dorr's story. It was the prism through which Americans understood some of the other constitutional crises we'll encounter. For many, he would always be a villain. One Maine newspaper in 1874 labelled him a "hot-headed [zealot]" and condemned him for "revolution and bloodshed." But for other Americans, he would always be a hero. That same year, one Michigan newspaper claimed that "by every principle of democracy, Dorr had the equity on his side." In 1912, Rhode Island's government came around to that view. That year, newspapers nationwide reported that it had built a monument to Dorr in Chepachet.[62]

Looking back almost two hundred years, we can see how easily the "Rhode Island Question" could have ended in calamity. Instead of being a scholarly lawyer, Dorr could have been a charismatic general who led a better disciplined and equipped militia. One of the cannons used in the attack on Rhode Island's armory could have discharged and the charter authorities' troops could have fired back. One of Dorr's men or one of the charter's militiamen might have fired a gun on accident at Chepachet and the other side could have responded in kind. President Tyler might have ordered federal troops to intervene and volunteers to the suffragist cause from other states might have materialized. Suppose, then, that one of those federal soldiers accidentally shot at Dorr's militia and one of Dorr's soldiers, inspired by Dorr's call to defy the federal government, fired back. The "national contest" Dorr described might have become a reality. In none of these scenarios is it easy to imagine Dorr prevailing. But in none of them is it difficult to imagine terrible bloodshed.

Above all, Dorr left difficult questions for his contemporaries and for us. He fought for the principle that the people—however defined—can implement their constitutional vision without working through existing political institutions. That principle can be used for good or ill. As I will discuss next chapter, antislavery Kansans self-consciously followed Dorr's example when they wrote a constitution in defiance of both federal and state authority. But, as we will see in part 2, southern rebels also made arguments like Dorr's. They cited a fundamental right to alter or amend government, raised an army, and sought the ultimate constitutional change: dissolving the US Constitution. None other than John Tyler supported their efforts. He advocated in favor of secession at Virginia's convention considering whether to leave the Union, served in the Confederate Congress, and became the only American president to be given a state funeral by an enemy of the United States.[63] We must ask whether society can really function the way Dorr envisioned. Can governments have the necessary stability if people can ignore the established political process and overthrow it at will? On the other side, it reflects poorly on Rhode Island that so many citizens had given up on the political process as a viable method of change that they felt compelled to hold an extralegal constitutional convention and form a militia to implement the constitution it produced. Politicians have frequently used constitutions to entrench their power and thwart reform. When they do so, they pose another question: is the only path toward constitutional reform the one walked by Dorr so many years ago?

3

Bleeding Kansas and a Parade of Constitutions

In 1855, Free-Staters wanted to write a constitution to keep slavery out of Kansas. To do so, they would have to fight a war against foes intent on killing them and destroying their towns while standing up to two presidents of the United States and the might of the federal government. History sometimes has a way of summoning just the right leaders to overcome such long odds. The American Revolution brought forth George Washington. In a moment that called for similar strength of character and leadership ability, Free-Staters got Charles Robinson and James Lane. Both had fled to Kansas after spending time in jail in other states.

A year earlier, due in large part to US Senator Stephen Douglas of Illinois, Congress passed the Kansas-Nebraska Act. Instead of declaring states above a certain latitude free, as had been the case under the compromise of 1820, the legislation emphasized popular sovereignty as the solution to the divisive question of whether a new territory would permit slavery. The people of the Kansas and Nebraska territories themselves would vote on what to do. The result, Douglas promised, would be that "slavery agitation should be banished from the halls of Congress and cease to be an exciting element in our political struggles."[1] Reaction to the Kansas-Nebraska Act divided along sectional lines.

David Atchison best represented the southern view and would ultimately go to Kansas to promote it. Atchison was clean-shaven and had thick, flowing hair. He represented Missouri in the US Senate for twelve years. He wrote, "If Kansas is abolitionized Missouri ceases to be a slave State, and New Mexico becomes a free State, California remains a free State." On the other hand, "If we secure Kansas as a Slave State, Missouri is secure, New Mexico, and Southern California, if not all of it, become Slave States; in a word, the prosperity or the ruin of the whole South depends on the Kansas struggle." After leaving the US Senate, Atchison did everything he could to protect slaveholder liberty. At one point, he even threatened to "*hang every Abolitionist that dared to show his face*" in the territory.[2] For Missourians like Atchison, the stakes were even higher than they were for other Southerners. If neighboring Kansas became a free state, Missouri slaves might be more likely to run away. Slave property would become much more precarious.

Abraham Lincoln, who would owe his rise to national prominence in part to constitutional instability in Kansas, best represented the northern consensus. In his Peoria speech in October 1854, Lincoln argued that the Kansas-Nebraska Act was "wrong in its direct effect, letting slavery into Kansas and Nebraska" and predicted that the act would allow slavery "to spread to every other part of the wide world, where men can be found inclined to take it." Anticipating objections antislavery Kansans would later make, Lincoln also argued that permitting slavery there would simultaneously disadvantage poor white workers and betray the promises of the Declaration of Independence.[3]

Kansas became the principal battleground for the nation's cold war over slavery. For Kansans, that war quickly became hot. Amid conflict between organized militia groups, both proslavery and antislavery Kansans turned to constitutions as a weapon to end the fight on their terms. But the bitter conflict ensured that Kansans failed to form a stable consensus on even the most basic constitutional questions. Who gets to write a constitution? What is the process to ratify it? Does Kansas have a constitution? If so, which of several is actually in force? Which, if any, actually represents the will of most Kansans? Who is the government and is it legitimate?

Southern Attempts to Dominate Kansas

Southerners could initially expect popular sovereignty to benefit them—if they acted quickly. By early 1855, there were 8,000 white settlers and 192 slaves. About 50 percent of settlers came from Missouri and another 7 percent came from other Southern states. Only about a third were from Northern states. But that ratio was changing. Free states in 1850 had almost 60 percent of America's population and many of those states were densely populated. Free states tended to contain more people who would have an incentive to settle in Kansas.[4] At the same time, vast portions of the South remained sparsely populated, meaning that many slaveowners would move to Mississippi, Texas, and Arkansas before they went to Kansas.

This population disparity helps explain why Northern states more aggressively encouraged immigration to Kansas. The New England Emigrant Aid Society (NEEAC) carried out the most prominent effort. The group's founder, Eli Thayer, believed that emigration from Massachusetts and other northern states could make Kansas a free state. Massachusetts's governor signed NEEAC's charter, and it had plenty of money. In addition to helping settlers move to Kansas, NEEAC helped provide weapons.[5]

Charles Robinson came to Kansas as a NEEAC agent. Robinson grew up in Massachusetts and practiced medicine there for many years. He moved to California after the gold rush and was indicted for murder; one newspaper later claimed that he had "knock[ed] out a sleeping man's brains with a bar of iron." While imprisoned and awaiting trial, he won election to the California legislature. Fortunately for him, he was not convicted. When he moved to Kansas, Robinson immediately became one of the two most important men in the Free-State movement. His life story spurred curiosity, and as a man who was "tall, well-proportioned, [and] commanding in appearance," he had the bearing of a leader. He could be intimidating, for a contemporary wrote that he had "cold, keen blue eyes that seem to look you through."[6]

For their part, Southerners complained that NEEAC settlers were "picked up and culled from the ignorant masses which Old England and New England negro philanthropy has stirred up and aroused to madness on this topic." These "masses" allegedly constituted a "Hessian band of mercenaries" who intended to "commence and carry on a war of extermination against Slavery." In calling New Englanders "Hessians," southerners deliberately invoked the German mercenaries the British used during the American Revolution whom the Declaration of Independence condemned for "cruelty & perfidy scarcely paralleled in the most barbarous ages." New England immigrants were tyrants and southern slaveholders were the founding fathers bravely resisting them. Though these New Englanders earned an outsized amount of southern ire, many northern settlers also came from midwestern states.[7]

To secure control before northerners could shift Kansas's demographics, proslavery advocates pressured the territory's governor, Andrew Reeder, into scheduling legislative elections as soon as possible. Reeder obliged by calling elections for March 30, 1855.[8] The promise of popular sovereignty was that laws for Kansas would be made by Kansans. But that presupposed agreement about who was a Kansan. Since 1776, state constitutions had tried to ensure that voters had a real "attachment to the community." That is why, by the 1850s, constitutions commonly required individuals to live in the state for at least six months before they could vote. Consistent with this consensus, Reeder ordered election judges to "reject the votes of all non-residents, who I shall believe have come into [Kansas] for the same purpose of voting."[9] But, this presented two problems. First, determining whether someone was a true Kansas resident was difficult because it was such a new territory. By definition, most of those attempting to vote would have ties both to Kansas and the states they came from. Requiring residency for six months before individuals could vote would disenfranchise many people who had recently come to the territory and genuinely intended to stay. Second, it would be practically impossible to decide whether every potential voter really had come to Kansas just to vote. Was it enough to ask a potential voter why they had come to Kansas? Was the election judge supposed to carry out an investigation? And who would ensure any such investigation was fair?

In any event, some immigrants intended to defy Reeder's proclamation. Missourians argued they had a right to do so because the upcoming election would decide "whether the government of this Territory shall be given over to the hands of Abolitionists and Negro Thieves, or to the true and honest men of the South." Northerners opposed to slavery understood the stakes as well. That is why a merchant observed northerners coming into his store with only a "carpet-sack and blanket" purchasing goods to use temporarily in Kansas, and then reselling those goods to him on their way out of Kansas.[10] Although both sides were willing to take votes from non-Kansans, slavery supporters benefited more from the practice. Many Missourians could cross the border to vote and return home the same day. But northerners would have to travel for days, if not weeks, to get to Kansas. That reality made a journey to Kansas just to vote in one election more unappealing for northerners than it was for Missourians.

On March 30, 1855, a combination of fraud, violence, and intimidation brought victory to proslavery forces. Missourians descended upon Kansas in large numbers. The *Herald of Freedom* reported that two hundred

Missourians went to one polling place "with the view of overbalancing the large number of free voters in that district." The whole time, they "expressed a determination to return to Missouri as soon as the election was over." Another district, which had only 369 voters according to the most recent census, recorded 1,039 votes. In other places, Missourians forcibly removed election judges who tried to prevent shenanigans. When one judge continued to resist, "a pistol was three times snapped in his face, and a club flourished over his head." When the judge still refused to resign and closed the poll to prevent Missourians from illegally voting, "the mob then selected a new board, with two drunken secretaries, who took possession of the ballot-box, and allowed no person to approach it unless he was right on the 'goose question,' a slang phrase used among the Missourians" implying they favored extending slavery to Kansas. Such behavior helped earn Missourians active in Kansas affairs the derisive nickname "Border Ruffians." In this atmosphere, many antislavery men refused to vote.[11]

Reeder had to decide what to do with the results. Reeder grew up in Pennsylvania and was a successful lawyer there. But as governor, he faced accusations of corruption for speculating in Native American lands. Critics referred to him as "Squire Reeder" instead of "Governor Reeder." In this case, however, Reeder demonstrated integrity. He called new elections for several districts where there had been widespread complaints. In a speech in Pennsylvania, he acknowledged that "the conduct of the people on the border counties of Missouri had astounded and amazed him by their reckless disregard of all laws, compacts and constitutions."[12] Outraged by these remarks, Benjamin Stringfellow, publisher of the proslavery *Squatter Sovereign*, went to Reeder's office and knocked him to the floor. In the altercation, the two pulled pistols on each other before officials could drag Stringfellow away. Even after the new elections, a proslavery majority remained. It began expulsion proceedings against the few antislavery legislators. Ultimately, those men resigned after seeing their cause was hopeless.[13]

The territorial legislature consolidated power and strengthened slavery. Over Reeder's veto, it moved the capital from Pawnee to Shawnee Methodist Mission, which was right on the border with Missouri. Putting the capital there would make it even easier for Missourians to influence Kansas politics. The legislature passed a slave code and then took measures to protect slave property. It imposed capital punishment on anyone helping a slave leave Kansas to get their freedom. It imposed a felony conviction and at least a five-year prison sentence on people who wrote, published, or circulated materials that were "calculated to produce a disorderly, dangerous, or rebellious disaffection among the slaves in this Territory, or to induce such slaves to escape from the service of their masters, or to resist their authority." The legislature hoped these laws would attract southern immigration. The *Leavenworth Herald* bragged that "the triumph of the Proslavery party is complete and overwhelming." It implored: "Come on, Southern men! Bring your slaves and fill up the Territory. Kansas is saved!"[14]

Beginning to view Reeder as an adversary, the legislature petitioned President Franklin Pierce to remove him.[15] The request was granted.

The Topeka Constitution

Elections seldom put an end to deep philosophical disagreements. This is especially true when the losing side genuinely believes that the winning side cheated its way to victory and that it faces oppression. Free-Staters therefore derided the territorial legislature as "the bogus legislature." They decried the laws "passed, and now attempted to be enforced by the aid of citizens of foreign States [as being] of the most oppressive, tyrannical, and insulting character." Their grievances were legitimate, but their options to redress them were limited. There was no realistic prospect of the legislature repealing proslavery laws it had just passed. Given their proslavery bent, courts were unlikely to protect the constitutional rights of antislavery Kansans.[16]

Free-Staters could only protect their interests by working outside the established political process. In short order, they called an extralegal constitutional convention. They regarded Thomas Dorr as both an inspiration and a warning. Free-Staters echoed his reasoning when they asserted that "the people of this country have heretofore exercised the right of changing their form of government when it became oppressive, and have at all times conceded this right to the people in this and all other governments." In linking their cause with Dorr, they defended his actions in large part. The *Herald of Freedom* even described him as "Gov. Dorr," suggesting a belief that he had actually been Rhode Island's rightful governor. But Dorr's fate wasn't encouraging. The *Herald of Freedom* acknowledged that "Gov. Dorr, and his party, were crushed out." He had been "ousted, thrown into prison, and finally convicted of high treason against the State." The only way to avoid this outcome was for the new government not to "come in conflict with the Territorial organization."[17] That left a critical question hanging over the convention: how would the territorial government react?

With the future uncertain, Free-Staters met in Topeka. As president of their convention, they chose James Lane, who was destined to become Robinson's rival for leadership of the Free-State movement. Lane was athletic and had a thin, clean-shaven face. He was the son of a prominent Indiana politician and was a lawyer with a penchant for breaking the law. He had served as colonel of an Indiana regiment during the Mexican War and was proud of his combat record. Upon returning to Indiana, he served in the state legislature and as lieutenant governor before winning election to the US House of Representatives. Once there, he initially opposed the Kansas-Nebraska Act before deciding to support it. One writer claimed that he was "illiterate, profane, and an adept at the use of slang phrases" who could "make you weep or laugh at his pleasure." Throughout his life, Lane demonstrated a short temper. In Indiana, he was fined $100 and briefly imprisoned for challenging another man to a duel. According to Robinson, Lane even challenged another delegate to a duel in Topeka. Lane's critics also charged that he had gone to Kansas to fulfill his ambition to become a US senator after his support of the Kansas-Nebraska Act made that impossible in Indiana.[18]

Delegates primarily broke into two factions: radical and conservative. The two groups even met separately at the beginning of the convention. Radicals were willing to use force to confront the territorial and federal government, while conservatives wished to avoid that. Aside from this basic division, delegates also disagreed on other fundamental questions.[19]

Nonetheless, they quickly agreed on a definition of the "people" that excluded Black and Native American people as surely as it excluded Border Ruffians. Although a few delegates had supported Black men voting, the Topeka Constitution restricted suffrage to white males over twenty-one and "every civilized male Indian [over age twenty-one] who has adopted the habits of the white man." Delegates limited the militia to white men. To prevent Missourians from pouring in to swing future elections, delegates provided that voters had to reside in Kansas for at least six months prior to the election.

Delegates excluded slavery from Kansas. They did so not primarily out of concern for slave liberty, but to secure their own liberty from slaveholders and Black people. Although a few delegates were ardent abolitionists, many others "were indifferent to the question of slavery and had been driven to act with the Free-State party because of the invasion of their own political and civil rights." In fact, Robinson alleged that Lane tried to buy a slave before the convention, and had "said in his first public speech at Lawrence he had as soon buy a 'nigger' as a mule." Most delegates were hostile to slavery because they believed it reduced "the laboring white man, who must everywhere constitute the great proportion of mankind, in the estimation of those who are not engaged in physical labor, to the same scale of admeasurement upon which the slave, alike with himself, receives his proportion according to his adaptation to physical labor." They didn't want white workers to "incur poverty, and even resort to clandestine means of subsistence, rather than incur the taunts and sneers of negro-owners, and negroes themselves, of being a 'poor white man.'" These sentiments explain why many delegates argued in favor of barring free Black people from Kansas; a popular referendum on the subject later passed.

To immunize its definitions of "the people" and "liberty" from change, the Topeka Constitution prohibited any constitutional amendments or conventions before 1865. Slaveholders seeing no realistic chance to change the law would be dissuaded from coming to Kansas, which would lead to a bigger Free-State majority over time. Free Black people would see no realistic possibility of finding equality in Kansas and choose to settle in other states like Massachusetts that permitted them to vote. Kansans would be free from both Black people and slaveholders. The delegates scheduled a ratification vote for December.[20]

As they left Topeka, crucial questions awaited them. How would Americans from other states view their work? Would the federal government intervene against them? Would territorial officials? There were ominous signs. A Missouri newspaper called the Topeka Constitution "A Revolution at Hand on Mexican Principles!" Closer to home, opponents invoked Dorr, though they wished to play the role of Samuel Ward King.

Perhaps inspired by his example, they called themselves the Law and Order Party. Reflecting their legal views, John Calhoun, a prominent proslavery Kansan, acknowledged that "'Tis the doctrine of the Declaration of Independence; 'tis the great charter of American freemen that the people have the right to rule." But then he argued that "if the laws are unconstitutional they must be repealed at the proper tribunal."[21] Of course, he refused to acknowledge that "the proper tribunals" were all hostile to Free-Staters.

Both Free-Staters and territorial government supporters adopted their positions on the proper way to make constitutions as much out of expediency as they did out of conviction. Some Free-Staters probably did share Dorr's conviction that the people could make a constitution without permission from existing political institutions. But others followed Dorr's path for a more practical reason: it was their only chance at political power. The legislature would never agree to call a constitutional convention that put slaveholder liberty at risk. Similarly, some slaveholders doubtless believed that Dorr's constitutional vision was dangerous and supported suppressing it in 1842. But others took the same position as People's Constitution opponents merely to preserve their power. Ask yourself what would have happened if Free-Staters had won a legislative majority earlier in 1855 and abolished slavery in Kansas. Would they have embraced the position that proslavery Kansans had a right to call an unsanctioned constitutional convention and put the resulting government in place? Conversely, would proslavery Kansans have embraced the position that only a legislature hostile to them could call a constitutional convention?

Territorial Government Response

The territorial government tried to suppress the Free-Staters before they could vote on the Topeka Constitution. By December of 1855, thousands of armed men stood ready to invade the unofficial Free-State capital of Lawrence. The need to recapture an escaped fugitive gave them the perfect excuse. In November of 1855, a Missourian killed a Free-Stater amid a dispute about who had title to certain lands. Armed Free-Staters worked to avenge the death. They burned the houses of two proslavery men and instructed several women to leave. Sheriff Samuel Jones arrested the ringleader, but some Free-State militia freed him and escorted him to Lawrence. In response, Jones asked Territorial Governor Wilson Shannon for military aid, which Shannon provided. Missourians began pouring into Kansas. Their real motivation was to crush the Free-State movement. One man testified before Congress that "several of them said they had come to serve Governor Shannon, if he would let them, and if not they would do their duty anyhow." Over one thousand Missourians established camp on the Wakarusa River. They brought weapons from Missouri's state arsenal to use in their attack on Lawrence.[22]

Lawrence responded by establishing a Committee of Public Safety, deliberately invoking the patriots who used groups of the same name to resist English rule prior to the American Revolution. The committee formed a regiment and appointed Robinson commander in chief and Lane colonel. The regiment had around eight hundred soldiers and two cannons. In addition, the *Herald of Freedom* noted that "many of the women were determined on shouldering the musket and fighting for their homes, and all they held dear."[23]

Major fighting appeared imminent after Free-Stater Thomas Barber died. He had ridden a few miles east of Lawrence when proslavery men ordered him to surrender. He refused and they shot him. The *Herald of Freedom* reported that when his body was brought into the Free State Hotel, "those who looked upon his cold and ghastly form pledged themselves anew before heaven that they would drive the demon, who could commit such barbarities in the name of law, from the Territory, or they would die in the attempt." In a eulogy, Robinson declared Barber "a [martyr] of freedom" and called for building a monument to him.[24]

Tensions increased even further when John Brown arrived in Kansas with his four sons and a stockpile of weapons. Brown descended from New England Puritans and lived like it. He was so strict about observing the sabbath that he forbade his children from playing on Sundays. Thin and wiry with a rugged appearance and a penetrating gaze, he looked the part of a minister telling worshippers they were sinners in the hands of an angry God. Brown developed a deep hatred of slavery as a youth when he watched an enslaved boy cruelly treated during the War of 1812. From that point one writer claimed, Brown "swore eternal war with slavery." It was therefore fitting that Free-Staters put Brown in charge of a militia company. He would become a major reason Americans spoke of Bleeding Kansas in the 1850s.[25]

Fortunately, negotiations began before widespread fighting erupted. Shannon met with Robinson and Lane. He "expressed regret that the people of Missouri were here in such numbers" and fretted that "he could not control them." Initially, Shannon demanded that Free-Staters recognize the territorial legislature's authority but chose not to press the issue when they refused. The negotiations ultimately resulted in a treaty where Lawrence pledged to help enforce the law against anyone Sheriff Jones was trying to arrest, but again refused to obey the territorial legislature. If Robinson is to be believed, at a peace party celebrating the end of hostilities, Lane proposed attacking the proslavery militia and "tried his best to procure the killing of Jones" which "would have opened the war in earnest."[26] No such attack was ever carried out. In the end, only Barber died during what became known as the Wakarusa War.

Bleeding Kansas Embroils a Nation

Free-Staters continued to defy the territorial government. After the peace treaty, in an election boycotted by proslavery men, Free-Staters voted to ratify the Topeka Constitution on December 15, 1855. They also scheduled elections for officials including the governor, supreme court judges, members of the legislature, and a delegate to Congress for January 1856. The territorial legislature forbade these elections. Free-Staters held them anyway and selected Robinson as governor. Any euphoria was short-lived.[27] On January 24, 1856, President Franklin Pierce claimed that what the Free-State movement had done "[was] of revolutionary character"—and he didn't mean it as a compliment. He declared that Free-Staters would be guilty of "treasonable insurrection" if they organized resistance against the federal government. On February 11, 1856, he threatened to send federal troops if Free-Staters didn't "disperse and retire peaceably to their respective abodes." They refused.[28]

Instead, Kansas would have two governments for the next three years. As 1856 unfolded, both governments pursued statehood. Both found support and opposition in Congress. Free-Staters had powerful champions in William Seward and Charles Sumner. But their petition for statehood hit a snag when it was revealed that the signatures on it were all in Lane's handwriting. After Stephen Douglas called the petition fraudulent, Lane challenged him to a duel, which Douglas declined. Ultimately, Congress refused to admit Kansas under the Topeka Constitution. However, Congress also failed to pass Douglas's bill to grant Kansas statehood under the proslavery territorial legislature.[29]

During the debate over whether to admit Kansas under the Topeka Constitution, the infamous caning of Charles Sumner happened. On May 19 and 20, 1856, almost as if channeling Dorr, Sumner argued that the Free-Staters had merely been faithful to the Declaration of Independence. He emphasized that "government is recognized as deriving its just powers only *from the consent of the governed*, who may alter or abolish it when it becomes destructive of their rights." What garnered the most attention was not his scholarly defense of the Free-State movement. It was his denunciation of Andrew Butler. His voice dripping with disdain, Sumner said that "the senator from South Carolina has read many books of chivalry, and believes himself a chivalrous knight, with sentiments of honor and courage." But that was delusional because Butler had "chosen a mistress to whom he has made his vows, and who, though ugly to others, is always lovely to him; though polluted in the sight of the world, is chaste in his sight—I mean the harlot Slavery."[30] Days later, Preston Brooks, a relative of Butler, came into the US Senate building. Waiting until the chamber emptied, he walked up to Sumner and accused him of publishing a "libel on my State" and of making "a slander upon a relative, who is aged and absent, and I am come to punish you." Brooks pummeled Sumner with a cane and "continued striking him right and left until the stick was broken into fragments, and Mr. Sumner was prostrate and bleeding on the floor."[31]

The situation was no more peaceful in Kansas. The territorial government renewed its attempt to destroy the Free-State movement. In April 1856, Sheriff Jones attempted to arrest a Lawrence man involved in the trouble that helped trigger the Wakarusa War. Jones failed, and got shot for his trouble. The incident gave the territorial government the pretext to commence another attack on Lawrence. By May, a territorial grand jury indicted Free-State officers and members of the Free-State legislature for high treason. The same grand jury also declared the *Herald of Freedom* and *Kansas Free State* to be nuisances. Robinson attempted to flee but was captured.

Soon, a proslavery army formed outside Lawrence. They carried a flag that said "Southern Rights" on one side and "South Carolina" on the other. In a speech to them, Atchison allegedly identified himself as a "border ruffian" and, to repeated cries and yells, asked, "Will every one of you swear to bathe your steal in the black blood of some of those black sons of—?" He then allegedly added, "I know you will never fail, but will burn, sack & destroy until every visage of these Northern Abolitionists is wiped out."[32]

Whether out of fear that they would lose a battle or a desire for the rest of America to see them as righteous victims, Lawrence's Committee of Public Safety resolved to offer no resistance. Healed from his wounds, Jones ordered Lawrence to surrender its arms and gave an ultimatum that if this weren't done in five minutes, the proslavery men would fire cannons at the town. The Free-Staters gave up some artillery pieces, but kept their private sidearms. The proslavery men then sacked Lawrence. They destroyed the two newspapers declared to be nuisances and burned down the Free-State hotel.[33]

Optimists might have hoped this was the climax of the violence in Kansas, but it was merely the prelude to more. On May 25, 1856, a company of men saying they belonged to "the northern army" came to James Harris's house in Pottawatomie armed with swords and pistols. John Brown was among them. They ordered Harris and the other men to surrender, confiscated his rifles and bowie knife, and ransacked the house for ammunition. They interrogated the men and eventually shot William Sherman dead. Testimony before Congress revealed that "Sherman's skull was split open in two places and some of his brains was washed out by the water. A large hole was cut in his breast, and his left hand was cut off except a little piece of skin on one side." In all, four men died that night. Brown insisted that he didn't personally kill any of them, but added that "I do not pretend to say that they were not killed by my order, and in doing so I believe I was doing God's service."[34]

Whether Brown hurt or helped the Free-State cause has generated debate ever since. Robinson himself best articulated the differing views. In 1873, he wrote the killing had "the effect of a clap of thunder from a clear sky. The slave men stood aghast. The officials were frightened. This was a new move on the part of the supposed subdued free men. This was a warfare they were not prepared to wage, as of the *bona fide* settlers there

were four free to one slave man."[35] In 1856, some Free-Staters undoubt-
edly believed Brown had exacted justified vengeance for what proslavery
forces did to Lawrence. Some proslavery men saw what Brown had done
and realized they had better think twice about persecuting Free-Staters
for fear of suffering the same fate as William Sherman.

Later though, Robinson claimed that "this blow [in Pottawatomie]
was not struck to punish criminals, or protect Free-State men, or to aid
in the cause of free Kansas, but to involve the sections, North and South,
in war."[36] Whatever Brown's true motivations, Free-State and proslavery
militia groups spent the next several years fighting.

After the Pottawatomie massacre, more radical Free-Staters began a
summer counteroffensive. In August 1856, Brown led forces to attack
proslavery settlements across the territory. They killed several men
and burned houses and farm equipment. This culminated in a bold as-
sault on August 16, 1856, that must have felt like sweet revenge. They
surrounded a proslavery fort and bombarded it with a cannon. With
the first shot, an officer cried, "This is the second edition of the 'Herald of Freedom.' How do you like it?" When the proslavery force flew
the white flag of surrender after suffering two dead and three wounded,
Free-Staters took as many as thirty-four prisoners. They were confined
in Lawrence in the same building out of which the destroyed *Herald of
Freedom* had operated.[37]

Proslavery forces retaliated. About four hundred of them encircled
Osawatomie on August 30, 1856. While Brown's men were eating break-
fast, the proslavery men attacked. Brown ordered his men to form a skirmishing line and engage the enemy. After two Free-Staters died in an
exchange of gunfire, Brown's men retreated, taking four more casualties
as they withdrew. One of them was Brown's son Frederick. Proslavery men
burned the town, sparing only one house where a sick family was unable
to leave. Though this was both a defeat and a tragedy for Brown, he earned
praise from northerners for his courage and coolness under fire. Years
later, US Senator John Ingalls of Kansas wrote that the Battle of Osawatomie was "our Thermopylae, and John Brown was our Leonidas, with his
Spartan band." Americans well-versed in classical history would have
viewed the comparison as a compliment. In ancient Greece as legend had
it, three hundred Spartan warriors led by King Leonidas bravely fought for
four days against a million Persian invaders before they all died.[38]

In Kansas meanwhile, the death count kept going up. By the end of 1856, as many as thirty-eight men had died. The deteriorating situation attracted national media attention. At the end of August 1856, the *New York Herald* lamented that "civil war exists in Kansas." Lest that sound exaggerated, the paper observed that "belligerents are arrayed against each other, fight each other, and treat for the exchange of prisoners according to the usages of a regular war" and compared the conflict to the one between Russia and allied powers in the Crimean War. It predicted that "the contagion of the war will be carried like an epidemic, and more rapidly, into the neighboring States, North and South."[39]

While fighting raged, the Free-State legislature planned to meet on July 4, 1856. In addition to linking their actions with the American Revolution, Free-Staters again imitated Dorr. The same day fourteen years earlier, Dorr had called the People's legislature into session at Chepachet. Daniel Woodson, temporarily serving as acting governor, commanded the Free-State legislature not to meet. It ignored him.

Then US troops showed up under Col. Edwin Sumner. Sumner had refused to intervene during the Buckshot War. But he had different orders this time. After informing the Free-State legislators that he acted at President Pierce's behest, he told them to disperse. Lest there be any thought of resistance, he explained that he would carry out his orders "even if it should demand the employment of all the forces in his command." Sumner took no joy in this. In fact, he described his duty as "the most painful of his life."[40] As a cousin of Charles Sumner, he must have lamented the irony that he was undermining the cause his celebrated relative had so vigorously championed.

Authorities eventually tried to bring down Robinson too. Although the treason charges were dropped in 1856, Robinson faced a fresh usurpation charge in 1857 for acting as governor. His trial raised two important questions for our purposes. First, who was Kansas's lawful government? If the Topeka Constitution were in force, then Robinson hadn't usurped anything. He had instead assumed the office to which he was legally entitled. Second, even if the Topeka Constitution weren't in force, had Robinson really usurped office? Although Free-Staters followed in Dorr's footsteps in many ways, there was a crucial distinction. Unlike Dorr, they had never tried to displace the government. They never carried out anything like Dorr's attack on Rhode Island's state arsenal. Perhaps at least in part because of these differences, a jury acquitted Robinson after deliberating all night.[41]

The Lecompton Constitution

In 1857, Kansas was in constitutional limbo. To escape it and strengthen their position, the territorial legislature called a constitutional convention.

Free-Staters refused to participate in delegate elections for two main reasons. First, they argued that the Topeka Constitution was still in force. In fact, one Free-State convention even resolved to "re-submit it to the people for ratification at the August election." Consistent with this position, Lawrence adopted its own charter that required town officials to swear to uphold the Topeka Constitution. It only backed down when Robert Walker, the latest territorial governor, appeared with militia outside Lawrence.[42] Second, Free-Staters didn't trust the election to be fair. Another Free-State convention concluded that the act calling the convention "is partisan in its character, clearly contemplates fraud, for the recurrence of which it offers inadequate security." The concerns were well-founded. The census used to allocate delegates favored proslavery counties. In the end, only about two thousand Kansans—one-fourth of the registered voters and one-tenth of the adult males—voted to call a convention.[43]

The resulting convention, held in Lecompton, was therefore proslavery. Most delegates described themselves as "Democrats," but others described themselves as "nullifiers," "Pro-Slavery," or "Ultra Southern Rights." Free-Staters denounced the convention as a "conclave of broken-down political hacks, demagogues, fire-eaters, perjurers, ruffians, ballot-box stuffers, and loafers" that constituted a "Traitors' Convention." They also excoriated individual members. John Calhoun, the convention's president, received special condemnation. He was a friend of both Abraham Lincoln and Stephen Douglas. But Free-Staters claimed that as surveyor general of Kansas and Nebraska, "his principal aim has been to advance ruffianism, annoy the Free State men, drink bad liquor and do the smallest amount of work possible." Even his looks were fair game for criticism. The *Kanzas News* claimed that "once in his life he might have been good looking, but the sensual, bullying, brandy-hued visage he now shows has but little title to anything in the shape of beauty."[44]

As delegates met, rumors swirled that Free-Staters would disrupt proceedings. Robinson claimed that Lane had formed a secret order and had proposed to "make war upon the convention and prevent the making of the constitution." A correspondent for the *New York Tribune* corroborated the story in large part, writing in his diary that "General Lane has ordered the Free-State forces of the Territory to assemble on Monday next, with arms and three days' supply of provisions, the purpose of which is to march on Lecompton and kill every member of the Constitutional Convention." If Lane did intend to break up the convention, he never followed through. The convention adjourned after four days pending the results of an election for the legislature and representative to Congress. The only progress it made was to select committees and convention officers. Perhaps somewhat surprisingly, Free-Staters agreed to participate in the legislative elections. Some may have believed Walker's promise of a fair election. Others probably calculated that they had a better chance of advancing their cause by capturing the territorial government than they did by trying to implement the Topeka Constitution.[45]

The October election predictably elicited allegations of fraud. Free-Staters won a majority of both houses of the legislature after Walker rejected some of the returns as fraudulent. A Kansas Supreme Court justice attempted to force Walker to issue certificates of election to proslavery men, but Walker refused. Free-Staters would be in control when the legislature entered its next session. For some proslavery men, the writing was on the wall: Kansas was destined to be a free state, especially since northern immigration by this point far outstripped southern immigration. But that writing was apparently invisible to the delegates in Lecompton. They resumed their convention amid the turmoil. When a group of Free-Staters came to protest, delegates feared that they had come "to break up the Constitutional Convention, by force." They responded by asking for US troops to protect them and their request was granted. In early November, the *Herald of Freedom* estimated that almost one thousand troops armed with artillery were guarding the convention.[46]

With security in place, delegates drafted a constitution. It went without saying that they refused to consider Black people as part of "the people" and excluded them from voting. But their most important goals were to secure slaveholder liberty and tie the hands of a legislature that would be hostile to their worldview. Some Americans today speak of certain Supreme Court decisions as "super precedents." Proslavery delegates believed that slavery was a super right. They claimed that "the right of property is before and higher than any constitutional sanction, and the right of the owner of a slave to such slave and its increase is the same, and as inviolable as the right of the owner of any property whatever." Recognizing that Free-Staters would run the territorial legislature, delegates prohibited it from emancipating slaves without their owners' consent and without compensating the owners. They also banned the legislature from preventing owners immigrating to Kansas with their slaves. Just as Free-Staters had, delegates banned free Black people from Kansas. The fact that they placed this prohibition in the Bill of Rights alongside guarantees to religious freedom and jury trials is telling. Ensuring that free Black people couldn't poison the minds of slaves was deemed essential to slaveholder liberty. To make their stance toward Black people even clearer, delegates insisted, as Virginia slaveholders had when revising George Mason's original Bill of Rights, that only "freemen" were equal.

Once the Lecompton Constitution was in place, change would be impossible. It forbade any amendments until 1864. Even then, it provided that "no alteration shall be made to affect the rights of property in the ownership of slaves." But why would a majority of voters, which by then wanted to prohibit slavery, ever ratify such a document? Delegates puzzled over this question before coming to an ingenious, if disingenuous solution. Instead of offering an up-or-down vote on the whole constitution, delegates would offer a choice between having the Lecompton Constitution with slavery or without slavery. But this "choice" was really an illusion. If Kansas voters chose the Lecompton Constitution without slavery, the only thing that would change would be that slaveholders from outside Kansas theoretically couldn't move there with slaves after ratification. The constitution wouldn't abolish slavery for slaves already there. And, the US Supreme Court might interfere with even this minimal limitation on slavery. Earlier in 1857, in *Dred Scott v. Sandford*, the US Supreme Court found that Congress couldn't restrict slavery in the territories because doing so violated a master's Fifth Amendment right to property.[47] If Congress couldn't prevent masters from bringing their slaves to a territory, could a territorial constitution? The Supreme Court might say "No." In that case, slavery would flourish in Kansas despite the wishes of most Kansans.

Flipping the Dorr script, Free-Staters compared the Lecompton delegates to Catiline and suggested *they* were the demagogues and insurrectionists. Free-Staters also complained that Lecompton delegates had "used the slave-driver's whip so long on Southern plantations, that they have fallen into the belief that all mankind can be driven as easily as the poor, degraded African race, whose liberty they have stolen, and whose hard earnings they have daily filched, and they would now attempt to whip freemen into a meek submission to their will."[48] While comparing their situation to that of slaves was excessive, they had a point that it was unfair for a constitutional convention to circumvent voters in this way. Yet, there was no consensus in the nineteenth century that a constitution had to be submitted to a popular vote. One renowned scholar of constitutional conventions rejected the idea "that the submission of a constitution to a vote of the people is imperatively required by some customary constitutional law of this country." Indeed, out of the original thirteen colonies which adopted constitutions during the American Revolution, only in Massachusetts and New Hampshire was there a binding ratification vote among the people.[49] President James Buchanan also defended the decision, citing the fact that the Kansas-Nebraska Act didn't require a popular ratification vote by its plain terms. Buchanan, it should be said, was eager to undermine the Free-State cause. In his first State of the Union message, he claimed the Free-Staters' "avowed object it was, if need be, to put down the lawful government by force and to establish a government of their own under the so-called Topeka constitution." Moreover, delegates faced outside pressure *not* to submit the Lecompton Constitution to a ratification vote from some quarters. A convention in one southern state complained that any "pledge to cause the Kansas constitution to be submitted to the people for ratification or rejection 'merits universal reprobation,' and is fraught with the rankest injustice to the South generally."[50]

Delegates scheduled the vote for the Lecompton Constitution with or without slavery on December 21, 1857. Free-Staters circulated rumors that "the Ruffians are coming over in large numbers to vote on the 21st, at the election on the Bogus Constitution." Ominously, the *Kanzas News* declared that "if an invasion is attempted, every Ruffian of them may find a last resting place on the soil he has desecrated by his presence." Another Free-Stater urged that "the free States must call their Legislatures at once together, remonstrate with the general Government, raise money, raise troops, and *by a loud demonstration cause the President to pause in his career.*" If that didn't happen, he predicted that "many a Spartan 'three hundred' can be found here to fill the pass, and who would infinitely prefer to fall, with arms in hand, to a shameful and ignominious existence." Perhaps John Brown would answer the call.[51]

Rather than fight, Free-Staters prevailed on Frederick Stanton, temporarily acting as governor in Walker's absence, to convene the territorial legislature. The legislature promptly called an election on January 4, 1858, where Kansans could vote on the Lecompton Constitution as a whole. That date coincided with elections under the Lecompton Constitution for the legislature, governor, and a member of Congress. At the same time, the legislature also passed a resolution seeking admission to the Union under the Topeka Constitution.[52]

Per usual, illegality and fraud marred the December 19, 1857, vote, and most Free-Staters boycotted. Still, proslavery forces could argue that Kansans had chosen the Lecompton Constitution with slavery. However, on January 4, 1858, those who voted overwhelmingly rejected the Lecompton Constitution.[53] The same basic question from 1855 lingered: did Kansas have a constitution or not?

Given their overwhelming turnout, Free-Staters also won elections for various offices under the Lecompton Constitution. Since the movement to implement the Topeka Constitution waned, this meant that Kansas potentially had an antislavery legislature and a proslavery constitution. From the federal government's perspective, the only redeeming feature of this arrangement was that the effort to put the Topeka Constitution in place ended. At least Kansas wouldn't have two separate governments. The legislature moved quickly to consolidate power. One of its first acts was to pass a bill placing Lane rather than Stanton over the territorial militia. According to Robinson, this increased the chances of conflict because Lane "became thirsty for blood and proposed a general massacre of pro-slavery men." Stanton vetoed the measure.[54]

Meanwhile, Congress had to decide whether to admit Kansas under the Lecompton Constitution.

The Leavenworth Constitution

Before Congress could make a decision, the territorial legislature passed a bill calling a constitutional convention. Legislators may have hoped a new constitution would convince Congress not to admit Kansas under the Lecompton Constitution. In a protest to Congress, the convention later argued that "the very existence of the Convention is conclusive evidence of the popular will."[55]

By this time, Kansas had yet another governor, James Denver. Denver vetoed the call for a convention, explaining, "I thought we had constitutions enough." Even Robinson agreed, and he didn't participate in the convention. Nonetheless, the legislature overrode the veto. Delegates met in Leavenworth. They were almost all from northern and midwestern states. Almost all identified either as Republican or Free-State.[56]

As the Topeka Constitution had done, the Leavenworth Constitution abolished slavery. In a contrast with the Lecompton Constitution, which held that "the right of property is before and higher than any constitutional sanction," the Leavenworth Constitution declared that "the right of all men to the control of their persons exists prior to law, and is inalienable." Lane, who may once have tried to purchase a slave, proposed adding this language after openly aligning himself with abolitionists. Unlike the Topeka Constitution, the Leavenworth Constitution made important strides toward Black equality in at least two ways. First, delegates rejected a proposal to segregate schools. Instead, the constitution simply provided for a "uniform system of common schools" that would "be open and free to every child in the State between the ages of five and twenty-one years." Almost a century before *Brown v. Board of Education*, the Iowa Supreme Court relied in part on similar language in the Iowa Constitution to find racially segregated schools unlawful. Second, delegates rejected a proposal to limit the franchise to "all white male citizens." Instead, the constitution permitted Black men to vote on whether to ratify it and required the legislature to hold a referendum on whether to permit Black men to vote going forward. Wyandot Native Americans could also vote. Delegates therefore embraced a broader definition of "the people."

Delegates broke from both the Topeka and Lecompton Constitutions by making their handiwork easier to change. Beginning in 1863, voters would be offered the chance to call a constitutional convention every ten years. As support for this choice, delegates could cite Jefferson. In a letter to Madison, Jefferson argued that "no society can make a perpetual constitution, or even a perpetual law" because "the earth belongs always to the living generation." As a result, Jefferson concluded that "every constitution then, & every law, naturally expires at the end of 19 years." Even today, many constitutions automatically give voters the choice to call constitutional conventions periodically. Surely, some Americans wish this were an option with the US Constitution even as others would dread the prospect.

The delegates also wrestled with the difficult question of what to do if Congress admitted Kansas under the Lecompton Constitution. When one man argued that it would be treasonous to implement the Leavenworth Constitution under those circumstances, he was met with cries of "treason then, let it be." Another delegate wisely suggested that Kansas could simply change constitutions once admitted. The legislature could ignore the Lecompton Constitution's prohibition on calling a constitutional convention until 1864. It could count on Free-Stater judges and executive officials to overrule any objections that such an action was unlawful. Moreover, there was no precedent for requiring Congress to approve new state constitutions, and there would be no such precedent until after the Civil War. In the eighteenth and nineteenth centuries, countless states had revised constitutions or adopted new ones without even a suggestion that there was a federal role in the process.

However, this strategy wasn't foolproof. Southerners were desperate to maintain a balance between slave and free states. They might take the position that once admitted under the Lecompton Constitution, Kansas must keep that constitution unless and until Congress approved a change. They would never have accepted that logic for themselves if they sought to, say, change the method of selecting judges in their own states. This is but another example of the slavery distortion that characterized the legal and political system during the era. Proslavery southerners were willing to undermine the very state sovereignty they would later cite as justification to secede from the Union.

The constitution was ratified after a "very light vote" where "few except those in favor of the Leavenworth Constitution, seemed to take interest enough in the matter to go to the polls." Antislavery Kansans then requested admission to the Union under the new constitution.[57]

While delegates were drafting the Leavenworth Constitution, Congress had been considering the Lecompton Constitution. The debate united the Republicans in opposition and divided the Democrats. It also brought rumblings of disunion from southerners when rapid approval for the Lecompton Constitution failed to materialize. One Alabama congressman threatened that if Kansas weren't admitted under the Lecompton Constitution, "secession must ensue, and he trusted Alabama would be the nucleus of a great Southern confederacy."[58] Free-Staters contemplated drastic measures of their own. Speaking for many, one Kansan called on Free-Staters to "swear before high Heaven that no earthly power shall force on us the Lecompton Constitution, until it has first been made the winding sheet of her freemen." Having exhausted peaceful ways to oppose the Lecompton Constitution, they were now justified in using force.[59] Congress managed to disappoint everyone and failed to admit Kansas under either constitution.

To retrieve the situation, Congressman William English offered Kansans a deal. They could receive four million acres in land if they voted to ratify the Lecompton Constitution with slavery. Refusing to ratify would mean forfeiting the land and admission to the Union until Kansas had 93,000 residents. On August 2, 1858, in the rare election that came and went without fraud or violence, Kansans decisively rejected the offer. Kansas still had no constitution.[60]

Kansas's constitutional crisis continued to affect national politics. Turmoil in the territory was discussed in *every* one of the seven famous Lincoln-Douglas debates. Douglas spent considerable time touting his opposition to the Lecompton Constitution and argued that his courageous stand had cost him politically. Lincoln would have no chance to oust him from the US Senate "were it not for the aid that he is receiving from Federal office-holders, who are using their influence and the patronage of the Government against me in revenge for my having defeated the Lecompton Constitution." Meanwhile Lincoln attacked the concept of popular sovereignty itself. The doctrine had promised to resolve the tensions over slavery. Yet, Lincoln taunted, "Is Kansas in the Union? Has she formed a Constitution that she is likely to come in under? Is not the slavery agitation still an open question in that Territory? Has the voting down of that Constitution put an end to all the trouble?" Members of the audience cried "No!"[61] Douglas narrowly won, but he was fatally weakened ahead of the 1860 presidential election. The debates transformed his rival Abraham Lincoln into a national star who could credibly compete for the presidency in 1860.

Kansas Finally Adopts a Constitution

The territorial legislature called another convention on March 4, 1859, and it was clear the resulting constitution would be less progressive on race than the Leavenworth Constitution had been. Only white males and Native Americans who were US citizens could vote for delegates.

Republicans and northerners dominated the convention. Absent from their ranks were both Robinson and Lane. Lane was briefly retired from politics after being acquitted of murder. What became known as the Wyandotte Constitution rejected Black equality and made sure Black people were not part of "the people." One delegate argued in vain that withholding the franchise from Black men was inconsistent with the section of the Bill of Rights that said all men are created equal. He was outvoted and the constitution permitted only white men to vote. Although this was a retreat from the Leavenworth Constitution, it was consistent with suffrage requirements in several other free states. At that point, only the New England states of Maine, Massachusetts, New Hampshire, Rhode Island, and Vermont allowed Black men to vote on the same terms as white men. Many delegates viewed the Indiana Constitution as a model when the convention began, and Indiana didn't let Black men vote at all. To emphasize that Black people weren't part of "the people," the Wyandotte Constitution also prevented Black men from serving in the militia. Foreshadowing some of the debates over reconstruction constitutions that will be covered in part 2, delegates rejected a petition for women's suffrage.[62]

Strategic considerations explain these choices in part. Supporters of the new constitution called the delegates "Apostles of Free Labor [who] work for the interests of the FREE WHITE MAN." No one could criticize the Wyandotte Constitution for racial radicalism because "the negro is an article in which they have no concern, and with which they do not propose to cumber the instrument they are drafting, for the glorious future of Kansas." At the end of the day, however, the *Herald of Freedom* found "little enthusiasm" for the Wyandotte Constitution.

Instead, many "who voted for the Constitution did so to put an end to the business of constitution making."[63] Nonetheless, Kansans voted to ratify in October 1859.

The path toward congressional approval was uncertain. Amid the intense focus on John Brown's raid into Harper's Ferry and subsequent execution for treason against Virginia, Congress delayed discussing the Wyandotte Constitution. When Congress did debate the new constitution, southern intransigence caused further delay. Then, Lincoln won the presidency in 1860, South Carolina seceded, and other southern states quickly followed. The nation was hurtling toward the Civil War. With southern representatives absent, Congress admitted Kansas under the Wyandotte Constitution in January 1861.[64] Years of constitutional crisis in Kansas were over, but that provided little comfort to most Americans. By then, they were in the midst of the worst constitutional crisis at the national level in American history. The Civil War had begun.

Aftermath of Bleeding Kansas

Kansans loyally supported the Union war effort. One of them was Powell Clayton. Clayton settled in Kansas amid the constitutional instability. His leadership of a Kansas regiment in the war led him to Arkansas, where he played a large role in the state's constitutional crisis that will be explored in part 2.

The two leading Free-Staters, Charles Robinson and James Lane, remained important figures in Kansas politics. Lane became a Union general. After Kansas's admission to the Union, he achieved his lifelong ambition of becoming a US senator. But as a man who had so relished violence, he came to a tragically violent end himself. He shot himself with a revolver in 1866 while experiencing a mental breakdown. Robinson fulfilled his long-standing goal of becoming governor. Any joy was short-lived. His long rivalry with Lane resulted in him becoming the first governor in American history to be impeached. Acquitted by the state senate, he served only one term in office. Though he had been a Republican for many years, he attempted a political comeback in 1890 as the Democratic candidate for governor. He lost and died soon after in 1894.[65]

During the 1850s in Kansas, disputes over constitutional ideals, factionalism, contested elections, and a willingness to use violence to achieve political ends had stewed in a cauldron and produced a terrible poison that infected the entire country. As we will see in part 2, Arkansas, South Carolina, and North Carolina would continue to drink that poison after the Civil War ended.

Part 2 Overview

While fighting raged during Kansas's constitutional crisis in the 1850s, the rest of the country engaged in an equally fierce contest over constitutional visions. Scholars have documented the debates over the relatively abstract question of whether the US Constitution was a proslavery or an antislavery document and the practically critical questions of whether the federal government had the authority to limit slavery and whether the US Constitution permitted secession. They have further recognized the Civil War as the worst constitutional crisis in American history.[1] Scholars have paid less attention to the significant role that debates over questions traditionally answered by state constitutions played in the process. In 1776, state constitutions took different positions on who "the people" were, how to define "liberty," and what the proper way to pursue constitutional change was. The Civil War therefore did not just result from different readings of the US Constitution. It was also a clash of state constitutions.

The South articulated a coherent constitutional theory while it put armies into the field. That theory rested on two fundamental premises: (1) the freedom to maintain white supremacy in every possible form, and (2) the right to use any means necessary to overthrow a constitutional order standing in the way of that objective. We might call this the spirit of 1861. Alexander Stephens's Cornerstone speech, the Confederate Constitution, and the secession ordinances southern states drafted upon leaving the Union best illustrate it. Stephens argued that slavery was morally right and that the founding fathers who had reservations about slavery's morality were wrong. While the Declaration of Independence said that "all men are created equal" and have an inherent right to "liberty," Stephens claimed the confederacy "was founded upon exactly the opposite idea; its foundations are laid, its corner-stone rests, upon the great truth that the negro is not equal to the white man; that slavery subordination to the superior race is his natural and normal condition." The confederacy, he proudly asserted, was the "first, in the history of the world, based upon this great physical, philosophical, and moral truth." The phrasing here is telling. The confederacy wasn't the first to recognize the alleged truth of Black inferiority—that distinction belonged to early state constitutions like Virginia's that embraced slaveholder liberty. But the confederacy broke new ground by making slaveholder liberty and Black subordination its very reason for being. The Confederate Constitution confirms Stephens's understanding of the proposed southern nation. When you read it, you would be forgiven for thinking that rebels had simply copied and pasted the US Constitution and replaced "United States" with "Confederate States." The Confederate Constitution's only real innovation—aside from giving the president a line item veto—was to explicitly mention slavery and clearly protect it.[2]

The secession ordinances imitated the Declaration of Independence in style. As the Declaration did, slaveholding southerners began by acknowledging that they were taking a momentous step, justified their decision with a core philosophical claim, listed specific grievances, and ended by defending their honor. The seceding states overwhelmingly listed maintaining slavery as the reason for their decision. Mississippi went so far as to say that slavery "is the greatest material interest in the world." Seceding states repeatedly complained about northern hostility to slavery which had manifested in all sorts of ways, from refusing to return fugitive slaves to electing Abraham Lincoln president. Slaveholders read Lincoln's statement from his famous "House Divided" speech that "government cannot endure permanently half slave, half free" as a threat to abolish slavery. Over and over again, the secession ordinances claimed that southern states were at risk of losing their liberty. By "liberty," they meant slaveholder liberty.

Losing slaves would mean more than losing valuable property. It would mean losing their definition of who "the people" were and, ultimately, their social status. South Carolina complained that some northern constitutions allowed Black men to vote, Mississippi claimed that the new Republican Party advocated "negro equality, socially and politically," and Texas believed Republicans demanded "the recognition of political equality between the white and negro races." This alleged insistence on Black equality was "debasing" to white people. This point of view becomes understandable when you recognize that Texas secessionists considered it an "undeniable [truth]" that America had been "established exclusively by the white race, for themselves and their posterity . . . that [Black people] were rightfully held and regarded as an inferior and dependent race, and in that condition only could their existence in this country be rendered beneficial or tolerable." Ending slavery and extending Black people political rights would "debase" white people by ending their unquestioned perch atop the social hierarchy. Secessionists also argued, as the Declaration of Independence had, that whenever any "form of government becomes destructive of the ends for which it was established, it is the right of the people to alter or abolish it, and to institute a new government."[3] Just as this principle gave the founding fathers the moral right to wage war against England, it now compelled secessionists to fight the federal government. Ironically, slaveholders who had forcefully rejected Thomas Dorr's argument that he could change Rhode Island's constitution outside of the prescribed political process were now doing the same thing.

Meanwhile, northern state constitutions took diametrically opposed positions. All abolished slavery and secured slave liberty. On the eve of the Civil War, five included Black men as part of "the people" and permitted them to vote and enjoy basic rights on the same terms as white men. Michigan, New York, and Ohio were headed in that direction and allowed Black men to vote in some circumstances.[4] Kansas provided the most recent warning that this constitutional vision threatened the South. While the Lecompton Constitution that slaveholders favored disenfranchised Black men, the Leavenworth Constitution allowed Black men to vote on its ratification, opened the door to them voting in other elections, and abolished slavery. True, it never went into effect, but it might be a preview of the future abolitionists had in store for white southerners as they gained power nationally.

The Civil War cost America more than six hundred thousand lives and left the South in ruin.[5] Its constitutional vision was also in mortal peril. By adopting the Thirteenth Amendment abolishing slavery, the Fourteenth Amendment guaranteeing all citizens equal protection of the laws, and the Fifteenth Amendment prohibiting racial restrictions on the right to vote, the US Constitution embraced the coalescing northern consensus on how to define "liberty," "equality," and "the people." At the national level, the Civil War's end had birthed a new constitutional order.

In southern states, however, the Civil War's end began an era of constitutional chaos. From 1864 to 1900, the US Constitution added three amendments. During that time period, Arkansas, Florida, Georgia, South Carolina, and Texas each drafted three different constitutions. Louisiana drafted four. Every southern state adopted at least one new constitution. In every state, at least one of these constitutions was dramatically different from constitutions that had come before. They took contradictory positions on how to define "liberty," "equality," and "the people." The constitutional debate in southern states focused primarily on the place of Black Americans in society.

At the founding, Thomas Jefferson predicted a race war unless Virginians abolished slavery and then sent Black people back to Africa. During the Civil War and Reconstruction, Jefferson's fears were realized. In truth, this was a one-sided conflict. As delegates to Texas's 1869 constitutional convention observed, "'the war of the races' [was] all on the part of the whites against the blacks."[6] One of the central battlegrounds for that war was the constitutional convention hall. A consistent pattern occurred throughout the South. Right after the Civil War, former secessionists who referred to themselves as conservatives, and later, Democrats, wrote constitutions that continued the spirit of 1861. These constitutions and legislation implementing them clarified that white people controlled political, legal, and economic affairs as they had before the war and that Black people would be treated like they were still slaves. White vigilantes murdered Black people with impunity.

This state of affairs enraged Republicans in Washington, DC. With Thaddeus Stevens playing an important leadership role advocating on behalf of Black people, Congress passed the Reconstruction Acts in 1867. The acts divided the South into five military districts and placed a military commander over them. To end military rule, states had to hold new constitutional conventions and allow Black men to vote for delegates. However, the acts disenfranchised men who had once taken an oath of allegiance to the US Constitution and then participated in the rebellion and made prospective voters promise to "faithfully support" the US Constitution. Many white men were unable or unwilling to take this oath while every Black man could. The constitutions had to allow all

men to vote except for those who participated in the rebellion and felons, and the constitutions had to be ratified by a majority of those voting
on whether to ratify. Congress had to approve these new constitutions.
State legislatures elected under the new constitutions had to ratify the
Fourteenth Amendment to the US Constitution. As justification for giving the federal government such unprecedented power over state constitutions, some Republicans pointed to the Guarantee Clause. Charles
Sumner called it a "sleeping giant."[7] It had slumbered while Dorr and
Free-Staters pursued constitutional change. Now Republicans awakened
it for the struggle against racial inequality. In many places, removing
white confederates from the political process and redistributing power
to Black voters was the only way to achieve new constitutions. It also
made those constitutions illegitimate in the eyes of many residents—the
ones with the most education, resources, and military training. Republicans had laid a foundation of sand for the new constitutions. But white
supremacists determined to continue slavery left no other place to build.

Every southern state except Tennessee began writing a new constitution in 1868. These new constitutions, drafted by men who referred to
themselves as radicals and Republicans, all repudiated the spirit of 1861.
This is evident from who participated in the drafting process. Where
only white men had written previous constitutions, Black men played an
important role in writing the 1868 constitutions. Where white delegates
who had drafted previous constitutions had frequently been slaveowners, white delegates in the 1868 conventions usually accepted Black
equality in important measure. Radicals and Republicans even began
these constitutions differently from the way delegates began earlier
constitutions. In several instances, they consciously linked their work
with the founding by incorporating some variation of the Declaration
of Independence's language that "all men are created equal" into their
constitutions for the first time. In other states—like Virginia—where
constitutions had limited such language to white people, they broadened
it to include Black people. To execute their vision of racial equality, the
1868 constitutions guaranteed Black men the right to vote and hold office. We might call this the spirit of 1868. To be sure, these constitutions
contained other important innovations such as creating public education systems. But it was the commitment to Black equality that generated the most vigorous disagreement and, ultimately, conflict. The spirit

of 1861 and 1868 were irreconcilable. Southern states during Reconstruction were again a house divided. The only question was who would be standing when it came crashing down.

As soon as the 1868 constitutions were written, conservatives began undermining them. They tried to defeat ratification by uniting white voters against the threat of "negro domination" and suppressing Black votes. They formed organizations like the Ku Klux Klan to wage guerrilla war against Republican governments and Black people. Years of armed conflict and efforts to overthrow the 1868 constitutions culminated in crises in just about every southern state that captured national attention. These crises were moments when the 1868 constitutional order broke down in dramatic fashion, providing Democrats an excellent opportunity to resurrect their old constitutional definitions of "liberty," "equality," and "the people."

In this second part, I describe crises in Arkansas, South Carolina, and North Carolina. In Arkansas, a minority coalition of Black and white Republicans sought to advance racial equality in the face of a hostile majority. The difficulty governing an unfriendly electorate led the Republican Party to break down into two factions. After a disputed election ended with two candidates claiming to have been elected governor, those factions, one of which was backed by the state's Democrats, formed competing militias. Those militias fought the Brooks-Baxter War while the federal government waffled about which side to support.

South Carolina had a Black majority and was the only state in American history to have a constitutional convention with a majority of Black delegates. The only way conservatives could reimpose their prewar constitutional vision of Black subordination was to bring the majority to heel. With a military precision that characterized their fight against the federal government, Democrats murdered and intimidated enough Black voters and committed enough fraud to make the 1876 election close enough for a dispute about who won. The aftermath of that election saw two men claiming to be governor and two bodies claiming to be the state house of representatives.

After conservatives succeeded in nullifying North Carolina's 1868 constitution, the coalition of Black and white voters that supported that constitution reemerged and formed the fusionist movement in the 1890s. At the state level, Democrats reacted by staging perhaps the most virulent white supremacy political campaign in American history to shatter the movement for interracial political cooperation. Meanwhile, Democrats in Wilmington conspired to overthrow a government they associated with Black political power, which culminated in an armed mob demanding the mayor's resignation at gunpoint after a day of bloodletting. If both these efforts succeeded, white supremacists could end Black political involvement in the state and eradicate the spirit of 1868 once and for all.

4

The Brooks-Baxter War

Few politicians have lost an election less graciously than Joseph Brooks. He refused to concede, petitioned the courts and the legislature to overturn it, and argued in the press that the election was stolen. When that failed, Brooks conspired with his political enemies and marched on the governor's mansion with armed followers to force his way into office.

Few politicians have been as determined to stay in office as Elisha Baxter. He threatened to declare martial law and disperse a court if it ruled against him in an election challenge, purged the state militia of political opponents, and turned on his own party when he didn't think it could keep him in power. When that failed to secure his position, Baxter tried to force every statewide official who opposed him to resign.

On April 16, 1874, a collision between an unstoppable force and an immovable object took place when Brooks found Baxter in the governor's mansion and kicked him out. If he thought his work was finished, he was mistaken. Baxter made a makeshift headquarters, gathered supporters into a militia, and plotted his return to power.

The Civil War sowed the seeds of Arkansas's 1874 constitutional crisis. It involved fighting and destruction all over Arkansas. And importantly for our purposes, it was a formative experience for all the major characters in the Brooks-Baxter War: Elisha Baxter, Joseph Brooks, John McClure, and Powell Clayton.

After losing the Civil War, conservative Arkansans still clung to the spirit of 1861. Arkansas's 1864 constitution only permitted white people to own weapons and prevented Black people from voting, holding office, or serving on a jury. They continued Arkansas's constitutional tradition of insisting that Black people weren't part of "the people" and defining "liberty" for Black people as narrowly as possible. The legislature refused to ratify the Fourteenth Amendment to the US Constitution. One legislator even drafted a resolution thanking Jefferson Davis for his service as confederate president and calling him a "martyr to liberty."[1]

Elisha Baxter became a fixture of the postwar establishment when the Arkansas legislature elected him to the US Senate. Clean-shaven with a gentle part in his hair, Baxter was born in North Carolina to an Irish father. Baxter was appointed to the US Military Academy at West Point but resigned when his father opposed him leaving home. In 1852, he moved to Arkansas and went into the mercantile business with his brother, which failed. Baxter then apprenticed as a lawyer and opened his own practice. Before the war, he served as mayor of Batesville and then as a legislator. He began politics as a Whig before identifying as an independent. He owned slaves but simultaneously believed slavery immoral. Baxter's wartime years are shrouded in mystery. He claimed that "at the outbreak of the rebellion, I believed that secession was unjust to the Federal Government and would prove disasterous [*sic*] to the people of the south and therefore adhered to the old Flag." Baxter further claimed he had been offered command of a Union regiment, but declined it because he didn't "feel it was [his] *duty* to make War upon the people of the South." Eventually, confederate authorities arrested Baxter and indicted him for treason. He managed to escape prison and evaded capture for eighteen days, all while living on raw corn and berries. It was at this time that he promised God to join the Union Army if he survived. In gratitude for divine intervention, Baxter later helped raise a Union regiment.[2]

Two wartime newspaper articles cast doubt on Baxter's claims. The first said that Baxter had been removed from his position as colonel of an Arkansas Union regiment and had schemed to become military governor of Arkansas. The second portrayed him as a coward who lied about who he was when arrested by men who knew him. After the war, Baxter's political enemies even alleged that he once became so excited during a speech supporting the rebellion that he fell through the bed of a wagon. He had only stopped supporting the confederacy, they claimed, when he lost a quartermaster position in a confederate regiment. Wherever his true loyalties lay, radical Republicans refused to seat Baxter in the US Senate when the legislature elected him in 1866.[3] But he remained hungry for high office.

The Spirit of 1868 Comes to Arkansas

Radical Republicans uprooted the power structure in Arkansas when they passed the Reconstruction Acts and required the state to draft a new constitution. Many whites committed to the spirit of 1861 could no longer vote because of their participation in the rebellion or refusal to uphold the laws and constitution of the United States. This gave Black voters electoral strength that exceeded their numbers. Though they made up only 25 percent of residents, Black people made up 35 percent of registered voters by the end of 1867. Because the allocation of delegates for Arkansas's 1868 constitutional convention was based on the number of registered voters, areas with large numbers of Black people therefore received more delegates and areas with large numbers of white former confederates received fewer. Of the seventy-five delegates elected, sixty therefore identified as Republicans.[4] This meant that the new constitution was guaranteed to embrace the spirit of 1868. The new constitution was also at major risk of failure before it was even written. Ironically, delegates faced the same obstacle as the Lecompton Constitution did. There, the census which allocated delegates for the convention heavily favored proslavery counties and many Free-Staters refused to participate in the election for delegates. As a result, proslavery delegates dominated the convention. But also as a result, most Kansans did not share the Lecompton Constitution's basic worldview and, for that reason, viewed the Lecompton Constitution as illegitimate. Similarly, the delegates to Arkansas's 1868 constitutional convention had different ideological commitments than most Arkansans. Could they succeed in gaining acceptance where the Lecompton Constitution failed?

Joseph Brooks and John McClure were both delegates to the convention. Joseph Brooks had a flowing beard, unruly hair, and a fierce stare. He was born in Kentucky but spent most of his youth in Ohio. Brooks became a minister and newspaper editor before the Civil War. When the war began, he personally presented a Bible to every member of the First Missouri Rifle Regiment and gave a "brief and affecting address" to a large crowd. The performance was a harbinger of the acclaim Brooks would receive for his public speaking. A follower claimed that his voice sounded like "the bellow of 'an old brindle-tail bull.'" Brooks eventually enlisted in the Union Army and became the chaplain of a Black regiment stationed in Arkansas by war's end. Brooks successfully operated a cotton plantation and championed racial equality. He favored taking land from rebels and giving it to freedmen. At one point, Brooks even claimed that the term "negro" was offensive.[5]

John McClure was born in Ohio where he became a lawyer at his father's insistence. McClure fought in the Union Army during the Civil War and was court-martialed for playing cards. McClure had a poor reputation at home in Ohio, which may have explained his decision to stay in Arkansas after the war. A letter to the editor of one Ohio newspaper claimed that "his legal abilities were all acquired in bar-rooms, at poker tables, and on the race-course." McClure was a Democrat before coming to Arkansas, but later joined the Republican Party. He had apparently struggled economically in Ohio, for the same letter to the editor described above said "he could have crammed all his wealth, if reduced to greenbacks, in the hollow of his rotten teeth." His efforts to improve his financial situation by managing a cotton plantation failed. McClure's critics claimed that he entered politics to ensure financial security. He would face allegations of corruption throughout his political career.[6]

Convention delegates made momentous changes to Arkansas's constitutional order. For the first time in Arkansas history, Black men were part of "the people." As another first in Arkansas history, the convention included eight Black delegates.[7] The new constitution therefore guaranteed Black men the right to vote. The constitution also committed to racial equality, holding that "[t]he equality of all persons before the law is recognized, and shall ever remain inviolate; nor shall any citizen ever be deprived of any right, privilege or immunity, nor exempted from any burden or duty, on account of race, color or previous condition." This provision was a marked contrast with earlier versions of Arkansas's constitution. Starting in 1836, Arkansas's constitution had insisted that "all free men when they form a social compact are equal and have certain inherent and indefeasible rights amongst which are those of enjoying and defending life and liberty; of acquiring possessing and protecting property and reputation and of pursuing their own happiness." This was similar to the language Virginia slaveholders used in 1776 to ensure that "liberty" and "equality" did not threaten slavery. A Black delegate, William Grey, linked the new focus on racial equality to the Declaration of Independence and the founding. "The original [contract] drawn up by the patriotic men of the Revolution," Grey said, was that "all men are created equal." Grey believed that "the hand of an angel guided the pen that wrote those words, and that they were recorded in heaven." As such, racial equality was not a dangerous innovation, but the only way to keep faith with the founding fathers and the Creator who inspired them.

While the constitution added Black men to "the people," it excluded many white men. The constitution denied the franchise to Arkansans the Reconstruction Acts prohibited from voting. McClure proposed going even further and introduced a resolution disenfranchising anyone who voted against ratifying the new constitution. It wasn't adopted. But the constitution did require that all voters swear an oath that they would "never countenance or aid in the secession of this State from the United States," and that they "accept[ed] the civil and political equality of all men before the law." The only way a disenfranchised Arkansan could ever vote again was to convince two-thirds of each house of the legislature and the governor to let him.

One white delegate called the oath "wicked," insisted that "the negro is not the equal of the white man," and claimed that allowing Black men to vote would inevitably lead to miscegenation. Another argued that it was unfair to simultaneously disenfranchise many white voters while allowing Black men to vote. Conservatives also appealed to the US Constitution and argued that since it didn't require an oath for voters, imposing one in Arkansas's was unconstitutional. Racists and former confederates weren't the only ones to dislike disenfranchising so many voters. Perhaps remembering what it was like to have no say in the laws governing him, a Black delegate expressed unease about disenfranchising former rebels and even argued that the Reconstruction Acts had disenfranchised too many of them. Still, the "assertions of gentlemen of the Conservative Party, that they are not willing to give [Black people] the right of suffrage under any circumstances," gave him no choice but to support the constitution.

Fifty years before the US Constitution guaranteed women the right to vote, delegates considered enfranchising Arkansas women. Speaking in favor, a delegate asserted that "man and woman are created equal." He even argued that "woman has a finer nervous system, or brain, a purer mind, and a more beautiful physique, than man." Most delegates treated the proposal as a joke, and it didn't become part of the constitution.

Conservatives did not think racial equality was a laughing matter. "For God's sake, let us build a wall!" between white and Black people, cried Joseph Bradley in introducing a resolution to ban interracial marriage. Bradley believed that interracial marriage was linked to the larger question about race relations that had "wrought the shedding of blood that has not yet grown cold" and which had "dissolved the American Government." He believed that banning interracial marriage would resolve that question by separating the races. Another delegate even went so far as to claim that banning interracial marriage was necessary to protect "poor white trash" from "further social degradation."

The occasional delegate defended allowing white and Black people to marry, but for the most part, delegates across the political spectrum believed interracial marriage was unacceptable. William Grey called interracial marriage an "outrage," but asserted that a ban was unnecessary because people wouldn't want to marry outside their race. He must have caused white people across the state unease when he acknowledged that they—often slaveowners—had raped Black women and suggested capital punishment for "any white man [who] shall be found cohabiting with a negro woman." Brooks claimed to dislike interracial marriage but asserted that nothing in the Bible prohibited it. Instead he asked his fellow delegates, "Will we cater to this prejudice of ignorance, superstition, and slavery, and allow ourselves to be thus distracted from the pursuit of the great end which we, in common, have before us?" That "great end" was helping to ensure civil rights for former slaves. McClure playfully suggested that Arkansans unable to protect themselves from getting into an interracial marriage without a constitutional provision banning it could go to court to have themselves declared incompetent. They would then be assigned guardians to personally prevent them from marrying outside their race. In the end, Arkansas's constitution did not bar interracial marriage.

The constitution made other noteworthy changes. It abolished imprisonment for debt and established a public school system that made no racial distinctions.[8] By creating a school system in the constitution open to all students, delegates made another important change in Arkansas's constitutional tradition. No longer was "liberty" purely about negative rights such as the ability to practice a religion without government interference. Instead, the state had embraced positive rights and taken on an obligation to promote the advancement of all citizens.

A Worrisome Ratification Battle

Now the constitution had to be ratified. Opponents must have feared that if they didn't defeat the constitution, there would be no chance to change it. The only way to amend the constitution to allow those disenfranchised to participate in politics was for a majority of both houses of the legislature to pass the amendment twice and in immediate succession, and then for a majority of voters to ratify.[9] Those who were disenfranchised—as were many white Arkansans—had no say in electing the legislators who would propose such an amendment. However, under the Reconstruction Acts, white Arkansans could vote on ratification without taking an oath that they believed in racial equality. As a result, such voters had a chance to vanquish a constitution they hated and hold out for a more favorable convention in the future.

The constitution's opponents employed a two-part strategy. First, they appealed to racial prejudice to unify whites. In the *Arkansas Gazette*, conservative delegates complained that the constitution "enfranchises the negro—places the ballot in the hands of a race totally incapable of self-government and thereby gives to stolid and brutish ignorance the political control of the state." They suggested that the constitution "encourages the social equality of the white and black races by requiring the legislature to tax you [white people] for the maintenance of free schools open to both races, and to which you are to be compelled to send your children." Finally, the oath that voters believed in legal and political equality was one "to which no white man can subscribe without a sacrifice of his manhood." They warned that "almost the entire white population of the state" was disenfranchised. But instead of becoming victims, the delegates expressed the hope "that the white men of Arkansas will be true to their manhood and promptly reject a constitution so destructive of their rights and utterly repugnant to the feelings of a free people."[10]

Second, they used force and intimidation to reduce Black turnout. The *Morning Republican* observed that "general terrorism" reigned in several counties where "violent and rebellious hordes of the 'white man's party' surrounded the polls . . . making loud threats and heavy demonstrations, and with instructions to 'spot' every man, white and black, who should have the temerity to vote for the new constitution." The paper claimed "indisputable information that many of the colored voters were kept or driven from the polls" because of the threats and violence. Nonetheless, it declared that the constitution achieved a majority by 1,649 votes although it also claimed that "had there been a full, fair, and quiet election, free from deception, force, and intimidation," the constitution "would have been ratified by [an] eight or ten thousand majority."[11]

For its part, the *Arkansas Gazette* claimed that "old men who staid [*sic*] at home during the war and took no part in it, and consequently were not required to take the amnesty oath, and were so told by the officer, had their names erased and were disenfranchised because they did not take the amnesty oath." Meanwhile "men who have not been citizens of this state six months were allowed to register and vote because they were mongrels." It also claimed that "timid men were intimidated and coerced to vote for the constitution by being told if they did not, they would be forever disenfranchised, their property confiscated and themselves banished or killed." Finally, it charged that election officials had opened up ballot boxes, thrown out votes against the constitution, and substituted ballots voting *for* the constitution. Nonetheless, conservatives claimed they had defeated the constitution by at least seven thousand votes.[12]

Irregularities really did happen. A. C. Gillem, the federal commander over Arkansas, found evidence that some men had voted multiple times. However, he was unable to determine whether they had supported or opposed the constitution. In the end, the official tally showed that 27,913 voted for ratification, while 26,597 voted against. Arkansas was finally readmitted to the Union.[13]

Three things deserve mention about the ratification process. First, voting was racially polarized. At the behest of the Reconstruction Acts, the federal government registered 43,170 white voters and 23,146 Black voters in August of 1867.[14] Black support for the new constitution was essentially unanimous, meaning that only a few thousand whites supported ratification. Second, a majority of Arkansans didn't support the constitution. With many whites unable to vote, ratification had been by a razor-thin margin. If all white men in Arkansas had been eligible to vote, the constitution would almost certainly have been defeated. A minority would now attempt to impose its constitutional vision on a majority willing to do anything to regain power. Third, the inability of all sides to agree on something as basic as whether a new constitution was in place was a bad omen for political stability.

Republican Party Dysfunction

During the ratification process, Republicans met to nominate candidates for office. Initially, Brooks sought the gubernatorial nomination along with James Johnson and Powell Clayton. Clayton was born in Pennsylvania and became an engineer before moving to Kansas. With a flowing beard and mustache and sober eyes, he looked older than his years and had a natural gravitas. Ironically enough for a man who ran the Republican Party in the state for almost fifty years, Clayton started his political career as a Democrat in Kansas. Clayton proved a brave and resourceful soldier. He won praise for his performance at the Battle of Pine Bluff, when his force of six hundred men faced four thousand rebels. Despite "a perfect tornado of shells, canister and bullets flying" all around him, Clayton "rode around the works and gave directions with as much coolness and composure as though he was directing the movements of some celebration instead of a battle." By war's end, Clayton was promoted to brigadier general. Afterward, he became a successful cotton planter before entering politics.[15]

Perhaps sensing that he had little chance against someone with a war record like Clayton's, Brooks dropped out of the race for governor and endorsed Clayton. The contest became one between a native Arkansan (Johnson) and a recent arrival (Clayton). Clayton won and Johnson settled for a spot as lieutenant governor. Native Arkansans reluctantly accepted this outcome, but their resentment would have fateful consequences.[16] The convention also nominated John McClure for the Arkansas Supreme Court. Republicans won and assumed control of Arkansas's government.

Republicans made progress in achieving their constitutional vision. The legislature built and funded public schools. The schools were segregated, true, but the fact that there were public schools at all extended opportunity to thousands of children who would not otherwise have received it. Republicans provided even more educational opportunities when they founded the University of Arkansas. Republicans also forbade race discrimination in public transportation. Anyone who discriminated against Black people risked fines of between $200 and $2,000.[17]

Conservatives turned to terrorism to defeat the new constitutional order. As violence swept the state, Clayton declared martial law in eleven Arkansas counties in the fall of 1868 and called out the state militia. In a speech defending this decision, Clayton noted appalling crimes. In Monroe County, Republican congressman James Hinds was assassinated, and vigilantes attempted to murder Brooks. In Crittenden County, the Ku Klux Klan murdered six men in ten days and drove men loyal to the Union from their homes. Union loyalists resorted to sleeping in the woods. The Klan's goal was political. Clayton explained that "men [were] repeatedly threatened with death, and many [were] compelled to vote against their wishes" because of the violence. The militia encountered heavy resistance. In one rebellious county, men fired on the militia and, when they finally retreated, "declared their intention to fight the militia and drive the militia out of the county."[18]

Still, even some Republicans were reluctant to use the militia. The *Morning Republican* noted, "In regard to the Governor's policy in this matter, there is a very radical difference of opinion among Republicans themselves." The paper argued that declaring martial law and mobilizing the militia was "having a very disastrous effect upon the most vital and important interests of the State" and called for "a most rigid and scrutinizing inquiry and investigation into all the facts and circumstances of our condition, the necessity for resorting to the remedy adopted, and the manner and extent to which that remedy has been prosecuted." Some of the unease resulted from stories about militia misdeeds. For example, the *Morning Republican* documented a case where four Black militia members were convicted of perpetrating "the fiendish and beastly crime of rape, upon several women residing in the vicinity of [their] camp." It didn't explain whether the victims were Black or white. If they were white, the incident would have been disastrous for perceptions of the Republican Party. Seeing Black men in uniform raping white women would have validated conservative predictions that the new constitution would lead to miscegenation and Black domination of the state. It is telling that the *Morning Republican* took care to inform readers that an all-Black firing squad carried out the execution.[19]

Republicans had a tenuous hold on power. Their coalition consisted of former slaves, white people who had relocated to Arkansas after the Civil War, and a modest number of native white Arkansans. Yet, at precisely the time they needed unity, they fell into factions. Native Arkansans believed Clayton was favoring outsiders over them for political appointments.[20] Watching outsiders receive so many appointments must have rankled. Native Arkansans had endured a hostile climate during the Civil War, and many had exhibited tremendous courage in opposing secession. They had bucked popular opinion and become pariahs in many cases. Watching northerners who had not made those sacrifices take so many offices couldn't have felt fair.

By early 1869, some Republicans openly aired their grievances. They complained that "in the bad management of our State government, under the *unwise* administration of Governor Powell Clayton, and in the rash, reckless and improvident legislation of the General Assembly," the "Republican Party of Arkansas has received wounds, from the effects of which the most energetic and untiring efforts of its *true* friends and defenders . . . can alone rescue it and save it from threatened defeat and overthrow."[21]

Lieutenant Governor Johnson led disaffected Republicans and participated in a plot to remove Clayton from power. When Clayton traveled to New York to request financial help for the state, the *Arkansas Gazette* reported that "the conservative republicans of the state have urged upon the lieutenant governor, who is said to be on his way here from his home in Madison county" to arrest "the absconding governor and such of his deputies and subordinates as have been aiding and abetting him in various violations of the constitution, and fraudulent and treasonable practices." The *Arkansas Gazette* claimed that launching a coup would make him "irresistible forever before the people of Arkansas." Johnson's supporters argued that the constitution had transferred authority to him. It provided that "in case of the impeachment of the governor, his removal from office, death, resignation, inability, or removal from the State, the powers and duties of the Governor shall devolve upon the Lieutenant-Governor during the residue of the term, or until the disabilities of the Governor are removed." The "removal" in this case would be Clayton's trip to New York.

Clayton foiled the plot when he returned to Arkansas before Johnson could act. Johnson responded by giving a speech calling Clayton a "despot" who "wields the scetpre [*sic*] of an emperor." A loyal lieutenant governor would have rushed to declare support for their boss amid reports of a coup. Instead, Johnson confirmed that he had been trying to replace Clayton for some time, stating that "a few of us last winter made an effort to organize a more moderate party." One of the new party's planks would be "to remove the political disabilities of the men who pay the taxes to support the government." Since this echoed Democratic complaints that the constitution disenfranchised so many whites, Johnson likely hoped to combine Democrats and dissatisfied Republicans into a new coalition. For his part, Clayton believed Johnson was trying to encourage his assassination.[22]

The Republican factions saw both a threat and an opportunity from disenfranchised white voters. On one hand, those voters were hostile to the new constitution with its emphasis on racial equality. They would do anything, including participating in military-style operations, to destroy the government. On the other hand, if one of the Republican factions could somehow win over those voters, they would broaden their coalition and cement their political power. Perhaps attempting to do exactly that for his faction of what were known as minstrels, Clayton suggested ending disenfranchisement in an October 1869 speech. Clayton recognized that ending disenfranchisement would require amending the constitution, a process that would take time. While many Democrats applauded the speech, many Republicans saw it as an effort to curry favor with Democrats so they would elect him to the US Senate. Tension ran so high that when a longtime friend questioned Clayton's motives, Clayton hit him.[23]

More radical Republicans who followed Joseph Brooks were known as brindle-tails. Like Johnson's moderate followers, they had already been suspicious of Clayton. To ensure Brooks's loyalty, Clayton may have tried to offer him a position as brigadier general of the state militia, which Brooks allegedly refused. To lower Brooks's political standing, Clayton supporters savaged him in the *Morning Republican*. They claimed that Brooks was a "degenerate hypocrite" who tried to use the Methodist Church as an "instrument to forward the cravings of his personal ambition" and that he sought to divide the Church, just as he was dividing Republicans, when the Church didn't grant him a prominent enough role. They alleged that instead of tending to his soldiers' spiritual concerns during the Civil War, he schemed to become commander of his district by lying about his superiors.[24]

Brooks's grievances against Clayton were likely personal as well as ideological. In the 1870 election, Brooks was declared the victor of a disputed election and sworn into the state senate. The senate soon reversed itself and seated his Democratic opponent. Clayton and his supporters did nothing to help. In fact, Clayton said he viewed Brooks as a political enemy and later claimed that Brooks had engaged in fraud to win the election. For Brooks, it must have been deeply frustrating to be one of the most prominent and outspoken Republicans in the state, and yet be shut out of elected office. By mid-1871, his loathing for Clayton led him to team up with Johnson's supporters and Democrats. He "denounce[d] the whole system of fraud, corruption, and official thieving which have characterized the administration of our public affairs" under Clayton. Although Brooks claimed he wanted only to purify the Republican Party, the *Morning Republican* noted that he was using "the same language and terms employed by the Gazette and the Democratic press of the State." Ignoring his longtime advocacy for racial equality, the *Morning Republican* alleged that "Mr. Brooks proposes to be the 'Moses' of the Democracy—he is to lead the slave-dealing, slave-whipping Democracy into the promised land." According to the *Morning Republican*, Moses wasn't the only Biblical character who compared unfavorably with Brooks. While the Apostle Paul stopped persecuting Christians when Jesus appeared to him on the road to Damascus to remove "the scales from his eyes," Brooks "journeyed to the rooms of the Democratic Central Committee, and the scales fell from his eyes and he cease[d] to persecute Democrats." To ensure Brooks's brand was toxic among Black voters, the *Morning Republican* even quoted Frederick Douglass as saying that "[Brooks's] career has been such as to completely disgust all true Republicans in Arkansas, and at the same time gain the highest [praise] of the Kuklux democracy."[25]

It is very possible that Clayton did propose ending disenfranchisement to gain Democratic support for a US Senate bid. With considerable support from Democrats, the legislature elected him to the US Senate in early 1871.[26] And he did eventually accept the appointment, suggesting that he had wanted to become a US senator all along. However, his election left him with a problem: his successor would be Johnson, who tried to oust him from office in 1869. This outcome was unacceptable, and not just because Clayton disliked and distrusted Johnson. Leaving the governor's chair to Johnson would hand control over the government to the growing coalition of conservative Republicans and Democrats. It would threaten to erode Clayton's standing as the most important man in the state's Republican Party. Clayton's efforts to avoid that outcome led to charges of bribery and impeachment proceedings against Johnson, McClure, and himself.

The 1872 Campaign

In the 1872 election, the same factions that had been pulling apart for several years maneuvered for position. Opposed by the minstrels, Brooks had no chance to win the Republican nomination for governor. But that didn't stop him from pursuing the high office he had craved since 1868. He won the nomination of the Reform Party, a group affiliated with liberal Republicans challenging Ulysses S. Grant for the presidency. In some ways, Brooks was an awkward choice for the conservative Republicans and Democrats he needed to unite given his past radicalism. As the *Morning Republican* taunted, "In 1870, Mr. Brooks was the most radical of the radicals; his platform was composed of disfranchisement for an indefinite period, confiscatory taxation, and a division of land among the 'homeless, houseless peasants' who thronged his meetings and hung upon his words." Now, to appeal to Democrats and conservative Republicans, he advocated eliminating disenfranchisement provisions in the constitution. Reviving attacks he had made the previous year, he portrayed the current minstrel administration as corrupt and wasteful. At least some erstwhile supporters must have wondered how sincere he was about his platform of "universal suffrage, universal amnesty, and honest men for office." Indeed, the *Arkansas Gazette* argued that "Mr. Brooks should be the last man whom democratic and conservative people should honor with their suffrages."[27]

Nonetheless, there were two reasons for them to be cautiously optimistic. First, it was public record that Brooks despised the minstrels, and conservative Republicans and Democrats could count on that animosity to keep him from falling in with the minstrels if elected. Second, Brooks's past radicalism might help him win more Black votes than another reform candidate could. After all, he had worked with the Freedmen's Bureau and vigorously advocated for Black people at the 1868 constitutional convention. In an interview several months after the election, none other than Powell Clayton asserted that "the democrats . . . have no love for him, and his adoption by the 'liberals' was an effort to capture the colored vote."[28] Because Black voters made up a substantial portion of the electorate, conservative Republicans and Democrats had reason to prefer a candidate who could be competitive with this demographic.

Meanwhile, the minstrels nominated Elisha Baxter. No less than Brooks, Baxter was a man whose ambitions had been repeatedly thwarted. Recall that he had won election to the US Senate, but was turned away and never got the chance to serve. Instead, he settled for a comparatively low position as a circuit court judge, crumbs thrown from carpetbagger Powell Clayton's table. The minstrels probably chose Baxter because as someone who had lived in Arkansas before the Civil War, he might have an easier time than an outsider winning votes from conservative Republicans and Democrats. The *Morning Republican* described him as "eminently conservative" and one of the "oldest citizens of the state." In case any conservative readers missed the attempt at outreach, the paper also described him as "a large property-holder, and thus deeply interested in the growing prosperity of the state [who] may be relied upon to zealously guard and protect the material interests of all of her citizens." Portraying Baxter as a "large property-holder" was an effort to remind readers that Brooks once advocated confiscating lands from rebels and distributing them to Black people and poor white people. The paper also reminded readers, if they didn't know already, that Brooks was a "carpetbagger" so reviled by many southerners. To further secure support from native Arkansans, Baxter's supporters touted an endorsement from a former confederate colonel, a tacit signal that former rebels and those who preferred antebellum days could safely support him.[29]

Both campaigns vigorously sought Black votes. Brooks's supporters reminded Black voters that Baxter had owned slaves and claimed that he had been a harsh master. Brooks's supporters also claimed that "in [his] capacity of quartermaster to his regiment . . . the supposition was, and is even to this day, . . . by the colored men who are now residents of Pulaski county, that he (Baxter) was instrumental in the murder of a number of colored men." The insinuation was not just that Baxter had murdered Black men, but that he had supported the confederacy. In short order, Black Baxter supporters denounced the claims as "base, foul and unmitigated slander on the good name of Judge Baxter, whom we esteem, regard and honor as one of the firmest, most reliable and trust-worthy friends and defenders of the colored people and their rights that can be found to-day in this state." Baxter's supporters also claimed that he had opposed a pre–Civil War bill forcing free Black people to leave the state or choose a master that one of Brooks's supporters proposed, a stance that would have taken some courage in an antebellum political climate dominated by slaveholders.[30] Allegations that Baxter murdered Black people have no evidence to support them.

Baxter's supporters accused Brooks of corruption. Without evidence, they claimed that Brooks had taken a bribe from Cairo and Fulton Railroad in return for championing its interests in the legislature. To contrast with this damning portrait of Brooks as a man without moral scruple for sale to the highest bidder, Baxter's supporters claimed that "his life has been one of unblemished purity," praised his "firmness and decision of character," and declared that "no right-thinking republican or democrat can hesitate to cast his vote for Judge Baxter, when comparing this high-minded, noble man to Joe Brooks." As evidence of his virtue, they claimed that he had been "torn from the bosom of his family, 'cast into prison,'" where "he lay like a felon, chained to his cell, in the penitentiary in Little Rock, because he was a union man."[31]

For as vicious and personal as their campaign became, Brooks and Baxter advocated similar policies. Like Brooks, Baxter advocated ending disenfranchisement of former rebels.[32] The lack of clear policy distinctions gave both men the room to play every side in Arkansas's political divides.

The election might have been one of the most corrupt in American history. Both in a lawsuit in the Arkansas court system and before Congress, legions of men testified that rampant fraud took place. One Brooks supporter who monitored voting testified that a county clerk simply threw out 133 Brooks votes and didn't count them. Others testified to even more brazen behavior. A man who supported Baxter said that someone had picked out Brooks ballots with a knife, destroyed them, and then replaced them with Baxter ballots. This would have been possible because voting procedures worked differently in 1872 Arkansas than they do today. Unlike modern elections where all the candidates appear on the same ballot and voters make their selection in the privacy of a voting booth, in Arkansas in 1872, the candidates had different colored ballots. Brooks and candidates aligned with him appeared on white ballots while Baxter and candidates aligned with him appeared on green ballots. It would have been easy for a corrupt election official to pick out the Brooks ballots or, as was alleged in another instance, burn them.

A sheriff supporting Baxter during the election even admitted to engaging in fraud. He altered a polling place so that Brooks voters couldn't see what happened to their ballots once they were submitted. Officials then put Brooks ballots voters had submitted into their pockets, reached back to a stack of Baxter ballots, and submitted them in place of the Brooks ballots. Before election day, the sheriff and other officials had met, "figured up and ascertained (knowing every man in the township and how he would vote) about how many Brooks tickets it would be necessary to change." Not content to change votes, the sheriff also ensured that Brooks votes which made it into the ballot box went uncounted because of supposed irregularities. Officials threw out ballots from a Brooks-leaning township because there had been no lock on the ballot box. The reason there had been no lock was because the sheriff did not deliver one "for the purpose of having that as one reason why the vote should be thrown out in case it went against us." Glaringly, there were no returns at all from three counties, and returns from more than forty precincts were missing.

Election officials also prevented Brooks supporters from voting in the first place. To give just one example, in one township, registrars looked at the voter rolls and muttered, "Well, you know how this man will vote." When they agreed that such a person was "a Brooks man" they struck him off the voter rolls and then provided no notice "to those men whose names were struck off to appear and show cause why their names should not be struck off." Baxter had an important advantage here. By law, the governor appointed a board of registration for every county, and the governor was Clayton loyalist O. A. Hadley. Hadley had an incentive to appoint registrars who would tilt the election to Baxter. To make the situation even more confusing, those denied registration tried to vote in separate "side polls" to establish that they had voted for Brooks and that they were legally entitled to vote. To be fair, Brooks's supporters participated in fraudulent schemes of their own. In one township, a Brooks backer testified that Brooks supporters had often voted twice "on fraudulent certificates under different names."[33]

Unsurprisingly, Brooks and Baxter disputed who won. While complaining that Brooks had engaged in fraud, the *Morning Republican* insisted that Baxter won by five to six thousand votes. It bragged, "The fraudulent swelling of [Brooks's] vote in some localities has failed to change the result, and we have defeated [him], horse, foot and dragoons, all along the line." Sarcastically, the *Morning Republican* told readers to "carry the news to Joseph," who had not conceded. Clayton insisted that Baxter had been duly elected as well. On the other hand, the *Arkansas Gazette* argued that "had we been given a full and fair registration, an untrammeled vote and an honest count, Mr. Brooks, under the peculiar circumstances growing out of the *do-nothing* democratic convention of the 10th of June, would have been elected governor of Arkansas."[34]

Arkansas's secretary of state certified Baxter as the victor in December 1872 with an official tally of 41,684 to 38,726. Brooks tried to overturn the election. His supporters appealed to Democrats to form a separate legislature that would recognize him as governor. McClure intervened to prevent this. He met with an influential Democrat and agreed to convince Hadley not to provide election certificates to Republican candidates in a disputed election. In exchange, about twenty Democrats agreed not to join Brooks's proposed legislature. On January 6, 1873, the state senate elected Clayton's brother John as its new president. With John Clayton acting as presiding officer, the legislators ratified the decision to certify Baxter as governor. McClure administered Baxter the oath of office.[35] In his inaugural address, Baxter pledged to be a unifier who would "confer the executive appointments upon honest, capable and sober men, whose commendable deportment shall constitute a guaranty that they will faithfully discharge the duties of any position in which they may be placed with a due regard for the rights of the people, irrespective of party affiliation."[36] He didn't know it at the time, but Baxter would ultimately create unity between Brooks, Clayton, and McClure.

The Republican Party Falls Apart

Baxter's new government did accomplish some long-standing Republican policy goals. In February 1873, Republicans strengthened Arkansas's commitment to racial equality by making it a misdemeanor criminal offense for school officials to provide unequal accommodations for

Black schoolchildren. But around the same time his baby daughter died, Baxter began alienating supporters. He upset McClure with his actions in regard to railroads. The state had issued bonds worth millions of dollars to support building railroads, but the railroads were having trouble paying off the debt. To ease their burden, a legislator proposed allowing companies to transfer stock shares to the state in exchange for the state repaying the bonds. To raise funds to pay the debt, the legislator also proposed a property tax. McClure strongly supported attempts to bail out the railroads, at one point even helping to draft amendments to the proposal, allegedly after taking into account Baxter's objections. After becoming editor-in-chief of the *Morning Republican* and chairman of the Republican State Central Committee, McClure directly criticized Baxter for his handling of the railroad issue in the paper.[37]

In the twenty-first century, it is strange to think about a judge so blatantly injecting himself into the political process. But we should remember that the ideal of judges staying out of politics is relatively recent. We have already seen that judges in Rhode Island publicly opposed the People's Constitution even though they might have to rule on its validity. We should also remember that in 1870s Arkansas, as is true today, many state court judges were popularly elected. They have constituencies to serve and must consider how the political climate will affect their ability to remain in office. That makes them unlike appointed federal judges who have life tenure protection and don't have to regularly face voters. Economic concerns rather than a dispassionate interest in economic development may explain McClure's behavior. The *Arkansas Gazette* reported that he had been paid to lobby for the railroad proposal in the legislature. The charge that a sitting supreme court justice was accepting money in exchange for supporting legislation is explosive but plausible. McClure admitted that he once agreed to keep the *Morning Republican* from attacking a particular railroad in exchange for $6,000, but then complained that he had only received $3,000. For his part, McClure claimed that Baxter told a legislator that he would support the railroad bill in exchange for $25,000 in bonds. Whatever the truth about the bribery allegations, McClure was angry enough that he "opened a warfare upon [Baxter] through the newspapers."[38]

The fight over railroads was also a fight between competing visions of the state's future. Republicans who wanted to continue supporting railroads with state funds hoped to build up infrastructure that would allow Arkansas to industrialize and were willing to endorse a more active role for government to do so. Aid opponents, in addition to worrying about corruption, preferred a smaller role for government and a primarily agricultural economy.

Baxter further upset Republicans by appointing Democrats to several offices including his former judgeship. Evidence of his overtures to Democrats comes from the *Arkansas Gazette*'s recognition on April 29, 1873, that although it didn't agree with every appointment he had made, many of them "were eminently fit and proper."[39] True, Baxter had said he would appoint able men regardless of party. But his Republican supporters probably thought that was just rhetoric. The spoils system of the time dictated that politicians reward supporters with whatever offices they could. Every Democrat appointed meant a disappointed Republican. McClure admitted that he did not approve of Baxter appointing Democrats "instead of appointing men who have claims upon the party for services rendered." Moreover, such moves would have worried Clayton. Baxter's outreach to Democrats meant he could forge a new coalition with himself at the head, threatening Clayton's prestige and control over state politics. The general used to being in command had to contemplate being relieved. In a conversation, Baxter told Clayton, "I always thought that your object was to hold the republican party intact without very much reference to the manner in which it might affect the State, and to hold yourself at the head of that party."[40]

Baxter's decision to appoint so many Democrats may have reflected an attempt to navigate Arkansas's changing electorate. With the end of disenfranchisement, thousands of Democratic voters who had supported the rebellion became eligible to vote. There weren't enough Republicans to reliably win elections in Arkansas anymore. Appointing Democrats to government positions could put Baxter in the good graces of all these new Democratic voters when election time came. That Baxter succeeded becomes apparent from how the legislature handled Brooks's April petition to overturn the gubernatorial election's results and the way the *Arkansas Gazette* began to cover him. Many Democrats in the legislature who had supported Brooks in 1872 refused to hear the petition. The *Arkansas Gazette*, after noting that it hadn't supported him in 1872, hailed Baxter for making "a noble stand against the corrupt plans of the railroad ring" and various other Republican policies. It was now "willing to take the governor on trust, and to render him, unsolicited and without reward, an honest and cordial support in his future administration, should his course remain unchanged."[41]

McClure and allied Republicans prepared to respond to Baxter's shifting allegiances. After claiming that it had only reluctantly supported Baxter over Brooks, the *Morning Republican* suggested that Baxter might owe his office to fraud. Rumors swirled that Republicans would file a quo warranto petition against Baxter alleging that he had been fraudulently elected, which would allow McClure to issue a restraining order preventing Baxter from exercising his powers. To prepare for such an eventuality, Baxter called up the militia and had it guard the executive mansion. A prominent Republican charged that the guards were "reckless young men, without any visible means of support, gamblers, unreconstructed men who have a bitter feeling to all northern men, and to all law and order, in fact."

In due course, on June 2, 1873, Republican Attorney General T. D. Yonley filed a quo warranto petition in the Arkansas Supreme Court alleging that Baxter was not Arkansas's lawful governor because he had "usurped, intruded into and unlawfully held" the office. If the move was intended to intimidate Baxter, it failed. He later admitted that he would never have obeyed a court decision granting the quo warranto petition. Instead, he called up the militia, prepared a martial law declaration, and planned to disperse the court if it ruled against him. In addition, Baxter had removed numerous Republican officers from the militia to ensure its loyalty to him. One of Baxter's supporters even allegedly threatened to have McClure and the Pulaski County's sheriff, whose job it would be to serve a writ on Baxter, hanged. Meanwhile, Baxter's attorneys argued that the Arkansas Supreme Court lacked authority to decide the petition. Brooks participated in the intrigue as well, filing his own quo warranto petition in the Pulaski County Circuit Court.

Little Rock threatened to erupt in violence at any moment. But then Clayton negotiated a deal. Some of the justices were skeptical of using quo warranto proceedings against Baxter for two reasons. First, two of them, M. L. Stephenson and Elhanan Searle, had won election on the same ticket as Baxter in 1872. If they decided Baxter had won through fraud, then wouldn't their positions be in question? Second, it was debatable whether the constitution gave judges the authority to decide who the state's lawful governor was under these circumstances. Arkansas's 1868 constitution provided that "contested elections [of the governor] shall likewise be determined by both houses of the general assembly in such manner as is or may hereafter be prescribed by law." This provision seemingly indicated that only the legislature should decide whether Brooks or Baxter had truly won, and it had rejected Brooks's petition. However, the constitution muddied the waters when it authorized the Arkansas Supreme Court to issue writs of quo warranto. Quo warranto proceedings have sometimes allowed courts to oust officials who lack a proper legal claim to their office. An official arguably couldn't lawfully hold office if they had only won through obvious fraud, even if the legislature failed to intervene. Ultimately, the justices agreed shortly after hearing oral argument that they lacked authority to determine who Arkansas's lawful governor was. But the justices resented Baxter calling up the militia and didn't want to be seen as deciding in his favor because they were intimidated. While he participated in deliberations about the case, McClure attacked Baxter in the press. The *Morning Republican* asserted that "the people at large may not be able to comprehend the subtleties of law—they may not know all about 'quo warrantos,' 'original jurisdiction,' etc.—but they know that Joe Brooks was made governor, and that Elisha Baxter was defeated. They know that at every step Mr. Brooks has been thwarted, and they feel that in defrauding him, they have been defrauded." If that weren't enough, it even claimed that it "heard a prominent leader in the kuklux organization say, the other day, that every kuklux in the state was the friend of Elisha Baxter."

Clayton asked the justices not to file any opinion "until he could make some effort to harmonize the quarrels that were existing between Judge McClure and Governor Baxter." Clayton did meet with Baxter. Clayton argued that Baxter had alienated too many Republicans by calling up the militia and filling it with Democrats. The two went back and forth for some time until the meeting came to a head. Baxter claimed Clayton threatened that unless Baxter agreed to disband the militia, the Arkansas Supreme Court would rule against him in the quo warranto proceedings. Clayton denied ever making such a threat, and stated during the meeting, "I do not know what the judges will do" but "it is my impression that you will have the benefit of the *quo-warranto* decision."

The claim that Clayton didn't know what would happen contradicts Stephenson's assertion that Clayton knew what they were going to decide, and that Clayton "asked [him] shortly after [Clayton's] arrival at Little Rock to postpone the filing of the opinion for a few days." Regardless of whether Clayton actually threatened Baxter, the two eventually came to an agreement. In exchange for disbanding the militia, McClure would cease operating the *Morning Republican* and stop attacking him.

Baxter did disband the militia. The Arkansas Supreme Court did reject the quo warranto petition over McClure's dissent. McClure resigned his position with the *Morning Republican*, writing, "I am assured by prominent and well-known republicans, not those who sympathized with Baxter, but by those whose sympathies were with me, that Elisha Baxter is desirous of acting in consonance with the wishes of the leaders of the republican party, and that he will in the future labor to perpetuate the supremacy of the tenets of Republicanism." He claimed to lack the necessary faith in Baxter to faithfully support him as owner of the *Morning Republican* and said he was resigning so that people who did believe in Baxter could support the paper. In short order, the Arkansas Republican Party declared that "by reason of the late change in the management of the Little Rock REPUBLICAN—the central organ of the party—certain personal embarrassments, which it is of no service now to recount, have been removed and that paper hereafter will not only reflect the general policy of the party, but will also be fully in accord with the present administration of the government of the state." The "personal embarrassment" was, of course, McClure. The *Morning Republican* asserted that "the differences existing heretofore among republicans, whether they attached themselves to the regular, the 'liberal' or the 'reform' organization, were not fundamental and nothing has occurred that should continue the separation."

The episode leaves open a fascinating question: what was Powell Clayton's role in the leadup to filing the petition? On one hand, he telegraphed Baxter that "the *quo warranto* proceedings against you have been inaugurated without my knowledge or approval, and are in my opinion unwise and highly detrimental to the interest of the State . . . I believe you are the legitimate governor of Arkansas, and as much as I regret to see our State disgraced abroad by distractions at home, I hope you will stand firm regardless of results." Moreover, he doesn't appear to have opposed Baxter's actions regarding the railroad bill proposal; Baxter later recognized that they "agreed to a great extent on railroad policy." These facts make it unlikely that Clayton wanted to remove Baxter from office. On the other hand, it is interesting that he never rebuked McClure for initiating "war" against Baxter. This may have been because they were friends and had a close working relationship. Or it may have been because Clayton was already suspicious of Baxter. Clayton would later claim that shortly after Baxter received the Republican nomination for governor in 1872, he "discovered duplicity in his dealings." While the two were traveling together to campaign, Baxter allegedly "worked with me during the day and at night . . . was having secret conferences with the Democrats, and was making pledges to them which he had no authority to make for the Republican party." As a knowledgeable and sophisticated politician, he must have heard the rumors of an impending quo warranto petition in May 1873 and never used his influence to stop it. In fact, newspapers at the time speculated that Clayton was hostile to Baxter and behind the effort to remove him.[42] Perhaps Clayton viewed the quo warranto petition as a useful shot across Baxter's bow to keep him toeing the party line.

Meanwhile, Brooks's quo warranto petition in the Pulaski County Circuit Court remained pending.

The Brooks-Baxter War

Baxter soon made Republicans regret their decision to end the quo warranto proceedings. In the fall of 1873, Baxter appointed fifty state legislators to public offices such as county prosecuting attorney and circuit judge. The move necessitated a special election to fill the seats. Because the 1868 constitution had been amended to end disenfranchisement, this would be the first election where many Democrats who had supported the rebellion could vote. Almost all of those elected were Democrats. It is hard to see this as anything other than a political maneuver on Baxter's part. He saw that he was losing support among Republicans and gaining it among Democrats. Appointing legislators to various offices earned him goodwill, and getting so many new Democratic legislators gave him new allies he needed to survive a future confrontation with Clayton.

The rapid transition of the legislature to Democrats was a clarifying moment. Republicans knew that they were facing powerlessness unless they took drastic action. Clayton, McClure, and Stephen Dorsey, the other US senator from Arkansas, met early in 1874 to discuss how to proceed. In and of itself, it is interesting that Clayton met with McClure given how the Republican Party had formally distanced itself from McClure. This may suggest that Clayton never believed McClure acted wrongly, or that he still valued his political instincts and friendship even after the previous year's events. At the meeting, the three preeminent minstrel Republicans strategized to put the legislature back in Republican hands. The purpose, which they would never have believed two years previously, was to have the legislature decide that Brooks had actually been elected in 1872. McClure figured that "if the matter [between Brooks and Baxter] was ever brought to a contest, or was ever brought to a point, were the facts ever disclosed in the case, Baxter would go out." The question is why McClure was so confident. In fact, he later claimed to have suspected that Baxter had not truly won the election before Baxter was even sworn into office. Could it be because McClure himself had directed or at least participated in the frauds? McClure denied doing so, but the possibility cannot be discounted.

Regardless, they were now so desperate that they were willing to work with a man minstrel Republicans had bitterly condemned in 1872. But there was no alternative. A Democratic legislature beholden to Baxter wouldn't impeach him and the Arkansas Supreme Court had permanently foreclosed courts from removing Baxter . . . or so it seemed. Changing the composition of the legislature and supporting Brooks in a renewed election contest was the only option minstrels had. Given how much of a freelancer Brooks had always been, going from a radical Republican to a reform Republican with Democratic support, they couldn't have thought he'd be easy to control. At best, he would have no choice but to rely on Republicans as he governed because he would upset the many Democrats who had come around on Baxter by riding into the governor's mansion at the head of the Republican Party. At worst, he would be just as willing to side with Democrats to advance his own personal interests as Baxter was. This framed the choice as being between a man hostile to Republican interests and a man who might be hostile to Republican interests. Better to take their chances with Brooks.

To get a Republican legislature in 1874, Clayton, McClure, and Dorsey needed Baxter's support. As governor, Baxter controlled the state's electoral apparatus and could make a thousand decisions that would help or hinder Republican candidates, such as whom to appoint as the registrars who would decide who could vote. To get that support, Baxter alleged that a Clayton agent offered him a federal judgeship and "as much money as I wanted" in exchange for participating in fraud that would elect Republicans to the legislature in 1874. Clayton denied that he had ever authorized such an offer. While it is impossible to know definitively what happened, it is certainly plausible that Clayton tried to offer a judgeship. As a US senator, he would have been able to push Baxter forward as a judicial candidate.

Clayton and Dorsey *did* meet with Baxter to secure his support for a successful Republican campaign. Baxter was willing to cooperate, but he had a price: the resignation of the lieutenant governor, speaker of the house of representatives, attorney general, McClure, and even Clayton's brother John—all Republicans.[43] All these men were in the line of succession should Baxter be impeached and removed. Baxter may therefore have seen their resignations as deterring any Republican legislature from impeaching him as there would be no prominent men who would be suitable candidates to take his place. Baxter probably also wanted payback, as McClure had fought him repeatedly and Attorney General Yonley had filed the quo warranto petition. Dorsey and Clayton couldn't accept this deal, as it would likely have resulted in Democrats replacing several statewide Republican officeholders.

With the plan to get a Republican legislature to make Brooks governor foiled, there was only one path forward. Brooks had filed a quo warranto petition himself in the Pulaski County Circuit Court, but it had flown under the radar as the Arkansas Supreme Court decided the attorney general's petition. Legally, the path was closed, as the Arkansas Supreme Court had emphatically declared that only the legislature could decide contested gubernatorial elections.

Shortly after the Arkansas Supreme Court rejected Yonley's quo warranto petition, Baxter's attorneys challenged the Pulaski Circuit Court's authority to hear Brooks's petition. The argument seemed a sure winner, but the Pulaski Circuit Court failed to rule on it for months. On April 15, 1874, Judge John Whytock called up Brooks's case without either of Baxter's attorneys present, decided that he had authority to hear the case, held that Baxter wasn't Arkansas's lawful governor, and awarded Brooks $2,218 in damages for lost salary. Whytock claimed that the Arkansas Supreme Court's decision denying courts authority to decide gubernatorial election contests didn't apply to him, since he was only deciding whether Brooks should get damages for wrongfully being denied office, not whether he should actually become governor. That McClure knew of, and likely encouraged Whytock's actions despite his denial, is apparent from the fact that he swore Brooks into office the same day Whytock made his decision. Notwithstanding his unbelievable claim that he only swore Baxter in because "he asked me," and that he would administer the oath of office to anyone who asked to be sworn in without investigating whether they were in fact elected, it is impossible to imagine a judge being that cavalier.[44] McClure wasn't surprised when Brooks came in to take the oath of office because he was expecting the decision.

Brooks then went to see Baxter with a copy of Whytock's decision. For a meeting during a hostile takeover, they were remarkably polite. Brooks and Baxter shook hands before Brooks told Baxter he was now Arkansas's lawful governor. Baxter responded that "I am entirely taken by surprise in the movement, am not now prepared to say what I shall do; but shall not surrender the office unless compelled to do so by force." After conversation in a "kindly tone," Brooks requested that Baxter vacate the office. At that point, Robert Catterson, whom Powell Clayton had struck in an argument over ending disenfranchisement of certain white Arkansans years earlier, and whom Brooks had put in charge of the state militia, ordered Baxter to leave the premises. Baxter did, and proceeded to Anthony House to set up a new headquarters where he plotted how to retake the government. Decades later, the *Arkansas Gazette* told a more dramatic tale. In 1893, it reported that when Baxter refused to vacate, "he was seized by several strong and armed men, and thrust bodily out of the executive office into the hallway, and the doors bolted in his face."[45]

That Clayton knew what Whytock would do or encouraged his actions becomes apparent from a telegram on April 16, 1874. There, he and Dorsey addressed Brooks as "Gov. Brooks," and informed Brooks that the Grant administration had refused to support Baxter.[46] After the 1873 quo warranto petition, Clayton had telegraphed Baxter that he didn't know about or approve of the attempt to oust him and that he viewed

Baxter as the legitimate governor. After Whytock granted Brooks's quo warranto petition in 1874, however, Clayton didn't condemn the decision or say that he didn't approve of it. If Clayton were truly surprised or dismayed, he surely would have said so. Like McClure, he was probably expecting the decision because he helped orchestrate it behind the scenes.

Both Baxter and Brooks tried to get the federal government to intervene on their behalf. As we saw in the Rhode Island and Pennsylvania crises, the US Constitution promised each state a "Republican Form of Government" and that it would protect them from "domestic violence." *Luther v. Borden*, a case that resulted from the Dorr Rebellion, indicated that federal courts could not decide who was Arkansas's lawful governor. It was up to the president or Congress. Dorr's rebellion informed how Americans made sense of the Brooks-Baxter War. Likewise, the Brooks-Baxter War caused Americans nationwide to relitigate the issues Dorr raised. The *New York Herald* spoke for many when it claimed that "the present condition of affairs in Arkansas resembles, in many respects, the situation in Rhode Island during the Dorr rebellion in 1842." As many newspapers did, the *New York Herald* also extensively summarized what happened in Rhode Island thirty years earlier. Michigan's *Jackson Daily Citizen* also compared the Brooks-Baxter War to the Dorr Rebellion and compared Brooks to Dorr. Both had been properly elected governor of their states, and both had justice on their side in trying to displace the existing government. On the other hand, Vermont's *Rutland Daily Globe* claimed that Brooks was a usurper just as Dorr had been.[47]

The federal government was indecisive. In responding to both Brooks and Baxter, US Attorney General George Williams refused to take a side and said that the Arkansas courts should determine who the governor was. This left more uncertainty. Would the Arkansas Supreme Court's justices stand by their earlier ruling that they lacked authority to determine who the governor was, or would the shifting politics change their votes? Clayton now opposed Baxter, and he had appointed two justices to the court and McClure as chief justice. They would not have been eager to defy their political patron. Indeed, three of the justices, McClure, Searle, and Stephenson, were among a group of Arkansas officials who told Grant that they supported Brooks. Sensing the danger, Baxter proposed calling on the legislature to decide who was governor. That was just as convenient as Brooks calling on the Arkansas Supreme Court to decide, since the legislature was in Democratic hands and many of the legislators owed him their seats. Grant sowed further confusion when he declared that he would take "any adjustment peaceably of the pending difficulties in Arkansas by means of the legislative assembly, the courts, or otherwise."[48] This set off a race between Brooks to get the Arkansas Supreme Court to rule that he was governor and Baxter to get the legislature to declare he was governor. Whoever succeeded first would ostensibly receive federal recognition.

Baxter issued a proclamation convening the legislature on May 11, 1874, to decide who was governor. Brooks faced a challenge in getting the Arkansas Supreme Court to side with him before the legislature met: courts don't usually just rule on issues; they do so in the context of a case between two (or more) parties. So, Brooks had to get a case before the Arkansas Supreme Court. Brooks first tried to get the Arkansas Supreme Court to declare him governor by appealing Judge Whytock's decision, which would give the court a case to decide. But that wouldn't work for two reasons. First, the court had given him everything he wanted, so he had no reason to be dissatisfied and nothing to appeal. Second, an appeal of Judge Whytock's opinion would require Baxter's participation since he was party to the lower court proceedings. Baxter could delay proceedings by refusing to appear or raising procedural challenges that consumed too much time. Brooks came up with an ingenious solution to ensure there was a suitable case for the Arkansas Supreme Court to rule on. He asked state treasurer Henry Page to provide $1,000 to the militia so it could confront Baxter's "insurrection." When Page allegedly refused on the grounds that Brooks was not actually governor, Brooks asked the Arkansas Supreme Court for a writ of mandamus to make Page pay. Page responded that Baxter was Arkansas's lawful governor, and that Brooks didn't have authority to request the money. This provided the Arkansas Supreme Court with a case between two parties it could rule on. We would today call this a collusive suit where two parties pretend to contest a legal issue so that a court can rule on it. The reason we know the suit was collusive was because Page's lawyer was Attorney General Yonley, the same man who had brought the quo warranto petition against Baxter in 1873.[49] Page likely didn't actually believe Baxter was governor. He simply went along with the charade so that Brooks could be declared governor.

Baxter's forces threw a wrench into the plan. Justices John Bennett and Elhanan Searle were riding a train to Little Rock so they could meet and decide Brooks's mandamus petition when Captain James Williams of Baxter's militia came into their car and said that no one could leave because there were horse thieves aboard. Williams then asked Bennett and Searle who they were, and upon learning that they were justices, said "I have come for you and I would like to have you go with me." Williams finally admitted after some more discussion that he was arresting Bennett and Searle "by the authority of Governor Baxter." Eventually, fifteen or twenty men came and escorted Bennett and Searle from the train. Instead of going to see Baxter as promised, they went to St. John's College. While Bennett was writing a letter to Baxter, Williams reappeared, promising to take Bennett and Searle to see him. They walked for some time until they were in an isolated area. No closer to Baxter, they began to fear for their lives. After spending a "pretty cold" night in the wilderness, they resumed their journey in the morning.

Brooks's supporters panicked. Without Bennett and Searle present, the Arkansas Supreme Court lacked a quorum to decide the mandamus petition. McClure quickly drafted a writ of habeas corpus ordering Baxter to release Bennett and Searle. A Pulaski County deputy sheriff served the writ on one of Baxter's commanders, only to be told that they didn't know where Bennett and Searle were. Clayton then asked for federal troops to get involved, and they began searching for the justices.

While the search was on, an order to kill the justices may have been out. As Lieutenant T. A. Summerhill of Baxter's militia informed them, "We have very positive information that the Federal troops and the Brooks men are after you for the purpose of your release, and my orders are very explicit not to allow you to be retaken alive at any hazard." Fortunately, Lieutenant Summerhill proposed to help the justices escape. He planned to take advantage of a superior's drunkenness so he could take command, get Baxter's soldiers to leave the area while the justices got horses, and then ride for Little Rock. Searle went along with the plan, but Bennett fled into the woods. Bennett traveled all night until at "about daylight he arrived at a negro's cabin, and knowing them to be true and reliable, he went in and explained to them his situation." The man then safely guided him into the city.[50]

With Bennett and Searle back in Little Rock, there were now enough justices to form a quorum and conduct business. They heard the mandamus petition on May 6, 1874, and issued their unanimous decision the next day. Judge Whytock had authority to determine that Brooks was governor, which made his decision valid and binding. Since Brooks was Arkansas's legal governor, he had the right to make Page provide state funds. The court didn't mention its opinion from a year earlier holding that only the legislature had authority to determine disputes over gubernatorial elections. Nor did it consider how explicit text giving the legislature sole authority to decide contested gubernatorial elections affected its ability to decide the case. Instead, it simply said, "We are of the opinion the circuit court had jurisdiction of the subject-matter, and its judgment appears to be regular and valid." Notwithstanding the decision's analytical weaknesses, it appeared to give Brooks the legitimacy he needed for Grant's support. He therefore telegraphed Grant as soon as the court issued its decision.[51] Baxter continued with his plan to convene the legislature. Both Brooks and Baxter sent representatives to Washington, DC, to plead their cases to the Grant administration.

While Brooks and Baxter jockeyed for federal support, militias loyal to them began fighting. Hundreds of Brooks's troops went on a dress parade in Little Rock. From his headquarters, Baxter addressed his men and they brayed for battle. The commander of a contingent of troops, King White, declared, "Give me permission and I will do the work. We will stay by you until you are governor of Arkansas." When a colonel with the federal forces in Arkansas asked White to disperse his men, White refused. Just as soon as White and the colonel finished speaking, someone shot at the colonel, which led to "a scene of the wildest panic." Baxter's soldiers "commenced discharging their pieces in every direction," and "in five minutes, the street from Main to Scott was deserted." Unfortunately, a "citizen highly respected for his worth and generally esteemed in the community" was killed by the gunfire. At least two others were wounded.[52]

The fighting escalated. In New Gascony, White ordered Brooks's forces in the area to disperse. When they refused, White himself opened fire, leading the Brooks men to take cover. The two sides traded fire for about half an hour, and two Brooks soldiers were killed and three were wounded along with a civilian caught in the crossfire. A Brooks soldier claimed he heard White say after the battle was over that he would "take no more Brooks men prisoner, but will slaughter then wherever he finds them assembling." He also alleged that "White's men are thieving from the colored people, stealing their arms and bed-clothes wherever they find them."

Two days later, two hundred Brooks cavalrymen attacked a group of Baxter men sailing down the Arkansas River. Six men were killed and six were wounded in the fighting. In total, twenty men died and many more were wounded in the Brooks-Baxter War.[53] The total would likely have been much higher had the fighting gone on longer.

The Arkansas Supreme Court's decision didn't lead to Grant supporting Brooks, so Brooks and Baxter tried to get a favorable legislative determination. After meeting with representatives from both Brooks and Baxter, US Attorney General George Williams proposed having the two men send their militias home and issue a joint call for the legislature to meet on May 25, 1874, and determine which one of them was Arkansas's lawful governor. Baxter rejected the proposal because he felt a joint proclamation legitimized Brooks's claim to power. Baxter, Brooks, and Grant negotiated the details of convening the legislature until Brooks suddenly questioned whether the legislature could decide the contest. Brooks asserted that many legislators actually had no right to hold office; indeed, if Baxter did not actually win in 1872, he lacked authority to appoint the legislators he had, and those legislators in turn lacked authority to decide a contested election. Brooks also argued that Grant was bound to respect the Arkansas Supreme Court's decision and even refused to disband his militia on the grounds that it was needed to protect the justices from assassination.

Grant soon ended the maneuvering. After taking advice from Williams, he proclaimed Baxter governor. He criticized "certain turbulent and disorderly persons" for "pretending that Elisha Baxter, the present executive of Arkansas, was not elected" and "combin[ing] together with force and arms to resist his authority." He ordered "all turbulent and disorderly persons to disperse and return peaceably to their abodes within ten days from this date, and hereafter to submit themselves to the lawful authority of [Elisha Baxter]." The first fallout of the proclamation was on the Arkansas Supreme Court. Stephenson resigned while McClure, Bennett, and Searle were impeached. All fled Little Rock.[54]

Brooks's supporters kept trying to put him in power. Just prior to Grant's proclamation, Clayton had introduced a resolution in the US Senate calling for three men to be appointed to "fully investigate into the cause of the disturbed condition of affairs [in Arkansas], and also into the question as to who is the lawful governor of said State by reason of having been elected to said office by the legal voters thereof." Later in May 1874, Congress passed a resolution requiring Grant to provide it all information in his possession about what had happened in Arkansas.[55] What became known as the Poland Committee began an investigation where it interviewed, among others, McClure, Baxter, and Whytock. That the committee continued working after Grant's proclamation suggests that Brooks supporters hoped Congress might overturn the decision.

While Congress investigated, peace returned to Arkansas. The legislature scheduled a vote on whether to call a constitutional convention. It was questionable whether this move was lawful. Most importantly, and unlike many other constitutions, Arkansas's 1868 constitution didn't explicitly authorize the legislature to call a convention. The only way to change the constitution specified in the text was for a majority of the legislature to approve an amendment in consecutive sessions and then for voters to ratify it. On the other hand, the 1868 constitution recognized that the people "have the right to alter or reform the [government] whenever the public good may require it." In the end, Arkansans arguably cured any legal objection to the legislature's act when they voted for a convention by an official tally of 80,259 to 8,607. Opponents charged fraud and there probably was some. Several counties showed zero votes against calling a new constitutional convention, which is unbelievable. However, even allowing for some fraud and intimidation, there is a plausible explanation for why a majority of voters really did favor a convention. Arkansas had just experienced a bloody crisis, and voters would logically have wanted to prevent something similar from happening again. For its part, the *Arkansas Gazette* suggested that many white voters came to the polls for the first time because they believed the election would finally be fair and that Republicans wouldn't manipulate the results.[56]

Democratic delegates dominated the convention and drafted the constitution to combat perceived excesses. The constitution limited the governor's powers by reducing his term of office to two years and reducing the number of appointments he could make. This would reduce the potential for would-be Powell Claytons to dominate Arkansas politics. The constitution required governors to have been a resident of the state for seven years before becoming eligible to become governor. This would prevent outsiders like Clayton from running for governor in the first place. The constitution also forbade the state from lending credit and limited its ability to tax. This would decrease if not eliminate arguments about railroad aid that had recently roiled the state. The overall goal was to restore as much of pre-Reconstruction Arkansas as possible. The constitution didn't restrict the franchise to white men, but it empowered an electoral coalition that ultimately would do so in the 1890s.

The delegates submitted the new constitution for ratification on October 13, 1874. Elections for regular political offices were also held that day. Republicans boycotted the election and argued that the new constitution was itself invalid. Voters ratified the constitution by a 53,890 margin and Democrats swept all the races.[57] With Republicans shut out of government completely, their only hope was that the Poland Committee overturned Grant's decision recognizing Baxter.

At least it seemed that way to everyone but Volney Voltaire Smith, Baxter's lieutenant governor. His father, allegedly hostile to Christianity, had been known as Delusion Smith, and had once contested an election for Oregon's US Senate seat. Although a new governor and lieutenant governor had taken office, Smith issued a proclamation claiming to be governor. He argued that because the 1874 constitution was invalid and because Baxter had relinquished his office, that left him as Arkansas's governor. Smith allegedly sold copies of his proclamation for five cents apiece. Augustus Garland, newly elected governor under Arkansas's 1874 constitution, announced a reward for Smith's capture, and Smith promptly went to Washington, DC, ostensibly to seek Grant's recognition. The effort failed. The final nail seemed to be pounded into the coffin on February 6, 1875, when the Poland Committee made its report. It concluded that "by a fair and honest return and count of the votes actually given at the election, Brooks was elected governor, and of right should have been so declared." However, it found that Arkansas's 1874 constitution was legitimate, which meant that the Democrats who won office in the most recent elections were properly in power.[58]

For a brief moment, Grant gave Brooks one last ray of hope. On February 8, 1875, he wrote a letter to Congress expressing the opinion that "all the testimony shows that in the election of 1872 Joseph Brooks was lawfully elected governor of that State [Arkansas]; that he has been unlawfully deprived of the possession of his office since that time; that, in 1874, the constitution of the State, was, by violence, intimidation, and revolutionary proceedings, overthrown, and a new constitution adopted and a new State government established." Why the change of heart? As the Poland investigation unfolded, Grant saw irrefutable proof that fraud probably accounted for Brooks's loss in 1872. This information was unavailable to him when he proclaimed Baxter governor. Political motives probably played a part, too. Democrats had taken over Arkansas and Baxter had been offered the Democratic nomination for governor before declining it. Continuing to stand by Baxter meant accepting Democratic control in Arkansas, which must have been distasteful given that other southern governments had been falling away from Republicans as Reconstruction ended.

If the letter invited the US House of Representatives to ignore the Poland report, it declined. The full House adopted the report by 150 to 81.[59] The Brooks-Baxter War was finally over. While at first glance, these events looked like the Republican Party had grown so dysfunctional that its factions were fighting in the streets, the reality is that the Brooks-Baxter War ended with white Democrats reconquering their state as they did across the South in the 1870s. At the end of the war, they were in power, and Black people and Republicans were out of power. They had even scrapped the 1868 constitution they hated, though they retained some of its features. Given the depth of their animosity to the 1868 constitutional order and majority in the state, they likely would have retaken Arkansas at some point.

After The Brooks-Baxter War

Powell Clayton finished his term in the US Senate before the Arkansas legislature sent a Democrat to replace him in 1877. In 1884, Clayton became the first white politician to lose a race for chairman of the Republican Party's national convention to a Black man after future President Theodore Roosevelt gave a speech seconding Mississippi Congressman

John Lynch's nomination for the honor. Nevertheless, Clayton remained a powerful figure in the Republican Party, serving as a member of the Republican national committee until 1912 and as ambassador to Mexico from 1898 to 1905. He died at eighty-one after a prolonged illness and was buried in Arlington National Cemetery with full military honors.[60]

John McClure gained widespread acclaim in a successful law practice and edited another Republican newspaper, the *Evening Star*. He also attempted a political comeback and came within 227 votes of being elected to the US House of Representatives in 1876. He died of natural causes, aged eighty-two, in 1915. In his obituary, the *Arkansas Gazette*, which fiercely criticized him during Reconstruction, called McClure a "fearless old fighter" who had managed to turn once bitter political enemies into friends.[61]

The two men who gave the Brooks-Baxter War its name died much sooner. Joseph Brooks served as Little Rock postmaster and died suddenly in 1877, aged fifty-six. Elisha Baxter tried and failed to win election to the US Senate in 1878. He practiced law and stayed active in the Methodist Church. He died in 1899 at age seventy-one. An obituary in the *Arkansas Gazette* said that he "was not a great lawyer, a great statesman, a great judge, nor a great soldier as greatness is usually measured by mankind, nor had he been a great reader of books . . . but he was incorruptible—one of the noblest of the Creator's work, an honest and a good man." Another writer offered even more praise when he called Baxter "the Moses that led Arkansas out of the wilderness of radical misrule and plunder—the leader who gave back to the people the ballot, the birthright of freemen."[62]

Arkansas didn't immediately disenfranchise Black men after the Brooks-Baxter War ended. It soon made up for lost time. In 1891, Arkansas adopted a law effectively allowing white Democrats to administer elections across the state. Arkansas also made it harder for the disproportionate number of illiterate Black men to vote by ending the practice of using distinctive colored ballots and requiring voters to instead be able to read a standard ballot to see where to mark their vote. With a whiter electorate in place, Arkansas ratified an amendment permitting only those who paid a poll tax to vote, which also disproportionately disenfranchised Black men. Over the next several years, the Democratic Party moved to primaries to select candidates and allowed only whites to participate. The few Black voters who could legally vote lost any practical influence. The Republican Party was no longer competitive, and they had no say in which Democrat would govern them.

Black people were no longer part of "the people." In what must have seemed a cruel irony, Arkansas's 1874 constitution continued to insist that "all men are created equally free and independent" and that no citizen "shall ever be deprived of any right, privilege or immunity, nor exempted from any burden or duty, on account of race, color or previous condition."[63]

5

A White Supremacist Revolution

South Carolina deserves the most credit—or blame—for starting the Civil War. It was the first state to secede. Open hostilities between the Union and confederacy began in the state when rebels fired on Fort Sumter in Charleston Harbor in February of 1861. Two of its sons, Wade Hampton III and Robert Smalls, spent the next years involved in the fighting. Both gained prominence because of their military records. Both believed they were fighting for "liberty."

Hampton made unthinkable sacrifices on behalf of slaveholder liberty. Like many southern planters, Hampton had the trappings of great wealth and the debt to go with it. Born in 1818, he received a college education and trained as a lawyer. But he never practiced and instead devoted his time to managing family plantations in South Carolina and Mississippi. After losing his first wife, he dealt with the grief by running for and then serving in the South Carolina legislature. There, he was initially a voice for moderation as calls for secession mounted. When secession was a done deal, though, he loyally supported South Carolina. He paid out of pocket to equip what became known as Hampton's legion and received a colonel's commission. When his unit marched to the frontlines, Hampton still had no military experience and had never heard a shot fired in anger. But as his enemies were about to find out, he could learn on the job. Six feet tall, powerfully built, and with a flowing beard, handlebar mustache, and tidy uniform, Hampton looked like the quintessential confederate cavalryman. At the Battle of Bull Run, he was shot in the face while leading a charge. He soon recovered and continued distinguishing himself in battle. By the war's end, he rose to the rank of lieutenant general. His military success came with a personal cost. His son Preston, who served under him, died in his arms. His home was destroyed during fighting in 1865. When defeat came, he experienced it as a personal humiliation. After the war, he was grieving, angry, and determined to win back the South Carolina he had lost.[1]

Roberts Smalls accomplished unthinkable exploits to advance slave liberty. In 1839, Smalls was born a slave. As a youth, he began plotting for his freedom. His prospects looked promising when his master let him work part-time as a ship pilot and keep a portion of his wages. By age nineteen, Smalls managed to save $100, almost enough to buy his own freedom. But by then he had fallen in love and started a family. What about his wife and children? With no chance of saving enough money to purchase all of their freedom, Smalls had to get creative. He decided to steal the ship he worked on and smuggle his family—along with other slaves—to freedom. When his wife Hannah found out, she told him, "It is a risk, dear, but you and I, and our little ones must be free. I will go, for where you die, I will die." Early one morning in May 1862, Smalls set sail. With the women aboard crying and praying, he steered the ship past a chain of confederate forts including Fort Sumter and managed to take down the confederate flag just in time to avoid being fired on by a Union vessel. Smalls won a $1,500 bounty for capturing the confederate ship. His family's freedom secure, and with a large sum of cash, Smalls would have been forgiven for getting as far from South Carolina as he could. Instead, Smalls worked to convince Abraham Lincoln to enlist Black soldiers in the Union Army. When he was successful, he became the first Black man to captain an American military vessel. With his thick goatee, mustache, and a face that somehow gave off both an air of focused determination and a penchant for mischief, he exuded the maturity and audacity that distinction required. Smalls was present in 1865 when the American flag was once again raised over Fort Sumter to mark the war's end. Unlike Hampton, Smalls greeted the confederate surrender with enthusiasm. He purchased his old master's house and started a school for former slaves.[2] Now that slave liberty had been achieved, he could begin working for racial equality.

There was not room for both Hampton's and Small's postwar visions. The struggle over whose would prevail was underway.

Preserving the Spirit of 1861

Conservative South Carolinians refused to accept the end of slavery lying down. But the obstacles in their path were formidable. South Carolina was majority Black and under federal military occupation. Federal

policy required them to accept abolition of slavery and repudiate secession before being readmitted to the Union. Worried about losing control
over their former slaves, conservatives declared war on the Black community. They were willing to use any means necessary to win. They
tried pleading their case to federal officials. They tried economic coercion. They tried terrorism. And they tried fraud and intimidation at the
ballot box. Their fanatical commitment to Black oppression reflected
deep-rooted constitutional values. Long before South Carolina cited
northern hostility to slavery to justify secession, its first constitution justified seeking independence because England had "proclaimed freedom
to servants and slaves, enticed or stolen them from, and armed them
against their masters." Its 1778 constitution guaranteed only "freemen" a
presumption of liberty. Secessionists even said that they believed in the
US Constitution's preamble, which attempted to "secure the Blessings
of Liberty." For them, "liberty" was slaveholder liberty. South Carolina's
1790 constitution held that "[a]ll power is originally vested in the people." "The people" were white.[3]

The spirit of 1861 animated South Carolina's 1865 constitution, written a few months after the Civil War ended. Governor B. F. Perry, whom
President Andrew Johnson appointed, argued "that this is a white man's
government, and intended for white men only." The constitution therefore restricted the franchise to white people and native South Carolinians.
Conservatives had kept their old constitution's definition of "the people."
Although they abolished slavery in theory, conservatives essentially re-
established it in fact. They even titled the act that became known as the
Black Codes "An Act to establish and regulate the Domestic Relations
of Persons of Colour, and to amend the law in relation to Paupers and
Vagrancy." The act aimed to keep Black people as agricultural laborers. It
prevented them from engaging in any trade other than animal husbandry
without getting a license from a court, which would be good for one year
only. The act referred to Black people who entered labor contracts as
"servants" and those who employed them as "masters." The law required
these "servants" to work from sunrise to sundown. The "servant's" workday was exactly the same as a slave's workday before emancipation. Black
people were unable to defend themselves against vigilantes prowling the
countryside to force them to work for their former masters since the law
generally forbade them from owning weapons.[4]

Conservatives also took illegal measures to maintain white supremacy. "Masters" often refused to pay their "servants" compensation due under their labor contracts and forced them off their land, leaving Black workers vulnerable to vagrancy charges. White people shut down schools that served freedmen through violence and intimidation. Black people were then unable to read the labor contracts they signed and enforce their meager rights in court. White vigilantes murdered former slaves with impunity.

Black people could not realistically challenge the conservative constitutional vision. There were two ways to change the 1865 constitution. One method was to call a constitutional convention, but only two-thirds of both houses of the legislature could do that. The other was for two-thirds of each house of the legislature to approve amendments in consecutive sessions.[5] Since no Black people could vote, no legislator had an incentive to change the law on their behalf. South Carolina's 1865 constitution operated as an impenetrable shield against Black political power and a powerful sword in support of white supremacy.

The Spirit of 1868 Comes to South Carolina

The situation in South Carolina changed when radical Republicans forced the state to hold a vote on calling a new constitutional convention. The prospect of replacing their 1865 constitution terrified conservatives for a simple reason: South Carolina was majority Black. Recognizing this fact, South Carolina's US Senator William Preston argued in 1842 that Dorr's theory of constitutional change would "ruin S. Carolina" because Black people "would revolutionize" the state.[6] Conservatives watched nervously as Preston's prediction came true. They knew conservative definitions of "liberty" and who constituted "the people" reflected a minority view that would lose in an honest democratic contest. The *Abbeville Press* spoke for many when it complained, "We are met at the very threshold of reconstruction by the spectre of negro domination—the elevation of the poor ignorant slave, to the high seats of legislation—the subjection of the property and intelligence of the country to the domination of its landless serfs." Conservatives held a convention to decide how to respond. The most prominent man there was Wade Hampton III.[7]

Some conservatives believed they could defeat the call for a convention through strategic behavior. States had to satisfy two conditions before they could hold a convention. First, a majority of registered voters had to cast a vote on the question of whether to hold a convention. Second, a majority of those who turned out had to actually vote in favor of holding a convention. An editorial in the *Anderson Intelligencer* argued that conservatives should abstain from voting. The editorial estimated that there were 125,000 voters in South Carolina; 45,000 were white and 80,000 were Black. It conceded that most Black voters would support calling a convention but said the only possible way to prevent a convention was for white people not to vote so that the required number of voters wouldn't participate. Another editorial in the same paper, however, argued for full conservative participation. It advised readers to "throw all of our energies into the pending canvass and secure a Conservative Convention" to "place the security of the state upon a safe foundation." The editorial ended by declaring that "[Black people] must be given distinctly to understand that they have forced upon the people of the South the formation of a white man's party, by the formation of secret negro societies, which are the sure hot-beds of a war of the races."[8]

The threat of violence didn't materialize when it came time to vote. Papers across the state reported calm at the polls, with one attributing the peace to officials closing barrooms and liquor stores. Perhaps, too, conservatives saw that there were enough Black votes to call a convention and believed efforts to intimidate or coerce enough of them to vote against calling a convention to end their second-class citizenship would be fruitless. Indeed, Black participation was high. The *Charleston Daily News* complained that "the different polls were thronged with an eager crowd of darkies, all anxious to display their rights as citizens by depositing their maiden votes."[9]

South Carolina's constitutional convention was in some ways the most egalitarian political gathering in American history. Although it has not taken a place in America's popular imagination in the same way as the Civil Rights Movement of the 1960s, it is a legitimate contender for the high-water mark in this country's attempt at multiracial democracy. While the 1787 US constitutional convention in Philadelphia that remains the subject of study today was all white, South Carolina's 1868 constitutional convention was majority Black. While many of the delegates to Philadelphia's convention had been slaveowners, a delegate to the 1868 South Carolina constitutional convention marveled that "perhaps more than half the members of this convention can testify that they were once held as slaves, bought and sold as property, and legally held as such, under the lash of the task-master—against the injustice of which there was no appeal, either in State or Federal courts."[10]

Delegates insisted that Black men were now part of "the people," and that racial equality was a fundamental constitutional value. The first provision in the 1868 constitution was that "[a]ll men are born free and equal—endowed by their Creator with certain inalienable rights, among which are the right of enjoying and defending their lives and liberties, of acquiring, possessing and protecting property, and of seeking and obtaining happiness." Earlier versions of South Carolina's constitution from 1776, 1778, 1790, and 1861 never said this. Nor could the slaveholders who drafted those constitutions have adopted such a provision with straight faces when they explicitly sanctioned slavery. For delegates to South Carolina's 1868 constitutional convention, their first substantive provision marked a deliberate and important shift in South Carolina's constitutional tradition. It also caused considerable debate. In response to the suggestion that this provision was not "strictly true and proper," one Black delegate argued that the provision recognized what was "meant by the framers of the Declaration of Independence." No less than in Arkansas, Black delegates in South Carolina framed themselves as the American Revolution's true heirs. One white delegate even positioned himself as so committed to racial equality that he proposed banning the words "nigger" and "negro" in the new constitution and allowing the government to imprison people for using the words.

South Carolina's 1868 constitution contained several specific provisions to ensure a broad definition of "the people." It removed any racial restrictions on the ability to vote. It severely limited the legislature's ability to disenfranchise felons. The legislature could only do so for those convicted of treason, murder, robbery, or dueling. A future legislature trying to undermine Black political power would be prevented from passing laws to make felons out of Black men for petty crimes and then using convictions to keep them from voting. Delegates had seen officials threaten vagrancy charges to force Black people to sign unfair labor contracts and likely feared seeing similar arrangements limit Black voting. Delegates ensured that there would be no property restrictions on the right to vote. Just three years after slavery, most Black people didn't own property, and many wouldn't for the foreseeable future. But a legislature hostile to their interests couldn't use this fact to disenfranchise them. In addition, poor white men who had been disenfranchised now had a chance to vote. Perhaps because they had such a large majority in the state, Republicans took none of the steps to disenfranchise white rebels that we saw last chapter. Finally, the constitution also instructed the legislature to prevent the coercion, bribery, and intimidation that characterized many elections during the era. Elections would instead be "free and open."

The progress in voting came with two caveats. First, men had to pay a $1 poll tax. Although the tax was a greater burden on those with fewer resources, the constitution forbade disenfranchising men because of inability to pay, and the money supported public education. Francis Cardozo argued that citizens should see the tax as an investment in their children's future. "Will you pay the poll tax to educate your children in schools, or support them in penitentiaries?" he asked. Second, delegates rejected a proposal to give women the right to vote. After "acknowledg[ing] the superiority of woman," William Whipper asserted that "there are large numbers of the sex who have an intelligence more than equal to our own, and I ask, is it right or just to deprive these intelligent beings of the privileges which we enjoy?"[11] While we should lament that so many Black men had been disenfranchised their whole lives, but then refused the opportunity to enfranchise women, we should remember that no one even raised the issue at South Carolina's 1865 convention.

Delegates also committed to a more expansive definition of "liberty" and insisted on human dignity in a way previous constitutions hadn't. South Carolina's 1868 constitution took steps to build a welfare state and reform the criminal justice system. The constitution obligated the state to maintain "institutions for the benefit of the insane, blind, deaf and dumb, and the poor." It also required counties to provide aid to the poor. At the convention, a delegate proposed ending capital punishment. While the effort failed, the convention did adopt a provision requiring the legislature to "form a penal code, founded upon principles of reformation." Criminal justice reformers today would likely be elated if they could argue that sentences violated the US Constitution because they didn't sufficiently consider rehabilitation. And yet the US Constitution contains no such provision. South Carolina's constitutional provision descended from earlier New Hampshire and Indiana constitutions and ultimately from enlightenment thinkers who questioned frequent use of capital and corporal punishment.[12]

At the urging of Robert Smalls, South Carolina's 1868 constitution established free public schools for all students regardless of race and required children to attend for at least twenty-four months. Before the Civil War, the wealthy elite sent their children to private schools while the rest of the state's children—white as well as Black—received no education. South Carolina lagged well behind northern states in educating its population. These provisions evidenced an important change in constitutional thinking. Like the US Constitution, South Carolina's earlier constitutions provided details about what the government couldn't do *to* citizens but said nothing about what the government had to do *for* them. South Carolina's new constitution—like many others from the period—embraced a broader vision of what constitutions should do.

Providing public schools generated debate about whether they would be integrated. Some were skeptical of the idea. One white delegate warned that "in attempting to enforce mixed schools, you bring trouble, quarreling and wrangling into every neighborhood." He predicted that fights between students would lead to fights between parents, with the result that "the State would be kept in a continual state of turmoil and strife." Just three years removed from slavery and secession, however, another white delegate stated that "I have seen white children sitting by the side of colored children in school, and observed that there could not have been better friends." Francis Cardozo, a Black man who received a college education in Scotland and served as a pastor of a church in Connecticut, made the most eloquent plea for integrated schools. The best way to fight racism, he argued, was to allow young children "to mingle in schools together, and associate generally" because "under such training, prejudice must eventually die out; but if we postpone it until they become men and women, prejudice will be so established that no mortal can obliterate it." Cardozo's arguments at the convention were similar to Charles Sumner's arguments twenty years earlier that segregated schools violated Massachusetts's constitution because they "[tend] to create a feeling of degradation in the blacks, and of prejudice and uncharitable-ness in the whites." And they foreshadowed *Brown v. Board of Education*'s finding almost a century later that segregated schools "[generate] a feeling of inferiority as to [Black people's] status in the community that may affect their hearts and minds in a way unlikely ever to be undone." Ultimately, delegates did not definitively resolve the issue.[13]

South Carolina's 1868 constitution was a progressive document for its time and improved upon the US Constitution in many ways. But it was a bridge too far for South Carolina's conservatives.

The Conservative War on the New Constitutional Order

Conservatives first attempted to defeat the new constitution by appealing to the federal government they had fought three years prior. Hampton and others submitted a petition to Congress. They described the new constitution as "the work of Northern adventurers, Southern renegades and ignorant negroes" and claimed that "not one percentum of the white population of the State approves it, and not two percentum of the negroes who voted for its adoption know any more than a dog, horse, or cat, what his act of voting implied." Conservatives complained that "there seems to be a studied desire throughout all the provisions of this most infamous Constitution, to degrade the white race and elevate the black race, to force upon us social as well as political equality, and bring about an amalgamation of the races." They ended the petition with a warning: "The white people of our State will never quietly submit to negro rule."[14]

Congress refused conservative entreaties. But conservatives persisted in their fight. To prevent Black people and Republicans from prevailing in the first elections after the constitution, many turned to coercion, intimidation, and violence. In testimony before a state legislative committee investigating a disputed election, one South Carolinian said that employers had resolved not to employ any man who voted Republican. This was a smart strategy as many former slaves still relied on contracts with their former masters to earn a living. Slaveholders had exploited Black labor to build their wealth, and then used that wealth to build white political power. Conservatives also used the legal system. One former slave was arrested and held without trial. Authorities released him when he agreed to vote Democrat. Sometimes, conservatives resorted to even more direct methods. In the spring of 1868, the Ku Klux Klan appeared in South Carolina for the first time. The Klan functioned as a paramilitary group. Chapters were organized into companies, each of which had a captain. Members swore to do whatever their leaders required. As one former member explained, the Klan strove "to kill out the leaders of the Republican party, and drive them out of the State." The *Edgefield Advertiser* described the Klan as "a secret organization, conservative in its character and breathing destruction to Radicalism." Therefore, it was "a powerful and lasting instrument of good." The paper spoke for many white South Carolinians when it urged: "Three cheers for the Ku Klux Klan!"[15]

The Klan worked to win the 1868 election for conservatives. After years of being denied a voice in the political process, Richard Johnson was excited to vote. But the night before the election, "the Ku Klux came through our plantation, and said if any of the colored people went to the polls the next day to vote, that they would kill the last one of them." Some Black men on the plantation were so determined to vote that they still turned up at the polls. But several decided not to vote at the last minute because "the Democrats had liquor at the box upstairs and were drinking and going on in such a manner that the colored people were afraid to go up." Eli Moragne was one of them. The day before the election, the Klan broke into his home, dragged him outside, stripped him naked, and then whipped him. He showed up despite the experience but was told that if he "voted the Radical ticket [he] would vote it over a dead body." Armed white men stood between him and the ballot box.[16]

Sometimes, Democrats engaged in violence without bothering to wear their Klan robes. William Tolbert, a Democrat who helped murder a Black Republican, observed that "committees were appointed, which met in secret, and they appointed men to patrol in each different neighborhood." This was done "to find out where the negroes were holding Union leagues." They had instructions to "break them up, kill the leaders, fire into them, and kill the leaders if they could." Committees were supposed to take ballots from Republicans and kill those who resisted. Republicans did resist because Tolbert described a scene where one Republican had been shot dead and others had fled. The violence was effective. At one precinct, Tolbert would ordinarily have expected between four and five hundred Black men to vote, but Democratic committee members in the area only allowed two Black men to vote before they started shooting. There were similar drops in Black turnout across the state. For example, in Abbeville County, around 4,200 Black men were registered voters, but only 800 actually voted in 1868's fall elections.[17] Republicans won the governorship and control of the legislature. But Democrats and conservatives saw that violence could be effective.

The campaign even saw targeted assassinations of Black public officials. At a Democratic meeting, members discussed what to do with B. F. Randolph. Randolph had proposed that "the forthcoming [1868] Constitution shall not itself make any distinction on account of color, and shall provide that no distinction whatever on account of color in any law, legislative or municipal, shall be made in this State." To add insult to injury for South Carolina conservatives, Randolph was not originally from the state and would have struck them as a "carpetbagger." He had served as a chaplain of a Black unit in the Union Army before becoming a Freedmen's Bureau agent. Randolph never demonstrated any hostility to white people. In fact, at the 1868 convention, he presented a petition to restore a white man's right to vote. Nonetheless, at the Democratic meeting, "some said, 'cut him up and feed him to the dogs,'" while others said that "they would box him up and express him to Governor [Robert] Scott [of South Carolina] as a present." Assassins found him aboard a train and shot him. While he lay dying, one of the murderers taunted, "You said yesterday that negro blood ran in your veins, and you was proud of it; now God damn you, it is running on the ground."

Authorities arrested D. Wyatt Aiken, a former confederate colonel and outspoken defender of slavery, for instigating Randolph's murder but then released him on a $5,000 bond. There is evidence for Aiken's guilt. A witness testified that he gave a speech in Cokesbury where he thundered, "Before the white man should be ruled by the nigger, they would kill the last one of them." Aiken "wanted the nigger to understand it was a white man's government, and that they intended to kill every leading Radical, and would not leave one on the face of the Earth." Another witness testified that Aiken "advised the colored men not to go to the polls on election day, for if they did, they would paint the old field with their bones."[18] Regardless, Aiken was never convicted of any crime.

The violence did stop temporarily, but that was a voluntary decision. Who did the Klan and other terrorists listen to? Wade Hampton III. Along with others, he issued a proclamation. "We beg of you," it implored South Carolina whites, "to unite with us in reprobating these recent acts of violence, resulting in the death of Martin, Randolph and Nance, by which a few lawless and reckless men have brought discredit on the character of our people, though provocation in these cases may have been given."[19] Their motive in issuing the proclamation was not to get fellow Democrats to see the humanity of Black Republicans. Rather, they worried more about the "discredit on the character of our people" that the violence threatened. Specifically, they may have believed the escalating violence would bring even more scrutiny from radical Republicans in Washington, DC. As one of the men who had petitioned Congress to save South Carolina conservatives from their new constitution, Hampton knew that they had to maintain the moral high ground to gain public sympathy, and assassinating politicians from the other party wasn't the way to do it. Tellingly, he and the other Democrats issued no such proclamation about other methods to suppress Black political power such as economic coercion or intimidation.

For many Black people, winning elections must have seemed like a Pyrrhic victory. A soldier from Kentucky told Congress in 1871 that "outrages" occurred daily. Disguised men would "go to a colored man's house, take him out and whip him," then "tell him that he must not give any information that he has been whipped" and "that he must make a public renunciation of his republican principles, or they will return and kill him." The soldier then testified that only one white man was ever officially investigated for participating in these whippings. But while the grand jury considered whether to indict him, "a number of young men came into court with pistols slung around them." The grand jury unsurprisingly found insufficient evidence to indict the accused. White Republicans faced violence too. After being whipped, an elderly man was ordered to come into town during a sheriff's sale and publicly "renounce his Republican principles" on pain of death. He complied with the demand even though a squad of federal soldiers offered to protect him.[20]

State authorities did try to respond. Amid Klan violence sweeping the state, Governor Robert Scott signed a bill authorizing a state militia. However, most whites refused to serve, a trend that became especially pronounced when Governor Scott rejected all-white militia companies offered by former rebels. In the end, as many as one hundred thousand men, mostly Black, joined by the fall of 1870. They often wielded state-of-the-art weapons such as Winchester rifles. White newspapers spread conspiracy theories about the militia. For example, after describing the militia sent to Edgefield as "the Corps d'Afrique," the *Charleston Daily Courier* claimed that it had come to the town to commence "the arrest of citizens on trumped up charges of being 'rebel bushwackers,'" and "'members of the Ku Klux Klan.'" It then suggested that the militia had tortured an innocent white man into admitting that he was a "bushwacker." Two things appear to have been truly offensive about Black militia units. First, they inspired pride among Black people. The paper complained that when a Black militia unit went to Edgefield, "the negroes of Edgefield became exceedingly jubilant, and determined to congratulate the colored soldiers on their great victory." Second, the militia gave Black men another economic option besides relying on their former masters. As the paper lamented, "Among the numerous evils which have resulted to the people of Edgefield from this invasion of the county by the negro militia, has been the desertion of the fields by the negro laborers."[21]

Violence between Black militia units and white people erupted in Laurens County right after the 1870 election. After a gun discharged during a fight between a police officer and a citizen, a white mob began shooting at militia in the town. Several Black men and a few white men died during the fighting and in the subsequent upheaval. One of them was Wade Perrin, a Black legislator. White men caught up to him, ordered him to dance, sing, pray, and then run away. While he was running, they shot him in the back. Between 2,000 and 2,500 armed white men occupied the town. They had confiscated militia weapons from the armory. Two different stories developed about what had caused the violence. The *Daily Phoenix* blamed Black people. In the months before the 1870 election, the paper reported, "the white people had been subjected to an organized system of disparagement, abuse, and threats of violence to person and property, which had produced that feverish state of feeling incident to a deep sense of outrage and injustice." Black people had allegedly become so unruly that "for weeks, whole families had not undressed for bed, so great was the apprehension of midnight negro risings, burnings and butcheries."

The *South Carolina Republican*, however, claimed that a white man deliberately attacked a policeman to provoke him into firing so they would have an excuse to shoot. This must have been a premeditated plot because "it was not three minutes after the first shot was fired before a line of white men had formed across the public square. . . . The white men came from every direction, out of the stores, the courthouse, and every other place, and what appears very singular is that every one *was fully armed*." After the white men had fired on the militia, the paper reported that "white couriers were dispatched on every road, to rouse the people, so that by night at least one thousand men were scouring the countryside on horseback, and in little squads hunting up Radicals." The incident attracted national media coverage. The *New York Herald* observed that "'The War of the Races' in South Carolina did not end with the rebellion, but occasionally bursts forth with its wonted fury."[22]

Governor Scott declared martial law in four South Carolina counties. But he also ordered remaining militia weapons in Laurens County transferred to Columbia. Removing the weapons ensured that the militia couldn't be a serious fighting force and made the martial law proclamation meaningless. A wave of Klan violence swept the state after Laurens. The scale of some of these attacks demonstrates the Klan's military discipline. For example, in the winter of 1871, authorities arrested twelve Black militiamen for allegedly murdering a confederate veteran in Unionville. Dozens of Klansmen rode into the town, broke into the jail, and shot five of the prisoners, two of whom died. When a judge ordered the surviving prisoners transferred to Columbia for their safety, as many as 1,500 Klansmen captured the town and blocked the exits. Having determined to lynch the prisoners, the Klansmen descended on the jail and demanded the keys. When the deputy refused, they marched his wife up to the jail, put a gun to her head, and threatened to shoot. The Klan removed the prisoners and murdered them.[23]

The violence diminished temporarily later in 1871, though there is disagreement about why. Some have suggested that aggressive federal measures were responsible. In 1871, the federal government stationed more troops in the state and engaged in a thorough intelligence gathering operation to learn more about the Klan. Federal legislation authorized President Ulysses S. Grant to use the military to enforce the law and placed congressional elections under federal supervision. What became known as the Ku Klux Klan Act allowed Grant to suspend the writ of habeas corpus when he deemed it necessary. After considerable debate, Grant suspended the writ in nine South Carolina counties on October 17, 1871. Over the next months, federal authorities arrested thousands of men for allegedly participating in the Klan and secured dozens of convictions and guilty pleas. These efforts were enough for one historian to claim that "the limited steps taken by the Federal government were adequate to destroy" the Klan.

Indeed, Klan violence was lower for the end of 1871 and some of 1872 than it had been earlier. At the time, however, law enforcement officials themselves were skeptical about whether their efforts had been effective. One prosecutor even suggested that "orders were given" from unknown persons to end the violence "for the present" and that the Klan would simply "wait until the storms blew over" to "resume operations." By the summer of 1872, Klan activity intensified, indicating that any benefits from federal intervention were limited.[24]

The Republican Party's Internal Challenges

Given the immense opposition it faced, South Carolina's government made important achievements. The state greatly extended educational opportunities. In 1868, 400 schools served only 30,000 students. But by 1876, 2,776 schools served 123,035 students. The state also expanded the University of South Carolina, even providing 124 scholarships to help poor students with tuition.[25]

Perhaps most importantly, South Carolina saw unparalleled Black involvement in politics during Reconstruction. During these years, 315 Black men served in political office. Six served in Congress including Robert Smalls. Two Black men served as lieutenant governor. South Carolina was a place where a parent could take a son who had experienced chattel slavery just three years previously to the legislature, point to a majority of the members, and say, "that could be you one day." The state that was the first to plunge the nation into Civil War because of its commitment to Black slavery was also the first to raise a Black man up to its supreme court. Jonathan Jasper Wright was born in Pennsylvania to free Black parents and managed to save enough money to attend college, a rare feat for both white and Black people in the era. He read law in his spare time while teaching to support himself. Upon passing the bar, he became the first Black lawyer in Pennsylvania. After the Civil War, he came to South Carolina to organize schools for freedmen.[26] Wright had a neatly trimmed beard and mustache, and his somber eyes betrayed a young man who was in a hurry or a man weighed down with cares, or perhaps both.

Corruption marred all of the progress. In 1870, the *Charleston Daily News* wrote that "the South Carolina Legislature enjoys the reputation, both at home and abroad, of being one of the most corrupt legislative bodies in existence." Corruption was so bad, the paper claimed, that "a remark frequently made among the white men in Columbia, Radicals and Democrats, was that two hundred thousand dollars, judiciously circulated among the legislators, would secure the passage of a bill repealing the Emancipation act, and putting all but colored legislators back in slavery." The paper then asserted that there was an organization known as the forty-thieves pillaging the treasury. The organization allegedly had a captain, three lieutenants, four sergeants, and twenty-eight privates. The group conspired to prevent the legislature from passing any "measure unless money was paid to the members of the organization."[27]

Although conservatives may have exaggerated corruption, it did plague South Carolina during Reconstruction. After John Patterson won election to the US Senate, authorities arrested him when a legislator said he had voted for Patterson after receiving a bribe. Critics called Patterson "Honest John," supposedly because he always made good on his promises to pay bribes. The legislature attempted to impeach Governor Scott for his behavior in issuing bonds. At the end of 1871, a Republican newspaper lamented that "1872 finds South Carolina financially in a bad way, with no one to blame but officials of our own party. This is a disagreeable statement to make, but it is the truth." William Whipper, who had argued for enfranchising women at the 1868 constitutional convention, asserted Scott bribed legislators to escape impeachment.[28]

All the corruption caused schisms in the Republican Party. Eventually Whipper, who would himself be accused of corruption, asserted, "It is my duty to dissolve my connection, not with the Republican Party, but with the men, who by dishonesty, demagogism and intrigue have defamed the name of Republicanism, and brought financial ruin upon the State." Disgruntled Republicans joined the new Union Reform Party along with some Democrats. In the 1870 campaign, the party's platform was "honesty against dishonesty—cheap, economical government against exorbitant taxation—reduction of public expenses against extravagant expenditure of the people's money—responsibility of officials for the faithful discharge of their duties against irresponsibility, selfishness and greedy absorption of power." The Reform Party failed to win the fall elections, though members alleged fraud and intimidation at the polls. Corruption in the Republican Party deprived it of unity precisely when it was most needed to overcome the massive resistance it faced.[29]

Some observers even claimed that corruption led to the Klan violence against Black people and Republicans.[30] But whatever else is true about the corruption in the South Carolina Republican Party, it does not explain the attempt to overthrow the constitutional order. We know this because conservatives and Democrats never gave the 1868 constitution or the Republican Party a chance. They schemed to prevent a constitutional convention in the first place, protested to federal authorities, and used terrorism, cold-blooded murder, and economic coercion to prevail in the 1868 general election. The reality is that, given their hostility to Black political advancement, they would have engaged in violence and attempted to defeat the new constitutional order even if every Republican official had been honest and efficient.

An Election During a War

1876 was the one-hundred-year anniversary of the American Revolution. No less than in 1776, a revolutionary spirit hung in the air. Democrats would engage in their most sustained effort yet to overthrow the government. They pledged their lives, fortunes, and honor to advance the principle that all men were not equal. And they had a plan. In 1876, they faced the same issue they had for the previous eight years: the state had a Black majority, and Black people reliably voted Republican.

General Martin W. Gary drew on how white Mississippians overthrew their government to provide a solution. He had fought with Wade

Hampton III in the Civil War and become a general. To win the 1876 campaign in spite of the forbidding math, he created a master plan. The plan called for the formation of Democratic rifle clubs who would wear red shirts at public meetings and on election day. The rifle clubs would be divided into companies and led by a captain. "In all processions the clubs [were to] parade with banners, mottoes, etc. and keep together so as to make an imposing spectacle." The clubs were to "attend every Radical meeting that we hear of whether they meet at night or in the day time." Democrats would be well-armed at Republican campaign events and "tell [Republican speakers] *then* and *there* to their faces, that they are liars, thieves and rascals, and are only trying to mislead the ignorant negroes and if you get a chance get upon the platform and address the negroes." In speaking to Black voters, rifle club members should "remember that *argument* has no effect upon them," that "they can only be influenced by their *fears*, superstition and cupidity," and to "treat [Black people] so as to show them, you are the superior race, and that their natural position is that of subordination to the white man." The plan paid special attention to election day. Each rifle club member was to have at least thirty rounds of ammunition and each club was to have three days' rations for the horses and men to be stored on the day before the election so that "they may be prepared at a moments [*sic*] notice to move to any point in the County when ordered by the Chairman of the Executive Committee [of the Democratic Party]." The plan contemplated an important role for individuals: "Every Democrat must feel honor bound to control the vote of at least one negro, by intimidation, purchase, keeping him away or as each individual may determine, how he may best accomplish it."[31] The Ku Klux Klan was back in a different colored uniform.

Democrats nominated Hampton for governor while Republicans renominated Daniel Chamberlain for reelection after a divisive process. Well-dressed with a thick, drooping mustache and a receding hairline, he looked like a distinguished law professor. Chamberlain was originally from Massachusetts. He had attended Yale and then Harvard Law School and carried student debt into the Civil War. Chamberlain then served as a lieutenant in the Fifth Massachusetts Negro Cavalry and saw action in Virginia. He originally came to South Carolina to settle a deceased classmate's affairs but remained afterward.[32]

The campaign would see politically charged violence ravage South Carolina. The situation became so bad that historians have referred to some incidents as "massacres." The seeds of the first were planted in the spring of 1876. Two months before a killing spree that received national attention, D. L. Adams, commander of a Black militia company, received warning that "the Democrats had made it up in their own minds, and they had organized all over the State, and also had about thirty men from Texas and Mississippi to come in this State, and they were feeding them, organizing all of the white men into certain different clubs, and before the election that there had to be a certain number of niggers killed, leading men, and if they found out after the leading men was killed [sic] that they couldn't carry the State that way, they were going to kill enough so that they could carry the majority." He later told Congress that some of these Democrats had kidnapped the company's drummer boy, whipped him, then forced the boy's mother to whip him again. Before the massacre, Adams also received a letter "specifying a dozen or two different names that was in the vicinity of Hamburgh [sic] that had to be killed." His name was on the list.

On July 4, 1876, Adams was leading his company on parade when white men driving a carriage refused to go around the parade and had to wait before being let through. The white people accused the company of deliberately blocking the road. Adams was summoned to court, but on the day of the trial, the white people in Hamburg "were getting drunk very fast" and "saying they were going to kill every God damned nigger in Hamburgh that day, and especially Doc Adams; that was myself." Adams was so afraid for his life that he went to the judge to explain that he would not show up for the hearing, not out of any disrespect, but because he didn't want to be lynched. M. C. Butler, who was representing the white plaintiffs, demanded that Adams surrender the militia's guns to him, which Adams refused to do. A crowd of white people then surrounded the militia in their drill room and shot at them for thirty minutes, at one point with a cannon. Then, the white people closed formation like a unit preparing to storm enemy fortifications. The militia returned fire briefly before fleeing the area.

While Adams sought safety, he heard white people going house to house and shooting the inhabitants. They referenced politics during the rampage. One said, "We are going to redeem South Carolina to-day!"

Another said, "By God! We will carry South Carolina now; about the time we kill four or five hundred more [Black people] we will scare the rest." At one point, Adams could see white people ransack his home. He lamented, "I saw them taking down my pictures and breaking up the furniture. They broke up everything I had in the world; took all my clothes, my mattresses, and feather-bed, and cut it in pieces and scattered it everywhere, destroying everything I had." The horrors were just beginning. As the night unfolded, Adams saw Black men in the town rounded up and white people debating what to do with them. Some of the white people "wanted to kill all, because if we don't, they will give testimony against us some day to come." Others wanted to kill only specific individuals. Eventually, Butler, who played a leading role in orchestrating the massacre, came by. Butler listed specific people he wanted killed. Four Black men died. Authorities indicted Butler, but never arrested him or forced him to stand trial. National media reports gave credence to Adams's description of the events. The *New York Herald* wrote that "this affair, apparently, was as unwarranted and unprovoked as it was barbarous." And even in protesting his innocence, Butler admitted, "Many things were done on this terrible night which, of course, cannot be justified"—before justifying the violence because "the negroes 'sowed the wind' and reaped the whirlwind."[33]

A potentially bigger massacre later happened in Ellenton, although historians and the press were unable to agree on how many died and who instigated the conflict. One account, sympathetic to the white people, held that two Black people had broken into a white woman's house, beaten her when she resisted, and then beaten a child trying to escape. Her husband then gathered associates to pursue the attackers. The group brought one of the assailants back who confessed to attacking her and identified the other assailant. Armed Black men fired on the posse raised to pursue that assailant, and three of them were wounded when the white men returned fire. At one point, the Black group agreed to talk with the white group and claimed they had not harbored the assailant. After both sides agreed to disperse, though, the Black group ambushed and shot a white man dead before burning a mill, gin house, and barn. After destroying a train, the Black men retreated to Ellenton under the leadership of Simon Coker, a Black legislator, and prepared to ambush white reinforcements. Three hundred white men were ready to charge into a group of Black people in a swamp when US troops intervened. The account only briefly mentioned that the white group had captured Coker and killed him.

The *New York Times* painted a grim portrait of Coker's death. It reported that a rifle club found Coker "quietly seated on his valise and waiting for a train." Upon seeing him, some members declared, "There's that—radical nigger, Coker." The club's captain told him, "I'm the nigger ruler, and you've got to go with me." The men dragged Coker aboard a car and forced him to get off when it arrived at Ellenton, then marched him into a field about one hundred yards away. When Coker insisted that he was a legislator, the captain responded, "Representative or no Representative, you are a radical nigger, and have got to die." He shot Coker twice while he was praying. Six other men fired their weapons until Coker was dead. The rifle club members then took Coker's watch, money, and gold shirt buttons. The story suggests that even if a burglary did occur, white people had simply used it as an excuse to pillage and murder. Rumors swirled that as many as three hundred died, although some casualty estimates were much lower. After the Ellenton massacre, President Grant proclaimed, "It has been satisfactorily shown to me that insurrection and domestic violence exist in several counties of the State of South Carolina, and that certain combinations of men against law exist in many counties of said State, known as 'Rifle Clubs,' who ride up and down by day and night in arms, murdering some peaceable citizens and intimidating others, which combinations, though forbidden by the laws of the State, cannot be controlled or suppressed by the ordinary course of justice." He ordered the rifle clubs to disperse.[34] They refused.

Instead, in Cainhoy, a US Marshall reported that Democrats had gone to Republican meetings in the area armed with Winchester rifles. They demanded that Republican speakers divide their time with Democrats at gunpoint; Republicans promptly agreed. At a meeting in October of 1876, Black Republicans came armed, but when informed of an agreement not to bring weapons to campaign events, stored some of them in a dilapidated building and others in nearby woods. In the evening, 150 Democrats came to the meeting from a steamboat. They seized the weapons in the building and carried them to the meeting. A Black candidate cried, "Those white men in that house have guns, and are going to shoot," before the white men shot a Black man dead. After that, Black men retrieved their weapons and returned fire. In the final analysis, six white men and one Black man died, making this the rare event during Reconstruction where more white than Black people died during an altercation.

Democrats told a different story. A newspaper claimed that after whites had found a stash of hidden arms, "the negroes advanced from the woods in regular skirmishing order, and fired upon the whites." It believed that Black men had massacred the white men. Another newspaper alleged that "the attack upon the whites was deliberately planned." We cannot know for sure whether Black people came to the meeting intending to kill white people. It is possible that they would want revenge for all the predations they had suffered over the years. But more likely, this was a rifle club executing Gary's plan and running into more resistance than expected. Regardless, Grant sent more troops to South Carolina after Cainhoy.[35] Perhaps Thomas Jefferson's most serious fear— race war—was being realized in South Carolina one hundred years after the Declaration of Independence.

A more traditional campaign unfolded at the same time as the red shirt reign of terror. As a confederate war hero, Hampton was popular among Democrats. He received adulation reserved in our era for charismatic presidential candidates. Over ten thousand voters marched in a procession in Charleston while "crowds of ladies waved handkerchiefs from every window." Hampton pursued a clever strategy during the election. In a speech on October 7, 1876, Hampton told his "colored friends to bear this in mind: I was the first to advise that rights of all kinds should be conferred upon colored men." Rhetoric like this helped Hampton distance himself from the red shirts and appeal to some Republicans disenchanted by all the corruption but unwilling to countenance murder. Hampton even claimed to know nothing about attacks on Black Republicans in front of Congress. But the assertion is untenable. He admitted that he was in touch with every part of the state. He was Gary's commander during the Civil War and a fixture of the conservative white establishment. He had been aware of violence against Black people in 1868 and wrote an editorial calling for the attacks to cease. He had even raised funds to hire lawyers for accused Klansmen. Hampton saw himself as chivalrous and benevolent and may not have personally approved of the tactics used to suppress Black votes, as one distinguished historian has argued.[36] But he did benefit from those tactics. The most charitable interpretation is not really charitable at all—he personally disliked the Gary plan, refused to use his influence to stop it, saw his chances to win increase as the number of Black voters decreased, all while presenting himself as a respectable moderate.

As election day approached, Democrats predicted that Republicans would steal the election. The *Anderson Intelligencer* claimed that a plan was afoot to "arrest the influential men and those who are active in this canvass all over the State [for the Democrats]" on false charges so they could intimidate Democratic voters. Indeed, fraud and intimidation did contaminate the results. The *News and Courier* reported that groups of Republicans would vote at one polling place, then go vote again at another. It also asserted that underage boys had voted Republican. No Black men would have been willing to vote Democrat after "one woman actually assaulted her husband" for doing so.[37]

On the other hand, Democrats themselves later acknowledged that they used fraud and violence during the election. "Pitchfork" Ben Tillman, who later played a role in provoking North Carolina's 1898 constitutional crisis (which we will explore next chapter), put it this way: "How did we recover our liberty? By fraud and violence. We tried to overcome the 30,000 majority by honest methods, which was a mathematical impossibility." A prominent historian observed that "there are reputable white men living in South Carolina who boast of having voted 18 or 20 times in the election. Parties of white men on horseback cast their ballots at many polls."[38]

Election Day Breeds Uncertainty

It was unclear who won the election. The *Port Royal Standard and Commercial* claimed that Chamberlain had been reelected governor by 5,332 votes. On the other hand, the *Pickens Sentinel* claimed that Hampton led by 3,000 votes. Key legislative races were undetermined. Fighting broke out in Charleston as ballots were being counted. The stakes were immense for the entire country. South Carolina's electors would be critical in determining the presidential race. South Carolina's US senator would help determine the course of Reconstruction policy in the South.[39]

The state would have to navigate a confusing maze of laws to escape the chaos. A statute charged the board of canvassers with tallying votes and declaring the highest vote-getter elected. However, South Carolina's constitution provided that "[e]ach House shall judge of the election returns and qualifications of its own members." The legislature also decided contested elections for governor. South Carolina's constitution required the secretary of state to forward returns to the legislature, which was to declare the candidate with the most votes elected. These procedural provisions lived in the shadow of substantive guarantees that elections would be "free and open," that all citizens had "an equal right" to elect officials, and that elections should be free from "power, bribery, tumult, or improper conduct."[40] Partisanship informed how both sides approached resolving the election. The board of canvassers had a Republican majority and three of its members had sought reelection. Republicans naturally favored a more expansive role for the board. Democrats might control the legislature if certain men were certified as victors, so they favored the legislature.

The board investigated irregularities in some South Carolina counties, and there were many. For example, Paris Simkins testified to Congress that in Edgefield County, the polls "were blocked and otherwise crowded by armed Democrats, who were uniformed in red shirts, and from one to two pistols buckled on the outside, and some with sixteen-shooters strapped to their sides, the major part of them being mounted on horses, and using threats of a violent nature to republicans who would present themselves for the purpose of voting the republican ticket." Simkins further testified that red shirts prevented between six and eight hundred Republicans from voting and that Edgefield County had reported three thousand more votes than would have been possible if only registered voters had each voted once. That outcome suggests that some South Carolinians really had voted multiple times. Several others testified to intimidation and fraud during the election. Democrats protested that the board of canvassers had overstepped its authority by investigating what happened during the election instead of simply counting votes. The South Carolina Supreme Court agreed and ordered the board to declare those who had won the most votes duly elected and leave contested elections to the legislature.[41] On one hand, the court was on solid ground because of clear constitutional text explicitly leaving contested elections to the legislature. On the other hand, the court failed to consider whether the election had lived up to the constitution's lofty promises of fairness in light of the fraud and violence. It also failed to consider whether the legislature must take these constitutional provisions into account when deciding the contested elections. To be fair, analyzing these issues in a principled way would have been difficult. How much fraud and intimidation does it take before an election is so unfair and unfree that a court can intervene? And how would a court tell? Even if there were good answers to these questions, would it be practical to expect a three-member court to fairly and thoroughly investigate an election in such a short time frame?

The board refused to obey the court's order and declined to issue certificates to candidates whose elections depended on votes from Edgefield and Laurens counties. The South Carolina Supreme Court responded by holding board members in contempt and fining them $1,500 each. They were imprisoned until a federal judge issued them a writ of habeas corpus. The secretary of state ultimately gave certificates to fifty-nine Republicans and fifty-seven Democrats in the house of representatives and certified a five-seat Republican majority in the senate. In spite of his ordeal with the South Carolina Supreme Court, he declined to issue certificates to candidates whose victories depended on votes from Edgefield and Laurens counties. The South Carolina Supreme Court in turn issued certificates to all candidates in the election who got the highest vote totals including the ones from Edgefield and Laurens counties. Meanwhile, a large crowd thronged Columbia.[42]

The dueling certificates soon led to dual government. It was unclear whether Republicans or Democrats controlled the house of representatives. When Democrats descended on the state house, the sergeant at arms and US soldiers defending the building refused them admission. Republicans proceeded as though they controlled the house of representatives. They elected E. W. M. Mackey as speaker of the house. Mackey was a native South Carolinian who had been a delegate to South Carolina's 1868 constitutional convention. He had parted hair along with a thick mustache and thin goatee. He looked older than his years and the coming month must have been extremely stressful for him. His members voted to unseat the Democrats from Laurens and Edgefield counties who had certificates from the South Carolina Supreme Court and seated their Republican opponents. Meanwhile, Democrats organized at Carolina Hall and elected William Wallace speaker of the house. Wallace was heavy-set with a goatee and mustache. The son of a general and grandson of a member of the continental army during the American Revolution, he had deep roots in South Carolina.[43]

Organizing two separate houses of representatives invited the difficult question of which one had a constitutional quorum. The constitution set the house's membership at 124. Neither the Republican nor the Democratic house had that many, but both argued they could form a quorum. Republicans argued that the house of representatives had only 116 members since no lawful elections had been held in Edgefield and Laurens counties—due to fraud and violence—and that they had a quorum with 59 members. But that ignored clear constitutional text. Democrats argued that the house of representatives must have 124 members and that they alone had a quorum with 63 members when members from Edgefield and Laurens counties were included. But that ignored the fact that those members likely wouldn't have won in an election that complied with constitutional requirements. When the South Carolina Supreme Court refused to decide the question of whether the election had complied with the constitution's guarantees of fairness in the electoral process, it may have thought it was avoiding a political question. Instead, it now faced an even more politically charged question: *who* constituted the house of representatives? The Wallace House or the Mackey House?

The Wallace House tried to force the issue. In early December of 1876, its members attempted to take over the state house. Wallace even went to the speaker's chair and gaveled the house to order. Hampton attempted to enter, but the Republican sergeant at arms stopped him. Mackey and the Republican sergeant at arms then went to the speaker's well. Mackey, who a newspaper reported was "trembling with excitement and gasping for breath," told Wallace, "You will please vacate this seat." Wallace responded, "I have been elected by a majority of the House of Representatives of the State of South Carolina, duly sworn in, in the Carolina Hall, on Tuesday, the 28th day of November, instant." Mackey replied, "I claim that I was elected Speaker of this House by a legal quorum of members legally sworn in. We do not recognize that any others than those sworn in here on Tuesday last are members of this House, and those men who are visiting this hall without our consent must keep order. I must again demand that you, Gen. Wallace, leave this chair." Wallace responded, "I have already declared that I am the legally elected Speaker of this House, and I must request you to retire." Both men ordered their sergeants at arms to enforce their orders to the other man to withdraw. Both a Democratic and a Republican sergeant at arms moved to enforce their orders while members of each body appeared ready for a brawl, but neither Wallace nor Mackey budged.

A fight was averted, but then the two sides tried to hold their legislative session at the same time. Both Wallace and Mackey recognized speakers. When two men spoke over each other, Wallace called the Republican speaker to order while Mackey called the Democratic speaker to order. Outside the state house, rumors of impending violence circulated. The *News and Courier* reported that Hampton received an anonymous letter threatening that a gang of Republicans were ready to start a fight in the state house. Meanwhile, five thousand Democrats had come to Columbia from across the state.[44]

The Mackey House inaugurated Chamberlain as governor on December 6, 1876. The *News and Courier* reported that he was "as white as a sheet and trembled visibly as he came to the front" and that only "one or two persons raised a faint cheer, but it soon subsided."[45] The South Carolina Supreme Court ended any celebration when it declared that the Mackey House was not the lawful house of representatives. Wallace had previously demanded that Mackey deliver returns for the election of governor and lieutenant governor. When Mackey refused, Wallace petitioned the South Carolina Supreme Court for a writ of mandamus to force him and the secretary of state to deliver the returns. All three justices wrote opinions in the case. Franklin Moses Sr. focused on the fact that South Carolina's constitution required 124 members of the house of representatives. Since 63 was enough for a quorum, Wallace was the speaker "of a legally-constituted House of Representatives of South Carolina." Jonathan Jasper Wright came closest to considering the larger issues of fairness in Edgefield and Laurens counties. In defending the rights of members from those counties to their seats, Wright wrote, "I presume the object of the government is, or should be, the protection and representation of the people." He reasonably worried that if the board of canvassers "have the right to throw out one County and thus defeat its representation, they can throw out one-half or all of the Counties in the State and defeat an entire election."[46] But Wright refused to consider whether the violence, fraud, and intimidation in the election had done precisely that.

The Mackey House did not retire from the contest. It elected D. T. Corbin to the US Senate. As the Law and Order Party did in Rhode Island, the Mackey House made it illegal to maintain "a government of the State in opposition to the legitimate and lawful government." But the Mackey House couldn't fund government because a judge issued a temporary restraining order preventing banks where state funds were deposited from paying out funds on the Republican state treasurer's order.[47]

The Wallace House inaugurated Hampton governor a week after the Mackey House inaugurated Chamberlain. In what must have been a bitter pill for Mackey to swallow, his own uncle administered the oath of office to Hampton. Though the atmosphere was initially "one of intense solemnity," there was "a spontaneous and universal shout" after Hampton was sworn in. Democrats fired rockets and cannons in celebration. Hampton then wrote Chamberlain demanding that he "deliver up to me the great seal of State, together with the possession of the Statehouse, the public records and all other matters and things appertaining to said office." Chamberlain refused the request, and some speculated that he would try to arrest Hampton.[48] The Wallace House also elected M. C. Butler, who had been indicted for his role in the Hamburg massacre, to the US Senate. Finally, the Wallace House passed a resolution authorizing Hampton to call upon citizens to pay one-fourth of the tax they paid the previous year which would be deducted from future taxes. This move raised $119,432.41.[49] When combined with the fact that the Republicans couldn't fund government due to the injunction, this infusion of money positioned the Democrats as the only party who could actually govern.

Chamberlain and Hampton both pursued recognition from the courts. Two issues distinguished their case from the earlier one recognizing the Wallace House. First, South Carolina's 1868 constitution required that both houses of the legislature be present when the speaker of the house opened and published the returns from the gubernatorial election. This protocol had not been followed here. Second, the constitution required that the legislature as a whole determine contested elections, and not merely one house of it. The problem was that the Republicans controlled the state senate while Democrats controlled the house of representatives. How could a divided legislature unify the state around one of the gubernatorial candidates? In *Ex Parte Norris*, the South Carolina Supreme Court made the question moot when it ruled for Hampton. It found the most important constitutional question to be whether Hampton received the most votes at the election. It treated the requirement for returns to be published in the presence of both houses as a technicality that could not defeat the claim of a candidate who had won the most votes. The decision was initially unanimous, but then Wright reversed course. After "mature deliberation," he concluded that Hampton wasn't the lawful governor. He believed that requiring both houses to be present when the election returns were submitted was an important substantive safeguard against illegality and fraud. This suggested that Wright worried that fraud and violence had in fact changed the outcome in Laurens and Edgefield counties. The *Charleston News and Courier* would later claim that Wright changed his vote after "he was subjected to a well organized system of espionage by his political masters who, by persuasion and intimidation, compelled him to sign an order revoking and cancelling the order that he had previously signed" and then simply signed his name to an opinion Chamberlain drafted.[50] There is little doubt that the justices faced intense lobbying behind the scenes given the case's stakes, but there is no hard evidence Wright acted to appease his "political masters." A more charitable explanation is that Wright faced incredibly difficult legal questions in a short time frame and came to believe his initial reaction was erroneous. If so, that invites criticism for indecision and praise for intellectual honesty.

While all of this happened, feverish negotiations happened in Washington about who won the presidential election. New York Governor Samuel Tilden had won the popular vote and was ahead in the electoral college. But he failed to secure the majority he needed because of disputes over electors from Oregon, Louisiana, Florida, and South Carolina. Amid a deadlock about whether the US House of Representatives or the US Senate should count the electoral votes, Congress formed a special commission to decide what to do. That commission awarded the disputed votes to Rutherford B. Hayes, and he became president. Historians have long suspected that Democrats and Republicans made a deal whereby Republicans kept the presidency in exchange for ending Reconstruction in the South.[51] The 1876 presidential election threatened a constitutional crisis at the federal level and remains the subject of scholarship today. Yet, a federal constitutional crisis was only a realistic possibility because of constitutional crises throughout the South during the era.

After Hayes became president, both Hampton and Chamberlain traveled to Washington, DC, to lobby him. Both met him in the White House and then wrote letters reiterating their request for support. Just as in Arkansas, Kansas, Pennsylvania, and Rhode Island, the president would have to choose sides in a state constitutional crisis. Ultimately, Hayes tacitly supported Hampton when he withdrew federal troops from the state house in Columbia. Prominent Republicans saw the situation was hopeless and publicly advised Chamberlain to step aside. Chamberlain acquiesced and turned over the office to Hampton on April 11, 1877, though he continued to insist that he had really won the election.[52] A persistent minority had defeated the constitutional order embraced by the majority.

In reflecting on the crisis, it might be tempting to focus on the 1876 campaign and the legal and political maneuvering that followed it. In and of itself, that tumultuous episode is a glimpse of what the Buckshot War might have become if it had dragged on longer. But the election dispute did not represent South Carolina's constitutional abyss. South Carolina was already there before the first ballot was submitted. The real story here is that South Carolina during Reconstruction was a battle-field for the race war white people waged against Black people. White people were always going to be at an advantage in this war. They had the military training and the financial resources Black people lacked. They were willing to use murder and terrorism as weapons. Black people were not. This observation is distressing because it suggests delegates to South Carolina's 1868 constitutional convention could have done nothing to avoid the fate their constitution suffered. No amount of creative drafting or generous outreach could have gotten white South Carolinians to tolerate a constitution premised on Black equality. For that matter, even if South Carolina's 1868 constitution had perfect procedures to resolve an election dispute and even if the judges and election officials had all been fair and courageous, Democrats would have refused to accept any outcome other than the total victory of white supremacy. If for some reason they failed to achieve that in 1876, they would have at a later date.

The only way to change this calculus would have been for the federal government to forcefully intervene in a way that northern public opinion would not have supported. Southern white people cared more about white supremacy than northern white people cared about Black equality.

The Spirit of 1861 and South Carolina's New Constitutional Order

Black suffering accelerated after 1876. Although Hampton did appoint some Black officeholders, their number precipitously declined by the 1890s. Wright resigned from the South Carolina Supreme Court. He spent his last years in poverty before dying of tuberculosis. Smalls and Cardozo, among others, were investigated for corruption and convicted. Cardozo went to prison. Democrats did not investigate the Ellenton or Hamburg massacres or the Ku Klux Klan activity that had taken place. Butler, who instigated the Hamburg massacre, went to Congress.[53]

While there was some lingering Black political involvement after the constitutional crisis, South Carolina's 1895 constitution ended it. The convention that produced it was far different from the 1868 convention. Only six Black people were delegates in 1895 while a majority of the delegates in 1868 were Black. Whipper and Smalls attended to defend their handiwork. Some of the white delegates openly used the word "nigger" at the convention, ironic since a delegate in 1868 had proposed banning the term. The overriding purpose for the constitution was to relegate Black people to second-class citizenship. Ben Tillman, who worked to suppress Black votes in 1876, urged white delegates to "unite as brothers" to establish a constitution ensuring that "we will not have to appeal to these people [Black people] as arbiters of our fate."[54]

They succeeded in reestablishing their pre–Civil War definition of "the people." The new constitution eventually restricted the franchise to those who could pass a test of reading and writing any section of the state constitution or demonstrate that they owned property worth at least $300. The constitution required paying poll taxes before voting. It greatly expanded the list of felonies for which someone could be disenfranchised. The provisions were race neutral on their face, but a scholar just one year later observed that "the object is, of course, to disenfranchise the ignorant negro, while retaining the illiterate white vote, and in this the scheme has not failed." The constitution also provided for segregated schools. A vicious cycle awaited Black people. Higher rates of illiteracy and lower rates of property ownership disenfranchised many of them, which led to a government that refused to adequately support educating Black students. The new constitution could only be amended when two-thirds of both houses of the legislature agreed to do so. With such a high bar to constitutional change and such a low number of Black voters, perpetual disempowerment was the outcome. South Carolina's constitutional experiment in multiracial democracy was over. Perhaps out of self-awareness, Democrats removed the 1868 constitution's provision that "all men are born free and equal" along with its prohibition on slavery.[55]

Whipper and Smalls did not go gently into the night. Struggling with asthma, Whipper warned that "when you treat a negro as an alien and stranger it will spread such a prejudice and lead to assassination, or what is now called lynching." Robert Smalls protested that "since Reconstruction times fifty-three thousand negroes have been killed in the South, and not more than three white men have been convicted and hung for these crimes." But if white people persisted in using the constitution to oppress Black people, "some morning you may wake up to find that the bone and sinew of your country is gone."[56] White southerners had voted with bullets before they deprived Black people of ballots. In the Great Migration that followed the rise of Jim Crow, millions of Black people finally responded by voting with their feet. They moved in large numbers to northern and western states willing to recognize some form of "equality" and to treat them as part of "the people." American politics would be forever changed.

The Aftermath of the Crisis

Some of the most prominent characters in South Carolina's constitutional odyssey died a few years later. William Wallace became a respected judge after serving as speaker of the house of representatives. The Charleston Bar paid tribute to him when he died in 1901. His opponent, E. W. M. Mackey died young in 1884.[57]

Daniel Chamberlain eventually regretted Reconstruction and soured on the Republican Party. Later in life, he claimed that "literary, scientific, or what we call the higher education" had been "a positive evil" to Black people and that they should focus on "simple manual labor of all kinds, which it is [the Black man's] lot to do,—lot fixed not by us, but by powers above us." Obituaries in South Carolina were favorable when he died in 1907. The *News and Courier* depicted him as "a scholar of the truest temper, a lover of his country of the broadest views" and declared that "at bottom he was always true, as we believe, to the highest welfare of his adopted State. New Englander by birth, he was a South Carolinian in spirit, and lived long enough to regain in large measure the respect of our people."[58]

Wade Hampton was reelected governor in 1878 and served in the US Senate. When he died in 1902, newspapers across the South praised what they saw as his gallantry in battle and nobility of character. At his funeral, another newspaper reported, "not less than twenty thousand people were there to testify their gratitude for the life that had ebbed away, while from far and near had come floral offerings that were expressive of the purity and beauty of his character."[59]

Robert Smalls received less acclaim when he died in 1915. In his final days, he must have wondered if his life's work had been a failure. Like Thaddeus Stevens, Smalls used his tombstone to send one last defiant message. An inscription declared, "My race needs no special defense, for the past history of them in this country proves them to be the equal of any people anywhere. All they need is an equal chance in the battle of life."[60]

Even though Black people robustly participate in politics today, South Carolinians still live with a constitution designed to make them second-class citizens. To this day, the South Carolina Constitution does not ban slavery. It does not declare, as many other state constitutions do, some variation of the idea that "all men are created equal." And it still allows the legislature to impose a literacy test on voters.[61]

6

The Spirit of 1868 Resurrected?

Wilmington, North Carolina, in November 1898 represented a crossroads for Thaddeus Stevens's constitutional vision. After "redeeming" governments across the South in the 1870s, Democrats began the process of putting Black people back in as near a condition to slavery as possible. The process, which was far along in most southern states, was halted in Wilmington when white Populists allied with Black Republicans. Black men maintained their right to vote and were a force to be reckoned with politically. They were officeholders. Their economic power was growing. Wilmington was proudly carrying the spirit of 1868 into the twentieth century. If its progress continued, it could serve as an inspiration to Black people presently living in places reconquered by the spirit of 1861. That is why two shadowy conspiracies had been quietly laying the groundwork for an armed coup d'état for months.

A short review of North Carolina's Reconstruction experience will give you a sense of déjà vu when you learn about what happened in Wilmington. After the Civil War ended and Congress passed the Reconstruction Acts, a new political coalition of white and Black Republicans drafted a constitution in North Carolina. They dominated the convention by a margin of 107 Republicans against just 13 conservatives.[1] Fifteen of the Republicans were Black. The Republicans made Black men part of "the people" and linked their focus on racial equality to the American Revolution. The 1868 constitution began its Declaration of Rights by emphasizing "[t]hat we hold it to be self-evident that all men are created equal; that they are endowed by their Creator with certain unalienable rights; that among these are life, liberty, the enjoyment of the fruits of their own labor, and the pursuit of happiness." These words did not appear in North Carolina's 1776 constitution. Conservatives recognized their inclusion as a significant step, for they complained that Republicans were taking the Declaration out of context; they understood the Declaration as referring merely to "the distinctions among white men, under the laws and Constitution of Great Britain." They further recognized that "the idea and provision of absolute equality runs through every clause of this Constitution."² Three changes illustrate the point.

First, delegates extended basic rights to everyone. They abolished slavery. But perhaps even more importantly, they made it clear that important liberties no longer depended on a person's social status. For example, where the 1776 constitution provided only that "no freeman shall be convicted of any crime, but by the unanimous verdict of a jury of good and lawful men," the 1868 constitution guaranteed that "[n]o person shall be convicted of any crime but by the unanimous verdict of a jury of good and lawful men in open court."

Second, the 1868 constitution made participation in politics much more democratic than it had been before. Every man, regardless of his race, could vote. Property requirements to vote and hold office were abolished. The constitution allowed voters to directly elect county officials instead of having a distant legislature select them. Removing racial and property restrictions on the franchise bolstered the coalition of Black and white people who had been dissatisfied with North Carolina's pre–Civil War political establishment. A thirty-year effort to break this coalition apart ultimately culminated in Wilmington's streets.

Third, the 1868 constitution guaranteed a right to public education, even commanding the legislature to make college tuition free "as far as practicable." In addition to committing to a more expansive definition of "liberty" as Arkansas and South Carolina did in 1868, delegates saw the right to an education as indispensable to their efforts to promote equality. In their appeal for ratification, they argued, "All may see the difference between the success in life of the educated and uneducated man, yet as often as not, the uneducated man has been gifted with the greater degree of intellectual power; the cause of his ill success is that it has not been developed." Therefore, they "propose[d] to 'level upwards,' to give to every child, as far as the State can, an opportunity to develop to the fullest extent, all his intellectual gifts."³

Conservatives fought the new constitution while it was still being drafted. Most unforgivably, it was both the product and enabler of multiracial democracy. Conservatives lamented that "Northern men in the Convention, claiming to be gentlemen, openly associate with these negroes [delegates to the convention], receive them into their rooms at the

Hotels, and confer, and consult, and jest, and converse with them, just as they would do with the most accomplished white man!" A minority report on suffrage complained that "the great mass of them [Black people] are so ignorant and prejudiced that they easily become the dupes of designing adventurers and demagogues, and through secret associations, introduced from Northern States, merely follow instructions, and reflect the views of those who control them."[4] Conservatives warned that the newly enfranchised Black voters "WILL RULE." Thus was born the cry of "negro domination" that white supremacists would use to drive a wedge between Black and white voters with aligned interests for the next thirty years. Conservatives warned that putting Black people in the dominant position would have catastrophic consequences. Black voters would elect legislators to tax the lands of white men so heavily that they would be forced to sell. Then, conservatives asked, "would not each negro get his forty acres very speedily?" White children would "be forced to go to school sixteen months with negroes." Even worse, the new constitution would force a seventeen-year old white girl to "recite with negro boys of twenty" who could "make love to her, and call her pet names." A Black delegate tried to defuse the explosive miscegenation issue by introducing a resolution, later passed, that "it is the sense of this Convention that inter-marriages and illegal intercourse between the races should be discountenanced, and the interests and happiness of the two races would be best promoted by the establishment of separate schools." But conservatives were determined to paint Black men as sexual predators and warn that they would be a menace so long as they participated in politics.[5]

Conservatives had little prospect of convincing Black voters to oppose a constitution conferring rights on them. So, to defeat the burgeoning coalition threatening their interests, they had to get white voters who disagreed with them on important issues to oppose ratification. But many white people in western North Carolina supported the Union during the Civil War and had lacked power before it. They were not natural allies. Conservatives attempted to exploit class resentments, arguing that wealthy white people would "have no fear of negro equality being illustrated in their own families" while poor white people would have to deal with integrated schools and Black rapists. They framed "*the struggle* [as] *narrowed down between the great mass of white people, especially*

*the poor white people, on the one side, and the negroes backed by a crowd
of hungry office-seekers, and such craven-hearted men of property as are
solicitous only for their own safety on the other side."* They even claimed
an entity called the "POOR WHITE MAN'S PARTY" existed to oppose
ratification.[6] Although many white voters across North Carolina held
racist attitudes, they also appreciated at least some of the new constitution's innovations. As such, the frightening picture of "negro domination" conservatives drew was not yet enough to sway a critical mass of
white voters.

In fact, and unlike in South Carolina, the constitution required white
support to pass. Whites had a voting majority of over thirty thousand
and could have voted down the constitution by themselves. Yet they did
not. As one article in *Tarboro's Southerner* explained, "No one doubted
that the white men of the East would rally almost as one man against
the Constitution and the only fear felt was from the indifference and
lukewarmness of the West. That apprehension has been sadly verified
and to the West alone can be attributed the success of the Radical-nigger
party." However, ratification came with an important caveat. Black people were in a precarious position because they had to rely on a majority
white electorate to uphold their equality. They had a similar percentage
of the population as Black people did in Arkansas, and we saw how that
ultimately worked out.[7] In the final analysis, only a minority of North
Carolinians genuinely believed in full Black political and legal equality.
Others who supported the 1868 constitution would grudgingly tolerate
some measure of racial equality so long as doing so served their interests. That meant that the constitutional vision of racial equality that so
animated convention delegates was ultimately a minority vision. They
were pushing a Leavenworth Constitution in a state where most residents preferred either a Topeka or Lecompton Constitution.

Wilmington Foreshadowed: Conservatives Overthrow the 1868 Constitution

Elected governor in 1868, William Holden stood between conservatives
and their constitutional vision. Refusing to give up after the constitution
was ratified, they embarked on a campaign to defeat it using the same
strategy they would attempt to use in Wilmington in 1898. They spread

inflammatory stories about Black people to arouse the sentiments of white people otherwise inclined to work with them, used violence with military precision to provoke a constitutional crisis, and then used that crisis as an excuse to remove a hostile elected official.

To generate outrage, conservatives returned to the same threat of Black men raping white women that they had used in arguing against the 1868 constitution. In April 1870, for example, the *Wilmington Daily Journal* reported a "gross outrage perpetrated by two negro ruffians in Cape Fear Township in this county upon two white women Tuesday night last." One of the Black men had allegedly "[sprung] upon [the mother and] placed his fingers on her throat and hurled her to the floor" while the daughter "was seized by the other ruffian and also borne to the floor." The article "shudder[ed] at the fiendish object which was evidently their intent," but at least they had escaped. Other white women might not be so lucky. It is probably no accident that these "outrages" were reported in the same issue and on the same page as an article complaining that the Fifteenth Amendment to the US Constitution, which protected suffrage for Black men, had passed.[8]

Meanwhile, the Ku Klux Klan worked to sway the 1868 elections. That year, the *Weekly North Carolina Standard* lamented that "the devilish K. Klux Klan have taken full possession of the town of Warrenton." The Klansmen were "out every night in disguise, halting peaceable citizens on the streets, showing their mysterious inscriptions, and [as a warning] digging graves about town and on the roads."[9] Their efforts in 1868 did not bear fruit, but that only made them more determined to influence the 1870 elections.

To do so, the Klan sowed terror among Republican and especially Black voters. They committed dozens of murders. In one case in the winter of 1869, thirteen Klansmen broke into a Black family's home, and shot four of the children and their pregnant mother. When they found a baby still alive, one of them "kick[ed] its brains out with the heel of his boot." The Klan then burned the house down. The Klan also assassinated Republican politicians. In February 1870, about one hundred Klansmen dragged Graham town commissioner Wyatt Outlaw, a prominent Black Republican, from his home and lynched him. They left a note on his body: "Beware, you guilty, both white and black." Conservatives argued that "the hanging of Outlaw was the work probably of a party of Blacks" who were "in disguise and whipped three other colored men."[10] In another case, Klansmen worked with a Democratic Party politician to hunt John Stephens, a state senator. While present at a Democratic campaign meeting, a "prominent Democrat of Caswell [County] approached Stephens with a smile, and asked him to go downstairs [into a courthouse] with him." Once inside the clerk of court's office, Stephens "was struck with horror when a rope, fixed as a lasso, was thrown over his neck from behind, and he was told by a spokesman of the Ku Klux crowd that he must renounce his Republican principles, leave the country, or die." When he refused, he "was then told that he must die." The Klan allowed him to "take a last look, from the window of the office, at his home" and he "beheld his little home and his two little children playing in front of his house." The Klan then "[threw him] down on a table," choked him, and cut his jugular vein. The Klan left his body "on a pile of wood in the room" before going upstairs where they "stamped and applauded Democratic speeches." The Klan even planned to murder Governor Holden but failed to follow through.[11]

As one North Carolinian testified to Congress, all of the violence had a political goal. Klansmen would frequently find Republicans, whip them mercilessly, and tell them that they had been targeted "because they were Republicans, and they must quit voting the Republican ticket." In counties with rampant Klan violence, "a perfect state of intimidation" meant that "you cannot get out the Republican vote."[12]

To bring the violence under control, Holden called out the militia and suspended the writ of habeas corpus. Critics called his actions the Kirk-Holden War, named after Holden and his commander of the militia, even though the only side killing was the Klan. Suspending the writ of habeas corpus might have been defensible, but violated the North Carolina Constitution, which declared that "the writ of *habeas corpus* shall not be suspended." Moreover, the actions of subordinates played into the perception that Holden was conducting a "reign of terror." Conservative newspapers reported that the militia arrested one man and hanged him by the neck to coerce him into confessing to Outlaw's murder. The steady drumbeat of negative coverage ensured that conservatives enthusiastically voted. The Klan violence ensured that many Republicans did not. As a result, conservatives won a majority in the legislature, which promptly impeached and then removed Holden for his actions in fighting the Klan, making him the first American governor to be removed from office.[13] Conservatives had successfully staged a coup. They never accepted the legitimacy of the 1868 constitution, and they managed to overthrow the government elected under that constitution. It is true that Holden exceeded his powers under the constitution. But conservatives had given him no choice. They worked with terrorists to bring government to a standstill and deprive citizens of basic rights. They had openly waged war on the constitution's values and then hidden behind the constitution's text to complete their triumph. North Carolina was "redeemed."

The 1870 elections also allowed conservatives to send five men to the US House of Representatives.[14] One of them was Alfred Waddell, who helped lead the effort to overthrow Wilmington's government in 1898.

Carrying out the Spirit of 1861

Once Democrats redeemed North Carolina, they enlisted the government in their effort to eliminate Black people from the political process. But the 1868 constitution still posed a hurdle because it guaranteed Black voting rights and "free" elections. Democrats turned to gerrymandering and byzantine voter registration requirements to circumvent these constitutional provisions. In municipal elections, for example, the legislature divided Wilmington into three wards. The first two had 400 voters and the last one had 2,800. Most of the Black voters were in the third ward, ensuring them less representation than they would otherwise have. The legislature also passed an act allowing any bystander to challenge a voter's eligibility. The voter would then have to provide witnesses that they were old enough to vote, that they had lived in the state for twelve months, and the relevant locality for ninety days. In addition, the registrar ruling on whether the voter was eligible had to know the witnesses and still had discretion to deem a voter ineligible if they were unsatisfied. White Democratic registrars had an incentive to rule as many Black Republicans ineligible as possible. Moreover, because of pervasive racial segregation, they were unlikely to belong to any of the same social circles as a challenged Black voter, meaning that many Black people would be unable to produce witnesses that they were eligible to vote that the registrar would know and trust. But the North Carolina

Supreme Court rebuffed these efforts. The court found it "too plain for argument" that such extreme gerrymandering contradicted the state constitution because it was a "violation of fundamental principles, the [proper] apportionment of representation." It was unimpressed by the legislature's argument that its division of Wilmington's wards was merely a race neutral attempt to "favor the intelligent and educated," instead of an attempt to discriminate. The court recognized that the new voter registration laws were "framed upon the idea of making the ballot as difficult as possible" and held that they violated the state constitution. And the court suggested it would continue to take Black voting rights seriously in the future, writing that "not only is freedom to vote and hold office secured in our present Constitution, but it is so imbedded in the hearts of the people that it was thought necessary to stipulate against any interference with it by a contemplated Convention to alter the Constitution."[15]

Indeed, the legislature had called a new constitutional convention in 1875 but explicitly forbade it from imposing an educational or property qualification on suffrage. Delegates took an oath to obey this instruction. As a result, Democrats could not wield two of the most powerful weapons against Black suffrage—ones that we have seen worked in Arkansas and South Carolina. However, Democrats found another ostensibly race neutral alternative; they added a provision disenfranchising felons, which remains in the current version of North Carolina's constitution. One Black delegate to the convention argued that "the measure was intended to disenfranchise his people" and was ruled out of order by the presiding officer when he called felon disenfranchisement "villainous." Another delegate argued that "such a law might influence partizan [*sic*] Judges to do a wrong for party ends." That is, a Democratic judge might work to ensure convictions of Republicans to prevent them from voting. This was plausible because delegates also amended the constitution to give the legislature authority to alter the number of judicial districts for trial courts however it wished.[16] The legislature (which was in Democratic hands) could therefore produce districts likely to elect Democratic judges, use the criminal justice system to disenfranchise Republican voters, and further entrench Democrats in power.

With the constitution amended, Democrats passed an election law giving justices of the peace the power to select registrars for each county.

The legislature selected the justices of the peace, so it essentially provided for Democratic registrars in each county who could be counted on to use election procedures to make it harder for Republicans and Black men especially to vote. As they had tried to do previously, the legislature allowed registrars to make any potential voter provide at least one witness testifying to his identity and age. By 1889, the legislature also required a valid registration to state a person's age and place of birth. This would have been difficult for many former slaves who often couldn't precisely identify their birthdate. They wouldn't have had birth certificates in the modern sense. So, they would have had to find a witness to support a specific date. Former slaves who had moved away from the plantation on which they were born (by choice or not), would have been unable in many cases to secure witnesses who could testify to when they were born. Even if they did live nearby, their parents or other relatives who could swear to when they were born might well be dead or have been sold to a distant location. That would have left them dependent on a former owner for help in participating in the political process they needed to use to escape slavery's legacy. Although the North Carolina Supreme Court had once thwarted similar measures, its composition changed after Reconstruction. Justices were selected by popular vote. Excluding Black voters from the political process led to Democratic justices unsympathetic to their plight.[17]

As one scholar observed, "Use of the gerrymander, disfranchisement for petty crimes commonly committed by Negroes, intricate election laws partially administered, and a liberal amount of 'judicious' cheating by election officials aided the Democrats in rendering innocuous the Negro vote in the State."[18] The spirit of 1868 was defeated.

The Spirit of 1868 Resurrected and the Democratic Response

North Carolina, like the rest of the South, was a one-party state after Reconstruction ended. But in the 1890s, the same coalition that had ratified the 1868 constitution reconstituted itself. During the 1880s and 1890s, the Populist movement gained traction. As the state industrialized, poorer whites felt like they were being left behind. The "very mechanics or factory operatives, descendants for the most part of the despised poor whites" felt themselves losing social status. In 1892,

Populists formed a third party and won 18 percent of votes statewide. The panic of 1893, when farmers suffered serious financial setbacks because the prices of various agricultural products collapsed, helped heighten their appeal. Populists were now a serious political force, but they needed more support to form a majority. With Democrats opposed, the only path to power for white Populists lay in working with the Republicans. That meant Populists needed Black votes. Ultimately, they decided to join with Republicans in the 1894 elections. This "fusion" ticket won statewide elections including both houses of the legislature.[19]

Democrats, remembering how they had been able to break a similar alliance a generation ago, trotted out the same trope of "negro domination" they used to generate opposition to the 1868 constitution. In one instance, Democratic newspapers extensively covered the house of representatives' decision to hire a Black doorkeeper in 1895. The *Goldsboro Weekly Argus* complained that "it has come to pass in North Carolina, that old, broken soldiers of the Confederacy, who have filled this place for years . . . are stood aside, be they Democrats or Populists, and this burly, billigerent [sic] bribe-taking negro [doorkeeper], is elected in their stead."[20]

Democrats also attempted to use Frederick Douglass to arouse opposition to the fusionists. They claimed that a fusionist legislator had proposed ending a day's session in honor of Frederick Douglass. To ensure this story produced the appropriate outrage, the *Henderson Gold Leaf* called Douglass a "negro miscegeationist" because he had married a white woman and described the decision to end the day early as "a cheap bid for negro votes." This was particularly egregious, Democrats claimed, because the legislature had rejected resolutions to honor George Washington and Robert E. Lee. In truth, the house of representatives had already adjourned out of respect for both Washington and Lee. But the allegations served a useful purpose. The fusionist legislature, Democrats told North Carolinians with racist views but who had fallen away from the Democratic Party, was celebrating the Black man they had warned would "make love to [a white woman] and call her pet names" and degrading two white patriots.[21] Such stories failed to dislodge the fusionists from power. They maintained their hold on the legislature in the 1896 elections and won the governorship too.

Still, Democrats knew they had to split white Populists from Black Republicans, and racial resentment was their strongest weapon. In the 1898 elections, Furnifold Simmons, chairman of the state's Democratic Party, organized one of the most racist campaigns in American history. Simmons was short with a thick mustache, and he spoke in a soft voice. His official portrait gives the air of someone eyeing you warily, or perhaps deliberating on the best strategy to turn a situation to his advantage. Simmons had a particularly strong stake in reestablishing white supremacy in North Carolina and defeating Populists. He had lost his seat in the US House of Representatives in the 1888 election to a Black man. He and his supporters "[felt] that one of the most useful men in the National Congress has been displaced by the incompetent negro." Simmons had considered running for his old seat in 1890 but withdrew from consideration after the farmer's alliance opposed him.[22] The 1898 elections gave him a chance to avenge his earlier defeats and clear a path to high office.

During the campaign, Simmons put "everybody to work—men who could write, men who could speak, and men who could ride—the last by no means the least important."[23] That campaign, which encouraged the coup in Wilmington, also used Wilmington as a villain to foment outrage. The *Wilmington Semi-Weekly Messenger* portrayed Wilmington as a place where "negro domination" was at its apex because "negro officials . . . are in the post office, in the custom house, in the city government, in perhaps every department, on the police, in [the] health department, and so on." It used this allegedly sorry state of affairs to challenge white men to rise up. After all, "there is not a decent, honorable, upright, worthy white man in all North Carolina who is so fallen in his manhood as to be willing to be overruled and mastered by the negro race." The paper even claimed that there was "a plot to turn North Carolina into a Negro state forever" and that Black people planned to "get control of the state, and force the whites to flee for life and at any sacrifice." The end result would be that "the Africans pour in as the locusts overran Egypt in the time of Moses, the commonwealth will be despoiled, plucked, and ruined." Of course, it was possible that instead of driving white people out, Black people planned to "dominate [white people] and play the role of master." To give credence to these rumors, the paper passed along a report from the *Atlanta Constitution* that Black people in other states were planning how to come take over North Carolina. Democrats knew that white people from western North Carolina had provided crucial support for both the 1868 constitution and the fusion movement and that many of them rarely encountered Black people. To win their support, they tried to encourage sympathy for white people in eastern North Carolina living under "negro domination." They needed to vote for white supremacy because allowing Black people to become school committeemen, police officers, and postmasters in the east had "made them insulting and arrogant . . . especially [to] the ladies who have to submit to insults from those savage negroes." "Negro domination" wasn't just a matter of Black officeholders. It also manifested in Black people "elect[ing] nearly all those who" held office in Wilmington and places like it, even if those officials were white. That is, Black voters were like "the owners" of a corporation who had selected white agents to do their bidding.[24]

The need to protect white women featured prominently during the campaign. Democrats suggested there was a rape epidemic that only extreme measures could prevent. Thus, papers across the state spread a story from a newspaper in Greene about a Black "devil in human form" who attempted to rape a "respectable white lady." The *Elizabeth City Fisherman* reminded readers that the alleged incident happened "in a county in which a black fiend was convicted and hanged last fall for a like offense." The paper asked readers, "What is the value of such punishment as an example and a warning to the negro when it is neutralized by the lessons taught in the every day practices of Republican politicians?" That Republicans had sanctioned raping white women left white Populists with a clear message: "There is but one party in North Carolina for the white man who has any self respect or any regard for the virtue of the women who should be dear to him. That party is the White Man's Party—the Democrtic [*sic*] Party."[25]

The effort to make Black male sexual predation a decisive issue received a boost when North Carolina newspapers passed along Rebecca Felton's speech in Georgia from a year prior advocating increased opportunities for white women. Felton was the wife of a Georgia congressman and an early feminist. In her speech, Felton asked male listeners, "Why not, then, gentlemen, throw open the doors of the university to women of Georgia . . . and allow the daughters of the farmers of Georgia to contest for those degrees, upon the same plane, and without favoritism, that are now conferred upon men?" Felton was particularly concerned about "the unprotected condition of thousands of women living upon the farms, many of them widows and orphan daughters of dead confederates." Perhaps the most significant threat facing them was Black sexual predators, who felt like they could rape white women with impunity because they were allowed to vote. "If it needs lynching to protect woman's dearest possession from cravening human beasts," she thundered, "then I say 'lynch' a thousand times a week if necessary."[26]

On its own, the speech played into themes Democrats wanted to emphasize. But then Alexander Manly made the speech into an even more explosive issue. Editor of the successful Black-owned *Wilmington Daily Record*, Manly challenged Felton's narrative. He insisted,

> Our experience among poor white people in the country teaches us that women of that race are not more particular in the manner of clandestine meetings with colored men, than are the white man with colored women. Meetings of this kind go on for some time until the woman's infatuation or the man's boldness, bring attention to them, and the man is lynched for rape. Every negro lynched is called a "big, burley [*sic*], black brute," when, in fact, many of those who have thus been dealt with had white men for their fathers, and were not only "black" and "burley," but were sufficiently attractive for white girls of culture and refinement to fall in love with them, as is very well known to all.

Manly ended his article by warning white people: "Don't think ever that your women will remain pure while you are debauching ours. You sow the seed—the harvest will come in due time."[27] There was a long history going back to slavery of white men sexually abusing Black women. Decades before, Harriet Jacobs had explained how masters began sexual liaisons with slaves in North Carolina. When a woman turned fourteen or fifteen, "her owner, or his sons, or the overseer, or perhaps all of them, begin to bribe her with presents. If these fail to accomplish their purpose, she is whipped or starved into submission to their will." And, there was a long history of sexual relationships between white women and Black men during slavery. In many cases, white women initiated those relationships and used their authority to force Black men to sleep with them. After explaining that white women "know that the women slaves are subject to their father's authority in all things [including sex]," Jacobs asserted that "in some cases they exercise the same authority over the men slaves." She went on to describe a situation where a white woman "selected one of the meanest slaves on [her] plantation" to be her sexual partner. The choice was deliberate, for the woman "did not make her advances to her equals, nor even to her father's more intelligent servants. She selected the most brutalized, over whom her authority could be exercised with less fear of exposure."[28] From the perspective of the twenty-first century, we can therefore see that Manly simply spoke the truth. But the truth was inconvenient in 1898. The editorial insulted the honor of white men by calling them rapists. It suggested white women were liars when they said they were raped. And it attacked poor white men the fusionists needed for support when it claimed that they were "careless in the matter of protecting their women." Democratic newspapers across the state quoted from the editorial and condemned Manly. Sensing the danger, Populists and Republicans denounced him.

Skillful orators stoked outrage across the state. The two most famous were Alfred Waddell and Ben Tillman. Waddell had once described himself as such "a young and enthusiastic Union man, and [so] desirous to do all that was in my power for its preservation" that he quit his job so he could buy a newspaper to promote his views. But when he heard that the rebels were about to open fire on Fort Sumter in Charleston, South Carolina, he rushed down to witness the occasion. Waddell joined the confederate military, but had no "record worth mentioning" and had to resign because of poor health. He won a seat in the US House of Representatives during the conservative wave in 1870. While there, he was a member of the Ku Klux Klan committee. In that capacity, he said of the committee's report that a "greater waste of paper and ink was never perpetrated, for it accomplished nothing, except perhaps the aggravation of sectional bitterness in the country, which was doubtless the purpose of those who instigated the investigation."[29] By the 1898 campaign, though, Waddell had long ago lost his seat in Congress. The campaign offered him renewed relevance.

In his most famous speech, Waddell appeared at the Wilmington Opera House in October 1898. The *Wilmington Semi-Weekly Messenger* claimed that there had never been "a more representative gathering of white men of Wilmington" and noted that many women attended. Waddell gave a fervent defense of white supremacy. "To seriously argue to an intelligent audience the soundness of the Ten Commandments as a code of morals, could hardly be more unnecessary not to say comical," Waddell claimed, "than to discuss the rightfulness and the expediency of maintaining the absolute supremacy of the white people in any part of the territory of the United States." Waddell ended with a warning: "Let [Black people] understand once [and] for all that we will have no more of the intolerable conditions under which we live. We are resolved to change them, if we have to choke the current of the Cape Fear with carcasses." Waddell received a standing ovation after the speech.[30]

US Senator Ben Tillman had helped overthrow South Carolina's Republican government in 1876 and then helped draft South Carolina's constitution in 1895 that ended Black political influence in the state. The man who had successfully called upon white men to "unite as brothers" at South Carolina's 1895 constitutional convention was a natural spokesman for white supremacy. In late October 1898, between seven and eight thousand white men attended a rally in Fayetteville where he spoke. The rally began with a procession led by a Wilmington band and "the imposing 'scarlet brigade' of hundreds of horsemen riding in column followed by a 'float' of ornate decorations, in which were seated sixteen of the pretty girls of Cumberland and Fayetteville." Tillman urged white Populists and Democrats to put aside their differences and "act decent and get together, run up the flag of white supremacy, and put North Carolina back where she will never slip up any more." Tillman believed it would be easier for North Carolina to accomplish this than it was for South Carolina. Because they were a minority during Reconstruction, South Carolina whites "grew desperate and donned red shirts and got out their shotguns and took the state." But Tillman "did not deem it necessary to advise the people of North Carolina to do that, for they are in a majority and can secure white government without that." Turning his focus to Manly's editorial, Tillman asked, "Why didn't you kill that nigger editor who wrote that? Send him to South Carolina and let him publish any such offensive stuff, and he would be killed."[31]

The white supremacy campaign ignored Tillman's suggestion to rely on peaceful methods. Red shirts deliberately held rallies in majority Black parts of North Carolina. They also beat would-be Republican voters and threatened their lives. The violence became so intense that Republican Governor Daniel Russell issued a proclamation stating that "certain counties lying along the Southern border of this State have actually been invaded by certain armed and lawless men from another State," and that "several political meetings . . . have been broken up and dispersed, by armed men, using threats, intimidation, and in some cases actual violence." Russell ordered the violence to stop and people from other states participating in it to leave. They didn't. US Senator Jeter Pritchard even asked President William McKinley to send federal marshals to preserve the peace. The request backfired. A Democratic newspaper, which somehow got ahold of Pritchard's letter, suggested northern soldiers might be sent to "'intimidate' white North Carolinians and aid the negroes in securing a permanent control of the state."[32] Many white North Carolinians resented federal occupation after the Civil War and Prichard's letter allowed Democrats to claim that fusionists were seeking to victimize them again.

As election day approached, Wilmington was a tinder box ready to explode at any moment. A *Washington Post* writer observed that "Wilmington might be preparing for a siege instead of an election. The citizens are armed and make no secret of the fact. There is a new Gatling gun in the local armory, and 2,000 Winchester rifles are said, on reliable authority, to be distributed among private residences." Whites had organized the city in military fashion with a lieutenant in charge of every block and a captain over six blocks.[33]

The violence worked. Before the election, the fusionists withdrew candidates in New Hanover County. On election day, many fusionist supporters were intimidated from voting by red shirts surrounding the polls and firing their weapons. Well before the election, Democrats had used means besides violence to suppress votes. In some cases, they offered Republicans money to vote Democrat. In others, economically powerful Democrats took a page from the Law and Order Party's playbook in Rhode Island and threatened to foreclose on the mortgages or immediately collect the debts of fusionists if they voted. When some Black voters did show up in one precinct, Democrats "came out there with a list [and] challenged pretty nigh every negro that was on the registration book" because they "had some crime or another marked against him." As a result, fifty fewer Black men than expected voted there. Even newspapers from outside the state noted low Black turnout. The *New York Evening Journal* reported that, although white men had "two 'rapid fire guns'" ready for deployment, "it is now thought that there will be no trouble, as the negroes are manifesting but little interest in the election." They were understandably "quiet in the Sixth or 'red shirt' district" and in "Richmond and Robeson they [were] not voting." Across North Carolina, fewer than half of registered Black voters actually voted. Red shirts even attempted to assassinate Governor Russell. While he was traveling back to Raleigh from Wilmington on election day, red shirts boarded his train and searched for him. Before boarding, they had been drunkenly hollering "Bring him out! Lynch him! Lynch the governor! Lynch the fat son of a bitch!"[34]

In addition to suppressing votes, Democrats also engaged in fraud. Harry Hayden, who wrote a favorable account of what transpired in Wilmington, noted that "there were some irregularities in this state-wide election, in this city and elsewhere in the state," because "the white citizens realized that victory had to be won by hook or by crook, otherwise they would have to continue to live under the intolerable conditions of the time." One of those irregularities involved a white supremacist voting nineteen times. In the end, Democrats won an overwhelming majority in the legislature.[35]

The campaign of 1898 was a constitutional crisis. It was more than a typical election where parties aired policy differences and competed for votes. It pitted two constitutional visions against each other: one that gave Black people freedom to participate fully in the political process and saw them as equal citizens and one that gave white people freedom to fully subordinate Black people and saw Black people as second-class citizens. Democrats used every means available to win the election so they could complete the wholesale revision of the 1868 constitution they had sought in 1875. Democrats had a necessary two-thirds majority in both houses of the legislature to impeach and remove Governor Russell and the state supreme court.[36] Democrats had used propaganda, bribery, fraud, intimidation, and violence to effectively overthrow North Carolina's lawful government. What remained was to cement the new constitutional order they had installed. They would work to achieve that objective in Wilmington.

Wilmington's Conspirators Put Their Plans in Motion

In our federal system, states are separate sovereigns who have substantial leeway to regulate their own affairs. One of the principles underlying this arrangement is the notion that at least some decisions that affect local communities should be made locally. A policy that makes sense in one place might not make sense in another. This same logic applies to cities, towns, and municipalities. That is why most state constitutions today explicitly describe some level of municipal government.[37] Many municipalities have charters which serve a similar function to constitutions in that they confer rights and structure the government. This all suggests that just as there might be federal constitutional crises and state constitutional crises, there might be municipal constitutional crises. That is exactly what happened in Wilmington in 1898.

After Democrats "redeemed" North Carolina, they worked to eliminate Black political influence at the municipal level. North Carolina's 1875 constitution gave the legislature almost unlimited power to change municipal governments. The Democratic legislature then granted itself the power to appoint justices of the peace and instructed those justices of the peace to select a county's board of commissioners. This ensured that a Democratic legislature in Raleigh dedicated to white supremacy selected local officers to govern predominantly Black and Republican areas of North Carolina. Democrats sought to diminish Black influence in Wilmington specifically by amending its charter so that the governor could appoint five "discreet and proper persons" from each of the five wards to be the board of audit and finance in Wilmington. At least three of the members had to approve levying any taxes. Even if Black people could vote in sufficient numbers to elect a mayor and aldermen, officials loyal to the Democratic legislature could veto whatever policy choices they made.[38]

When fusionists took power, they restored a semblance of local rule in Wilmington. 1897 amendments to the charter substantially diminished the powers of the board of audit and finance and allowed voters to select one alderman from each district for a total of five and permitted the governor to choose the other five. The amended charter also required the city to hold elections every two years. The cumulative result of these changes was to provide Black people a greater say in Wilmington's affairs, although many wanted even more reform. At the time, Black voters sought political influence commensurate with their economic advancement. By the 1890s, Black people had successfully entered the medical and legal fields and started businesses. Black homeownership rates in Wilmington were higher than in other parts of the country. Black people from around the state came there in search of economic opportunities. Some white people alleged that "Negroes were given preference in the matter of employment, for most of the town's artisans were Negroes, and numerous white families in the city faced bitter want because their providers could get but little work as brick-masons, carpenters, mechanics." The result was that "Wilmington was really becoming a Mecca for Negroes and a City of Lost Opportunities for the working class whites."[39]

Given how much white Democrats resented growing Black political and economic influence, it is unsurprising that they refused to accept the outcome of Wilmington's 1897 elections. In March 1897, two Black men were elected to the board of aldermen and Governor Russell appointed one more to the board. Republicans controlled a majority of the board. Democratic officeholders declined to leave their positions after the election. They argued that changes to Wilmington's charter were unconstitutional, which would have meant that the elections were illegal. To assure themselves power, Republicans met early one day after the election, swore in the new members, and elected Silas Wright mayor.

After the Republicans met, the Democratic mayor and six of the Democratic members of the old board met with Democratic candidates claiming they had actually won seats on the board in the 1897 election. A crowd watched as the board agreed they were duty-bound not to turn over the government to the Republicans because of impending litigation over the constitutionality of changes to Wilmington's charter. The Democrats then purported to elect a city clerk, treasurer, and police chief. After this meeting, the three Democrats who had legitimately won election in 1897 met with five who claimed that they had won seats on the board. A justice of the peace swore them all in. The group purported to elect one of their number mayor. Three mayors and three boards of aldermen claimed to govern one city.

In April 1897, Democrats instituted quo warranto proceedings against Wright, alleging that he was not Wilmington's lawful mayor. A lower court concluded that the 1897 charter was unconstitutional and that the Democratic board of aldermen and mayor in power before the election continued in office. But the North Carolina Supreme Court reversed, giving Republicans the unquestioned legal right to govern Wilmington.[40] A potential crisis was averted. But a real one was impending.

Although Wilmington's board of aldermen was not up for reelection in the 1898 campaign, a conspiracy of nine men, later dubbed the secret nine, planned "a city wide protective campaign that was to be conducted co-ordinately with the state-wide 'White supremacy' movement." The group was allegedly concerned about Republican misrule and an epidemic of Black men raping white women. The secret nine divided the city into eight sections and placed a captain over each section and designated two of them to be the contacts to keep the larger group secret. "Every member of this group realized the gravity of the situation knowing full well that it was absolutely necessary to keep the existence of such a body secret, for had it been known that such a committee existed, every member would have been arrested and placed in durance vile to answer the charge of inciting to rebellion." At the same time, another group, called the secret six, was also scheming.[41]

To spur their revolution, the secret nine spread rumors that Black people were planning an uprising. The *Wilmington Semi-Weekly Messenger* asserted that "Sambo is seeking to furnish an armory here with sixteen repeating rifles to kill whites and promote a race war of extermination." It repeated a story where "negroes summoned to work the public road, told the white roadmaster that they hoped the time was not far off when they could use their axes and hoes to kill white people." A separate group of conspirators even hired two Black detectives who warned that Black men were allegedly planning to burn Wilmington if Democrats won the election. White people responded to these rumors by purchasing thousands of weapons.[42]

The secret nine worked to keep violence from exploding *before* the election. They had "planned the Revolution, which they scheduled to start on November 10, 1898, the day after the statewide elections." So, when a group of red shirts came to conspirator Hugh MacRae threatening to lynch Manly and burn the *Wilmington Record*'s office for writing the editorial responding to Rebecca Felton's speech, MacRae begged them to "desist in their plans."[43] They had deliberately schemed to overthrow Wilmington's government after the statewide elections took place. As I will show, that counterintuitive timing was probably deliberate.

The conspiracy bid for public support at a mass meeting of one thousand people in Wilmington's courthouse after the election swept Democrats into office statewide. The meeting included "Wilmington's very best citizens, including ministers, working men, lawyers, doctors, merchants and all classes of our people." At the meeting, Alfred Waddell read aloud the "White Declaration of Independence." The style mimicked Thomas Jefferson's Declaration of Independence. Both began with grand statements of principle before listing specific grievances. Contrary to Jefferson's assertion that "all men are created equal," the White Declaration of Independence claimed that "the Constitution of the United States contemplated a government to be carried on by an enlightened people; believing that its framers did not anticipate the enfranchisement of an ignorant population of African origin; and believing that those men of the State of North Carolina, who joined in forming the union, did not contemplate for their descendants subjection to an inferior race."

Notwithstanding that only a minority of the board of aldermen were Black and that the mayor and police chief were white, the Declaration asserted that "[w]e, the undersigned citizens of the city of Wilmington and county of New Hanover, do hereby declare that we will no longer be ruled, and will never again be ruled by men of African origin." The Declaration proceeded to list specific grievances. It said it was unfair for Black people to rule white people when white people paid 95 percent of taxes. It complained that Black people received nearly all jobs in Wilmington and demanded that those jobs go to white people. It demanded that the *Wilmington Record* shut down and that Manly be banished. Hundreds of white men signed their names to the White Declaration of Independence after Waddell read it. Ministers encouraged citizens who were preparing to kill innocent Black people, steal their property, and destroy the spirit of 1868 once and for all. The meeting ended by calling on Wright and his police chief to resign because of "their utter incapacity to give the city a decent government and keep order therein."[44]

Waddell and a committee of twenty-five white men then summoned prominent Black leaders to a meeting. There he read aloud the White Declaration of Independence to them. He then gave them an ultimatum to indicate in writing by 7:30 a.m. on November 10, 1898, that they would accommodate its demands. The clear implication was that if they did not, terrible consequences would befall the Black community. Yet there was no way that the Black leaders could actually comply. For example, the White Declaration of Independence said "we will not tolerate the action of unscrupulous white men in affiliating with the negroes so that by means of their votes they can dominate the intelligent and thrifty element in the community." How could Black people control whether "unscrupulous" white people wanted to ally with them politically? How could they tell white employers whom to hire? And how could they instruct the mayor and police chief to resign? The one demand they could hope to satisfy was that Manly leave the city. In fact, he already had.

The group wrote a response promising to use their influence to get Manly to leave Wilmington. An attorney tasked with delivering the letter decided to mail it instead to Waddell's house when he saw red shirts firing their weapons. Waddell didn't receive the letter before his deadline. Apologists for the destruction and killing in Wilmington would later claim that the attorney's decision to mail the letter instead of deliver it was fateful. Violence had only been unleashed, they suggested, because Waddell was unable to inform angry white people that the Black community's leadership was seeking to help expel Manly.[45] But the historical record makes clear that the violence had been planned far in advance.

On the morning of November 10, 1898, Waddell led an armed mob toward the *Wilmington Record*'s building. For a man with an unimpressive war record, the chance to command what looked like a military formation must have been thrilling. Waddell claimed that he intended only to destroy the press which had produced Manly's editorial. When a few men threw kerosene lamps on the ground and set the building on fire, Waddell claimed that he cried "Stop that fire! Put it out!" and that he "at once had the fire alarm bell rung." But when firemen rushed toward the scene, "some of the men [in the mob] discharged their fire arms in the air and the children in the negro school nearby were thrown into a state of great alarm." After the fires were extinguished, Waddell claimed he told the crowd "Now you have performed the duty which you called on me to lead you to perform. Now let us go quietly to our homes, and about our business, and obey the law, unless we are forced, in self-defense, to do otherwise."[46]

Soon afterward, a group of armed Black men and a group of armed white men confronted each other. The *Wilmington Semi-Weekly Messenger* claimed that a Black man fired at the white men with a pistol and that the white men had been compelled to "fire a volley from shotguns, Winchester rifles, and revolvers." Two Black men died instantly. In a public relations coup, white Wilmington residents managed to convince many Americans that Black residents were the aggressors and that they were the victims. *The Daily Picayune* in New Orleans claimed that there "is no doubt that the negroes are responsible for the precipitating of the race war" and cited an affidavit from a "thoroughly reputable" Wilmington resident as proof. This justification for the violence is belied by the way white people behaved after this incident. Red shirts began hunting down Black people and murdering them indiscriminately, often shooting them in the back while they were fleeing. Black men occasionally fired back but were no match for the overwhelming force arrayed against them. Scores of Black families hid in the woods outside Wilmington, afraid for their lives. While there were rumors that Black men planned to attack white homes and businesses that day, this fear cannot explain all of the people murdered. Even a favorable account of the coup later admitted that "of course, there were some ignorant whites, 'poor-bockers' or 'poor white trash' as they were and are still called down South, who did some dastardly deeds under the cloak of this Rebellion." To this day, there is no agreed upon death count. There were estimates as low as fourteen and as high as one hundred. An official North Carolina report in 2006 made no conclusive findings.[47]

While white people slaughtered Black people in the streets, Waddell and his committee of twenty-five met and selected eight white supremacists to serve as aldermen. The aldermen in turn selected Waddell to serve as mayor. They sent messengers to instruct Wright and the current board of aldermen to resign. The police chief later testified that they had "gotten word at the city hall that they were coming over [to] demand the offices, and take them by force; if we didn't resign, they would take them by force." Eventually, Waddell led two hundred men armed with Winchester rifles into the city hall and its corridors. Waddell ordered Wright to call a meeting of the board of aldermen and Wright complied. The board members resigned one by one and approved their replacements. Wright offered his resignation last, and the new board of aldermen accepted it. The new board members swore to support the US Constitution and the North Carolina Constitution. The US Constitution promised a "Republican" form of government to each state and equal protection of the laws for all citizens. The North Carolina Constitution insisted that all men were created equal and had the right to life and liberty, and defined "levying war against [the state] as treason." The aldermen had trampled underfoot the same documents they now promised to uphold. As their first act, the new aldermen fired the three fusionist board members who were absent. As their second, they accepted Wright's resignation and replaced him with Waddell. Waddell later insisted that "there [had] not been a single illegal act committed in the change of government. Simply, the old board went out, and the new board came in—strictly according to law."[48]

With a new government in power, the secret nine drew up a list of prominent Black and white Republicans to banish from the city forever. The Wilmington Light Infantry, which had served in the Spanish American War earlier in the year, sent soldiers to arrest some of the men to be banished. Many of them "were run out of the state for the simple reason that they were Republicans and refused, at the bidding of an irresponsible mob, to surrender their right to franchise." They were forbidden from ever returning on pain of death. Those banished included Silas Wright and his police chief. Many other Black people not on the list decided to leave Wilmington as well in subsequent days. Almost overnight, a majority Black city became a majority white one.[49]

Democrats had overthrown Wilmington's lawful government and nullified its charter. They celebrated by holding a parade. At 3:00 p.m. on November 11, 1898, five military companies marched through the streets while whites cheered them. They carried two rapid fire guns and a Hotchkiss cannon along with them. Once all the violence had served its purpose, Waddell proclaimed that "no further turbulence or disorderly conduct will be tolerated" and that "no armed patrol except those authorized by the Chief of Police will appear on the streets." After all, "justice [was] satisfied."[50]

The coup in Wilmington was more than a municipal-level constitutional crisis. It was a warning. A correspondent for the *New York Herald* recognized that the coup in Wilmington "has triumphed where John C. Calhoun failed." Calhoun famously argued before the

Civil War that states could nullify federal law. He hadn't prevailed when objecting to the so-called tariff of abominations in the 1830s and the Civil War had theoretically spelled the end for his philosophy. But the events in Wilmington meant "henceforth the constitution of the United States, so far as the 15th Amendment is concerned, will be a dead letter in the Carolinas." For that matter, the North Carolina Constitution was rendered dead letter too. It had promised "free elections" and independently guaranteed suffrage to men who weren't felons. If Black people ever voted again to "endanger white supremacy, then once more the shotgun." The message for Black people was clear: stay out of politics or suffer through another Wilmington.[51]

The Disenfranchisement of Black North Carolinians

Democrats moved quickly to disenfranchise Black men after their electoral triumph. During the election, they had actually denounced it as "the silliest of all falsehoods" that they would "disenfranchise niggers and poor folks if they get into power." But even newspapers from out of state suspected these assurances were given in bad faith. The *Indianapolis Freeman* predicted that "if the Democrats succeed in North Carolina, then follows a reign of political terror. The iron shackles of disfranchisement will be forged and riveted about every colored man." It encouraged Black men to vote in such a way as to avoid a constitutional convention where they would be deprived of rights as had recently happened in Mississippi in 1890 and South Carolina in 1895.[52]

Democrats were in power again, but so long as Black men voted in meaningful numbers, another fusionist alliance was possible. To disenfranchise Black voters, they needed to amend the North Carolina Constitution again, which required a majority of North Carolina voters to agree. They had several options. First, they could impose a property qualification. Since Black people had less wealth than white people, more of them would be disenfranchised. Nonetheless, many whites would also lose their right to vote. Those whites would be unlikely to support a constitutional amendment taking the franchise from them. Enough people might vote against such an amendment that it would lose even if Democrats resorted to fraud and voter suppression. Second, they could impose a literacy test, which would again have disenfranchised a disproportionate number of Black voters because they were more often illiterate than white voters were. The third was to combine a literacy test with a grandfather clause. That is, allow North Carolinians to vote if a descendant had been a lawful voter prior to a date when Black people could vote. Doing so would ensure most poor white men could still vote while filtering out a healthy number of Black voters. In the end, Democrats chose this option. A report from prominent journalist Josephus Daniels, who worked at the behest of the Democratic Executive Committee and who had actively participated in the white supremacy campaign, convinced them. He had visited Louisiana and concluded that a literacy test along with a grandfather clause disenfranchised most Black men while allowing poor whites to continue voting in the state. In due course, the legislature proposed a constitutional amendment requiring prospective voters to pay a poll tax and be able to read and write any section of the constitution. The amendment included a clause allowing anyone who could vote prior to January 1, 1867, and anyone who descended from someone who could vote prior to January 1, 1867, to continue voting until December 1, 1908.[53] No Black people were eligible to vote prior to January 1, 1867.

The amendment was now in voters' hands. Some Populists energetically opposed it. Although they may have held racist views, they knew a future fusionist coalition could never arise if the amendment excluded Black people from politics. To arouse white opposition, they argued that the Democrats were trying to impose "the yoke of political slavery" on illiterate white people. They claimed the amendment would disenfranchise sixty thousand white voters. Worst of all, disenfranchised white voters would be unable to vote on any future constitutional amendment guaranteeing their right to vote again.[54]

Other Populists supported Black disenfranchisement. An article in the *Progressive Farmer* claimed that "despite all the 'chin music' we have had, the question to be decided is, [i]s the negro as a voter desirable or profitable to the State?" Drawing on the same religious rhetoric a Pennsylvania delegate used to justify disenfranchising Black people before the Buckshot War, it argued that "the Almighty never intended that the negro should rule the white man" because God, "by the mouth of Noah pronounced the negro the servant of the white man."[55] Some Populists who supported the amendment believed that eliminating Black voters would prevent Democrats from using "negro domination" as a wedge issue in future campaigns. Populists would then have a greater opening to win racist voters who would no longer feel compelled to vote Democrat to preserve white supremacy.

The question of whether the proposed amendment would violate the US Constitution figured prominently in the campaign. It was one thing to violate the North Carolina Constitution in the effort to secure white supremacy. It was another to defy the federal government. If a court ruled that the grandfather clause violated the US Constitution, the poll tax and literacy tests would be left. While these tools would still disenfranchise many Black voters, they would also disenfranchise some white voters. And there was the possibility that a well-educated and financially successful Black man would be able to vote while a poor and uneducated white man would not. Such an outcome would have outraged white opinion across the state. One provision that might have forbidden the amendment was the Guarantee Clause. Could a government that disenfranchised so many of its citizens really be "Republican"? Yet, *Luther v. Borden* had indicated that it wasn't the place of courts to ask the question. And Justice Harlan's recent effort in *Plessy v. Ferguson* to use the Guarantee Clause to invalidate Louisiana's Jim Crow legislation requiring Black people and white people to ride in separate railroad cars had failed to garner a majority. That left a concern that because the Fifteenth Amendment forbade racial discrimination in voting, a grandfather clause that as a practical matter only allowed white people to vote would be unconstitutional. To avoid coming into conflict with the Fifteenth Amendment, George Brown, who served on a trial court, proposed altering the amendment to declare that it should be judged as a whole. If a court found part of the amendment unconstitutional, it would have to strike down all of it. That would ensure no white voters lost their right to vote. Democrats in the legislature took the suggestion.[56]

Brown had helped develop a constitutional amendment and defended its substance despite the fact that he might have to rule on its validity. A Black voter challenging the amendment in his courtroom would be forgiven for wondering whether the outcome reflected Brown's legal judgment or his political preferences. Brown would later serve on the North Carolina Supreme Court.

To maximize support, Democrats followed the same strategy they had in 1898. They used men who could write, men who could speak, and men who could ride. The Democratic platform warned that majority Black areas of North Carolina were "a smoldering volcano which might break forth at any time." White women were still "afraid to travel the road unprotected or to be left at home alone." At one point, in an issue alleging that Republicans planned to initiate violence if the amendment passed, the *Orange County Observer* even reprinted excerpts from Manly's column that helpfully produced so much outrage in Wilmington.[57]

Once more, Democrats urged voters to rally around the flag of white supremacy. A number of prominent orators gave speeches across the state extolling the virtues of white supremacy, often accompanied by red shirts. Perhaps the best was future governor Charles Aycock. At a campaign event in Wilmington, hundreds of enthusiastic whites including many red shirts participated in a torchlight parade in the evening before several Democrats gave speeches in favor of the amendment. Aycock made a speech of "great earnestness and eloquence" that "made a profound impression" on listeners. Aycock argued that "the white man civilized the world and was a ruler by instinct and inheritance, and that the negro was not." He also suggested that the literacy test in the amendment would be a "great stimulus to education" because it would ensure that state officials properly educated white boys so they wouldn't be disenfranchised.[58]

When it came time to vote on the amendment, Democrats took no chances. One fusionist newspaper claimed that Furnifold Simmons had instructed registrars not to register eligible voters likely to vote against disenfranchisement. In one county, that had resulted in Democrats refusing to register 400 eligible voters and intimidating 250 others into not voting. When some men nonetheless voted against the amendment, "they put tickets in the wrong box purposely, and in the count threw them out." In another county, a writer reported that one Black man was shot three times and that "the election . . . resulted in the entire suppression of the colored and white Republican vote, so far as I can learn." These techniques resulted in even majority Black counties voting to support the amendment, which would have been unlikely if there had been a fair vote. The amendment passed statewide and virtually eliminated Black people from political life. The number of registered Black voters went from 126,000 in 1896 to 6,100 in 1902.[59] Most of those would have been too terrified to actually vote.

The Spirit of 1861, Thaddeus Stevens, and Wilmington's Aftermath

In some ways, Black people now had less political power than they held when slavery was legal. Earlier in the nineteenth century, free Black men could vote in North Carolina. Yet, in a cruel irony, North Carolina's constitution continued to insist that "all men are created equal."[60] The coup in Wilmington made this new constitutional settlement possible. Black people knew that if they ever asserted themselves politically, they could be murdered or banished. And even if they managed to elect a government responsive to them, white people would simply overthrow it. Seen in this light, the chaos on November 10, 1898, served a purpose. And it may help explain why the conspiracy put the coup in motion *after* Democrats won the 1898 statewide elections and *before* the next municipal elections. Their protestations to the contrary, Democrats knew they were planning to amend the constitution to disenfranchise Black men. What better way to convince them not to vote against the amendment than what they did in Wilmington?

Shortly after North Carolina disenfranchised Black men, Alabama, Georgia, Texas, and Virginia followed its lead.[61] In doing so, they often looked to Wilmington for inspiration. When Hoke Smith ran for governor of Georgia on a platform of white supremacy, he "told of conditions in North Carolina prior to the disenfranchisement of the negro, and touched on the methods to which white people of Wilmington were compelled to resort in order to rescue their fair city from the control of the negroes, who had captured it." Furnifold Simmons, along with others who had been involved in Wilmington's coup, advised white Georgians on how best to disenfranchise Black people.[62] Every southern state now purged Black people from the political process. In 1861, the South began a war to protect slaveholder liberty, preserve its definition of "the people," and win a free hand for white supremacy. Fifty years later, it succeeded thanks to state constitutions. Armed mobs failed to kill Thaddeus Stevens during the Buckshot War. But red shirts, Klansmen, scheming politicians, and ordinary racists succeeded in killing his constitutional vision.

Alfred Waddell continued to serve as mayor of Wilmington until 1905. When he died in 1912, an obituary lamented that "the South lost one of its cleanest and purest types of the chivalrous gentlemen." The architect of the white supremacy campaigns, Furnifold Simmons, achieved the political power he craved when he was elected to the US Senate. After serving for many years, he unsuccessfully sought the presidency in 1920 and was ultimately defeated for renomination to the US Senate in 1930. He died in 1940. The requirement to pass a literacy test to vote still survives in the current North Carolina Constitution, though it is no longer enforced.[63] It wasn't until the 1960s that Black people became a meaningful force in North Carolina's politics again. Wilmington is still majority white.

Conclusion

The preceding chapters leave us with three important lessons. First, illegal violence has shaped more of our constitutional law than we would like to think. Second, the contest between different constitutional visions often has winners and losers. The real losers historically have been not the elites whose constitutional advocacy has received the most attention from scholars but the vulnerable among us whose constitutional defeats have received the least. Third, state constitutional crisis is a constant risk in the American project that deserves our vigilance.

Lesson 1: The Unsavory Part of American Constitutional Development

State constitutional history reveals that much of our constitutional settlement results from treason, insurrection, rebellion, and sedition. Lest this seem like the revisionist claim of a scholar imposing modern standards on past conduct, let us turn to a prominent dictionary from 1860 to understand these terms the way participants in many of our stories would have. That dictionary defined "treason" as "the offence of attempting to overthrow the government of the state to which the offender owes allegiance." It defined "insurrection" as "the open and active opposition of a number of persons to the execution of law in a city or state." It observed that a "rebellion" is "open resistance to lawful authority." And it described "sedition" as "a factious commotion of the people, or a tumultuous assembly of men rising in opposition to law or the administration of justice, and in disturbance of the public peace."[1] There is clear overlap among these terms. Importantly, something doesn't become less "treasonable," less of an "insurrection" or "rebellion," or less "seditious" if those who participate believe they have legitimate grievances.

With these definitions in mind, we can now see our constitutional development more clearly and explain how that history affects us today.

Several of our chapters involve sedition, treason, insurrection, or rebellion. Dorr led armed men in an attempt to displace Rhode Island's government. Free-Staters actively, and in some cases militarily, prevented the proslavery legislature from enforcing its laws. Joseph Brooks raised a militia and took physical possession of Arkansas's state house. Conservatives and Democrats overthrew Republican governments in North and South Carolina. In this, they merely followed the same pattern observed in other southern states during Reconstruction. Conservatives and Democrats had simple goals. They wanted an end to Black equality. They wanted to maintain as much of slaveholder liberty as they could. They believed only whites were part of "the people." It was a genuinely held constitutional vision that they believed gave them the right to launch coups d'état. In Mississippi and South Carolina, with their Black majorities, this constitutional vision could not succeed in a fair election. The same may have been true in other states like Alabama, Florida, Georgia, and Louisiana where Black and white people were nearly equal in population, and some white people may have been willing to accept a measure of Black equality alongside other innovations the 1868 constitutions made.[2]

Across the South, conservatives and Democrats did not achieve their constitutional vision through the reasoned deliberation we associate with the Philadelphia convention. They did not offer a Bill of Rights or engage in respectful dialogue to address concerns from political opponents as Federalists did in the 1780s. No, conservatives and Democrats killed those who got in their way. They waged war on the Black community. At the very least, they engaged in insurrections and rebellions by preventing Republican governments from enforcing law and order during Reconstruction and by trying to remove them by force. And if we accept that southern slaveholders owed the US government allegiance despite profound disagreements about what "liberty" meant in 1861, and if we accept their view that Black slaves had a duty to obey laws passed by antebellum southern state governments they believed to be unfair, then conservatives and Democrats in the 1870s owed their state governments similar obedience. If "levying war" against the federal government from 1861 to 1865 was treason—and the US Constitution says it is—then conservatives and Democrats equally committed treason against state governments.[3]

Insurrection, rebellion, sedition, and treason allowed conservatives and Democrats to remove Republican governments and render constitutional guarantees of racial equality dead letter. They could then call legally sanctioned constitutional conventions to turn the tenets of white supremacy into constitutional texts. Southern secessionists in 1861 and southern Democrats in the 1870s had the same constitutional vision. Both were willing to engage in sedition, treason, insurrection, and rebellion to accomplish that constitutional vision. The only difference is that they lost in 1865 and won in the 1870s. Several of our state constitutions—including ones some Americans still live under—are the handiwork of traitors and insurrectionists. When it comes to writing and revising constitutions, the pen has played an important role. So has the sword.

Furthermore, you are living with at least three consequences of the fact that violence did so much to make our state constitutions. First, it explains why state constitutions are easier to change than the US Constitution is. The US Constitution requires two-thirds of both the House of Representatives and Senate to propose an amendment and three-quarters of states to ratify, or a convention called by two-thirds of states to propose an amendment and three-quarters of states to ratify. Since the Bill of Rights, there have only been seventeen amendments. States, by contrast, use several methods to change their constitutions. Many allow a majority of both houses of the legislature to propose amendments and a majority of voters to ratify. Eighteen states allow residents to bypass the legislature and place amendments on the ballot themselves when enough people petition to do so. A majority of residents can then ratify. Fourteen states give voters the chance to call a constitutional convention at periodic intervals, say, every ten or twenty years. Overall, states today have fewer gatekeepers to constitutional change, and the gates themselves are easier to go through. To make that truth concrete, consider abortion. Wherever you stand, you'll have an easier time getting a constitutional amendment reflecting your moral conviction on that issue at the state level than you will at the national level. Some states have already amended their constitutions after the US Supreme Court overturned *Roe v. Wade*, and, depending on where you live, your state might realistically do so soon. On the other hand, no one closely following our polarized politics expects an amendment to the US Constitution on abortion anytime soon.

None of this was inevitable. In the late 1700s, it was possible to amend the US Constitution but impossible to amend several state constitutions. In the nineteenth century, state constitutions that did permit amendments made the process comparatively difficult. Connecticut provided one example of a common model. A majority of the house of representatives had to vote to propose an amendment in one session. At the next, two-thirds of both houses of the legislature had to approve the amendment. Finally, a majority of Connecticut residents had to vote to ratify. Alabama provided another model. There, two-thirds of both houses of the legislature had to propose an amendment. A majority of voters had to approve the amendment. Then two-thirds of both houses of the legislature had to ratify the amendment. As the nineteenth century progressed, states generally abandoned requirements that legislatures approve amendments in consecutive sessions and that legislative supermajorities approve amendments.[4]

As New Jersey's experience shows, a key motivating factor in this collective decision was a fear that citizens unable to formally amend their constitutions would resort to violence. Like many other states at the founding, New Jersey's 1776 constitution specified no method of amendment. Its 1844 constitutional convention initially planned to require a supermajority of both houses of the legislature to propose amendments. But one delegate persuasively argued that if you "shut the door against them, and tell them that they cannot make amendments without the consent of two-thirds, [then] the scenes of Rhode Island [the Dorr Rebellion] would be enacted over again." New Jersey settled on allowing a simple majority of both houses of the legislature to propose amendments in consecutive sessions and then a majority of voters to ratify. The need to make constitutions relatively easy for a majority to change to avoid constitutional instability became the received wisdom by the nineteenth century's end.[5]

Second, violence and resulting constitutional instability at the state level explain why you will not see a federal court use the US Constitution's Guarantee Clause to prevent partisan gerrymandering. In *Luther v. Borden*, the US Supreme Court suggested that whether a state had a "Republican Form of Government" as the US Constitution guaranteed was a political question that it lacked authority to answer. This view hardened over time as *Taylor v. Beckham* demonstrates. Kentucky's

1899 gubernatorial election saw an extraordinarily close contest between Republican William Taylor and Democrat William Goebel. Both sides complained about fraud with one newspaper editor imploring onlookers to "stop the steal." After conducting a hearing surrounded by around five hundred men, several of whom were carrying guns, election commissioners certified that Taylor had won. Goebel challenged that decision in the legislature. One day before the legislature ruled in his favor, an assassin shot Goebel, who survived long enough to take the oath of office. With the threat of conflict between the state militia and armed Democrats looming, Taylor sued to stop Goebel's lieutenant governor from becoming governor. He failed in state court and appealed to the US Supreme Court. There, he argued that the legislature had denied Kentucky voters a "Republican" government when it installed his opponents even though they received fewer votes than he did. The court cited *Luther* for the proposition that "it was long ago settled that the enforcement of this guaranty belonged to the political department" and discussed the case at length.[6] Federal courts still treat Guarantee Clause cases as political questions.

During Reconstruction, Republicans called the clause the "sleeping giant" of the Constitution. During the 1960s, Supreme Court Justice William Douglas suggested that it guaranteed a fundamental right to vote. Today, that clause arguably has a role to play in disputes about voting rights and gerrymandering. If a state is evenly divided between political parties, the government should reflect that fact. But politicians have managed to gerrymander legislative districts to give one party a supermajority of the legislature in many states. That supermajority can override vetoes from the governor. It can impeach and remove judges and executive officials at will. It can overcome a filibuster and pass whatever bills it wants without having to negotiate with the minority party. It has the votes to expel members from the minority party. State constitutions may have provisions promising a separation of powers, but as a practical matter, a legislative supermajority can exercise total control of the government. Could we really describe a government so distorted by gerrymandering as "Republican"? The Supreme Court could have considered this question in *Rucho v. Common Cause* in 2019. There, Maryland Republicans and North Carolina Democrats challenged gerrymandered districts. In 2012, Democratic congressional candidates won more votes in North Carolina than Republican candidates did. Yet, the legislature drew congressional districts projected to elect ten Republicans and three Democrats. Democrats running Maryland's government utilized the expertise of a self-described "serial gerrymanderer" to draw districts which elected seven Democrats and one Republican to Congress. Sensing that a Guarantee Clause claim would fail, the plaintiffs brought First Amendment, Equal Protection, and Elections Clause claims instead. But the Court quickly realized that the true "objection [to gerrymandering was] more properly grounded in the Guarantee Clause."[7] As such, it extended the principle that Guarantee Clause claims are political questions to other constitutional provisions.

Luther v. Borden was based largely on pragmatic concerns. Rhode Island had seen two competing governments raise militias to consolidate power. The state came perilously close to a bloody civil war. Whatever the charter government's flaws, it had managed to restore peace. Finding that the charter government was not "Republican" and holding that the people's government was still in place would have had dramatic consequences. It would have voided everything Rhode Island authorities did for over two years. It would have left unelected Supreme Court justices telling the elected branches to remove a state government. And it would plausibly have meant renewed hostilities between Dorr's supporters and Rhode Island's government. This hesitation set a precedent that *Taylor* drew upon. And the facts there must have given the court similar qualms. Lawyers sometimes say that bad cases make bad law. A corollary is that extreme cases make extreme law. To my mind, refusing to even entertain gerrymandering claims based on a doctrine developed out of fear that a wrong decision might lead to a civil war illustrates the point.

Third, the history of state constitutional instability and violence helps explain why we respect the US Constitution more than we do our state constitutions. One recent survey revealed 55 percent of Americans believe that God inspired the US Constitution. That raises the possibility that Americans are more likely to believe the US Constitution is divinely inspired than they are to know that their state has a constitution. This is at least partially related to how American constitutions have handled crisis and resistance. In 1850, former Vice President George Dallas explained that the US Constitution had "endured every variety of test—the rude shock of foreign war, the rough handling of conflicting parties, the noiseless yet ceaseless cankers of the spirits of monarchy, monopoly and money—and answered every purpose for which a free and virtuous community . . . could contemplate."[8] You are unlikely to ever hear any politician lavish such praise on a state constitution. And that was before the US Constitution made it through the Great Depression, Civil War, World War I, World War II, and the war on terrorism. The US Constitution has survived its crisis moments. State constitutions have often failed theirs. The US Constitution has withstood an effort to overthrow it while state constitutions often have not. That reality raises an uncomfortable question for many of our state constitutions. Do they deserve respect?

The question becomes particularly acute for certain populations and in certain places. When a slave descendant reads the North Carolina Constitution all the way through, they will learn that it *still* contains a literacy test. When they research where the provision came from, they will inevitably learn about the insurrection in Wilmington and subsequent campaign to disenfranchise Black voters. When they research the ratification vote, they will find the results tainted by fraud and violence. Why should that person respect a constitution designed to take rights from their ancestors? That was only made possible by racially motivated murder and terrorism? Yet intellectual honesty requires asking hard questions of the US Constitution too. In tolerating white supremacist coups d'état in southern states, the federal government turned its back on progressive constitutional experiments and left constitutional guarantees unenforced. The US Constitution promises states a "Republican" form of government, requires states to give all citizens "equal protection of the laws," and forbids race discrimination in voting. These texts may have remained intact after white supremacists overthrew southern governments, but did their principles? Would a former slave living under a Jim Crow constitution and seeing the federal government refuse to intervene conclude that the US Constitution had really "answered every purpose for which a free and virtuous community . . . could contemplate"?

And if state constitutions have proven more unstable than the US Constitution because of their inability to withstand racial tension and racialized violence, that may be because the US Constitution was morally ambiguous about slavery and race in a way that state constitutions were not. Both abolitionists and slaveholders could celebrate the US

Constitution. Frederick Douglass spoke for many abolitionists when he called the US Constitution a "GLORIOUS LIBERTY DOCUMENT." Douglass appealed to the preamble, which had declared an intent to "form a more perfect Union, establish Justice," and "secure the Blessings of Liberty to ourselves and our Posterity." Pointing to the fact that the US Constitution never mentioned the word "slave," he asked, "If the Constitution were intended to be, by its framers and adopters, a slaveholding instrument, why neither *slavery, slaveholding,* nor *slave* can anywhere be found in it[?]" And yet, slaveholders could read that same US Constitution as proslavery. To justify secession, Georgia argued that northern states had "persistently refused to comply with their express constitutional [obligation]."⁹ That constitutional obligation was to return fugitive slaves to their masters. Georgia could also point to the fact that the US Constitution had refused to abolish slavery or even to declare that "all men are created equal" in 1787. Before the Civil War, the US Constitution was a Rorschach test. Americans could plausibly see two very different things in it.

State constitutions took clear stands on who were part of "the people" and what "liberty" meant. They either expressly prohibited or expressly permitted slavery. These commitments guaranteed that people who disagreed questioned the legitimacy of those constitutions. The result was repeated constitutional crisis and frequent violence. When Free-Staters abolished slavery in the Topeka Constitution and allowed Black men to vote on ratification of the Leavenworth Constitution, they contributed to constitutional conflict in Kansas. When Republicans used state constitutions to fight white supremacy during Reconstruction, a white supremacist backlash was inevitable. The price of constitutional justice was frequently constitutional instability. But the alternative—constitutional stability at the cost of constitutional injustice—might be equally bad.

Lesson 2: Catastrophic Constitutional Loss

Sometimes, constitution drafting involves a compromise that leaves both sides better off. At the Philadelphia convention, big states preferred that representation in Congress be based on population while small states preferred that each state get equal representation. Both sides got part of what they wanted: the US House of Representatives gives states seats based on population while the US Senate gives each state equal representation. Fundamentally, by agreeing to a new constitution better than the old Articles of Confederation, both big and small states achieved the more powerful central government they needed to confront the nation's challenges. Sometimes, one side loses out on its constitutional vision in the short term but receives an olive branch from the winning side and retains a stake in the constitution succeeding. Antifederalists worried about a too powerful federal government could console themselves with a Bill of Rights. James Monroe opposed the US Constitution at Virginia's ratifying convention and later became president of the United States.[10] But sometimes constitution drafting imposes total defeat on one side. That was the case at the state level with issues like slavery and suffrage. A constitution permitting slavery necessarily meant loss of liberty and dignity for Black people. A constitution denying racial minorities and women the right to vote shut them out of the political process. There were no silver linings. They suffered catastrophic constitutional loss.

The cruel irony is that these were precisely the groups who most needed a constitutional victory. When you picture the loser of a constitutional contest, you might think of a convention delegate giving an impassioned speech drawing on Thomas Jefferson's writings to argue that a state constitution should permit citizen-sponsored amendments and then watching that proposal go down to defeat. And indeed, that is a loss. Intellectually, that delegate's constitutional vision has not carried the day. If we move from a constitutional convention to a constitutional coup d'état, you might think of Daniel Chamberlain. And indeed, he lost an office and money after being forced from power. In the end though, the people with the wealth and status to gain office and have their constitutional views receive attention from historians generally have a cushion other Americans lack. For as much as he suffered, Thomas Dorr got out of prison, went home to a mansion, and was nominated for office after leading his rebellion. Conservatives who saw the South's 1868 constitutions reject their racial views still wielded economic power and remained prominent in society. To the extent losing slaves caused them financial problems, they had the option of doing an honest day's work themselves. After losing the governorship in 1877, Daniel Chamberlain put his Harvard Law degree to use and earned good money as a Wall Street lawyer and law professor.[11]

The people who suffered catastrophic constitutional loss were those living at the margins of society. The Irish immigrants who supported Dorr remained without a vote when Dorr left prison. Former slaves in southern states during Reconstruction went from having a voice in politics to having no voice in politics. Losing a constitutional provision declaring that everyone has unalienable rights to life, liberty, and property coincided with literal loss of life, liberty, and property to Klansmen and red shirts. Elites have generally thrived no matter how a state constitution changes. Whether nonelites have a chance to thrive has very much depended on whether a constitutional vision guaranteeing them rights and a chance to participate in the political process survives.

Lesson 3: State Constitutional Crisis Is a Threat We Should Take Seriously

Our constitutional story is still being written. And it is in such a precarious place that many Americans worry about whether our constitutional order will hold. They are right to do so. And as much as it pains me to say it, they may not be worried enough. The threat to constitutional stability could occur just as much at the state level as it could at the federal level. You might think it unlikely that a group of citizens would draft a constitution without government sanction and seek to forcefully put it in place, that one political party would cooperate with terrorists to overthrow a duly elected government, or that two political rivals would raise militias that fight in the streets over control of state government. But in the past several years, we have experienced events most of us thought unlikely. In 2014, no presidential candidate in the modern era had refused to concede defeat. Would you have believed someone who told you that in a few short years, a president would lose reelection by over seven million votes, claim to be the victim of massive voter fraud, and tell supporters to "fight like hell" on the same day Congress was certifying electoral votes? Would you have believed someone who told you that the US Supreme Court would then have to decide whether a state could bar a presidential candidate from the ballot because he had engaged in insurrection? If you saw all this coming, your crystal ball works better than mine. The rest of us would do well to consider what else threatens our constitutional order that we would normally be inclined to dismiss.

As the US Supreme Court abandons an expansive reading of the US Constitution—especially on divisive issues like abortion—state constitutions will grow in importance. Litigants who previously would have brought claims under the US Constitution will have to turn to state constitutions. Those who oppose those claims will have to focus on state constitutions too. With increased visibility will come increased pressure. Scholars and judges have pushed us to understand how important state constitutions are for years. In an excellent recent book on the subject, Judge Jeffrey Sutton urges us to consider the possibility that there might be fifty-one viable solutions to constitutional law disputes instead of one. We should pay more attention to how our fifty state constitutions can contribute to debates about liberty instead of assuming that nine Supreme Court justices have all the answers. Lawyers trying to win cases should think about how state constitutions could help them. To demonstrate the point, he tells us that if a basketball player were fouled and had a chance to shoot free throws to win a tied game, it would be madness for him to take only one of his two shots.[12] Yet that is frequently what happens because the legal profession has become so focused on the US Constitution and neglected to even study state constitutions. Let me add two sobering realities that raise the stakes of discussions about state constitutions. First, we have fifty-one chances at constitutional crisis in this country, not just one. Second, a constitutional crisis in any single state could cause a national constitutional crisis. In the 1780s, a popular cartoon portrayed the states which had ratified the US Constitution as pillars holding up the nation. Ominously, the whole structure still risked collapse because two states had yet to ratify.[13] The cartoon offers deep wisdom for our time. Knock out any pillar in our constitutional order and the whole thing could come crashing down. Disagreements about how to handle Bleeding Kansas brought Congress to a standstill. It helped cause the Civil War. South Carolina was at the center of the disputed 1876 presidential election. A similar crisis in the future would be just as likely to affect the outcome of a presidential election—and this in a badly polarized nation.

In assessing the risks of constitutional crisis in the future, we must recognize several constants. We will always have close elections. There will always be politicians who put their interests before the community's. There will always be strong disagreement about what constitutional texts should say and how to interpret what they do say. There will always be people dissatisfied by a constitution who fervently desire change.

As with marriages, some constitutional problems are solvable, and others are not. A married couple with different food preferences can usually find a way to compromise on what to eat for dinner. They might even do so in a way that makes both partners happy or at least satisfied. But they will not easily solve a disagreement where one partner strongly desires children, and the other partner is equally adamant that they do *not* want children. Similarly, one state resident who believes the retirement age for judges should be seventy and another state resident who believes the retirement age should be seventy-five can probably find a compromise and both be satisfied with the final decision. But they will have a difficult time finding a satisfying compromise if they have fundamentally different definitions of "the people," and "liberty."

One solvable problem in constitutional design is resolving election disputes. We can prevent at least some future Buckshot Wars. Fundamentally, these happen when too many state residents believe the election wasn't fairly run or that the official count isn't accurate. A simple web search will reveal several candidates for state office in recent years who refused to concede in a timely fashion and instead made wild charges of corruption or fraud. Those of us worried about a politician taking things a step further and using violence to force their way into office are left with a simple question. How can we make sure that a critical mass of residents on the losing side of an election trust the results? One fix that citizens across the political spectrum can support—I hope—is to invest more in local media outlets that provide balanced and thorough reporting about state and local elections. That would allow state residents with different partisan affiliations to trust the same sources.

Substantively, many Americans have different fears about the electoral process. Some worry about long poll lines and the difficulty of finding time to vote while juggling work and caregiving responsibilities. Others worry about voting fraud. While reputable media outlets have repeatedly found that fraud in American elections is rare, and that it did not change the outcome in the 2020 election, that message has struggled to gain traction. We should continue to provide accurate information about the historically low amount of fraud in our elections and emphasize all the advances in election integrity we have made over the years such as universal adoption of the secret ballot. However, we should also acknowledge that human nature has not magically improved since the nineteenth century. There are still individuals who will resort to dishonest means to win an election if they can get away with it. In a 2018 congressional election, for example, operatives for a congressional campaign gathered incomplete absentee ballots, forged signatures, and even filled in votes on them. North Carolina's board of elections found the scale of misconduct large enough that it ordered a new election. Several defendants pled guilty to crimes for their involvement in the scheme.[14] Such incidents are uncommon, but every time they occur, they sow distrust. In the coming years, I hope that responsible state policymakers can come to a grand bargain on election reform that takes concerns about voting access and election security seriously. These changes would decrease the number of disputes state constitutions have to resolve.

We should then make tweaks to ensure that better state constitutions are in place to handle those disputes that still result. Most states elect a secretary of state who manages statewide elections.[15] Election contests often end up in court. That should prompt us to consider how we select judges and whether they should openly affiliate with a political party the way they do in so many states. Judges and secretaries of state must often raise money for campaigns and please party members to avoid a primary challenge. State residents understandably wonder if those officials make decisions that result in one candidate winning instead of another based on their best understanding of the law or what would best serve their political goals. Even if many judges and election officials in our current system behave with integrity, it would be a mistake to ignore the risk their incentives create in the future. And it would be downright foolish to ignore the risks to the public's perception of fairness that these incentives raise. Seeing that a judge or election official is expressly nonpartisan and had no short-term incentive to favor one candidate over another would encourage a voter to consider trusting an election outcome they dislike. Finally, states should reconsider having the legislature as a whole decide contested elections. As Pennsylvanians in 1838 and South Carolinians in 1876 could attest, this is a recipe for disaster when an election dispute drags on and there is a question about which legislators properly hold office. State constitutional law scholars should work with citizens and policymakers to formulate alternatives, such as a special commission whose members come from both parties and are picked ahead of an election.

Alas, I fear good constitutional design alone cannot resolve every constitutional difficulty. These are questions about our identity as Americans and conflicting answers are liable to produce a constitutional identity crisis. We still have important disagreements about who "the people" are and whether voting is a right or a privilege. To this day, millions of Americans are disenfranchised because they have felony records. Even once they are released, they often must navigate a confusing maze of laws and pay a substantial amount of money to regain the vote. A map illustrating whether states make it easy or difficult for those with felony records to regain the ability to vote looks a lot like the map of states that seceded in 1861 to protect slaveholder liberty. A conservative delegate to North Carolina's 1875 constitutional convention who supported felon disenfranchisement as a way around the Fifteenth Amendment to the US Constitution would be elated to see that the policy still disproportionately keeps Black North Carolinians from voting.[16] If you agreed with Dorr that voting was a "natural right," the case for disenfranchising a person with a felony conviction who has completed their sentence and reformed becomes weak. If, on the other hand, you believe voting is more like a privilege that can be withheld if a person is insufficiently deserving, then the case for disenfranchising those with felony convictions might become stronger. Whatever your perspective, the issue remains contentious. You might be tempted to say that at least we have made extraordinary strides toward racial equality such that we are less divided on who "the people" are than we were in the past. That prompts me to observe that we have alternated between strongly rejecting and vigorously contesting whether racial minorities were part of "the people" for almost two hundred years and agreed that they were for only about fifty. Not until after the Civil Rights Movement in the 1960s did every state consistently embrace minorities as citizens with the same rights as everyone else. In other words, racial equality as we know it is an anomaly in American history. There is no guarantee that it will become the norm.

As our debates over abortion show, we remain intensely divided on what "liberty" means. Both those who want to ban and permit abortion access have passionate views on the subject, often view those who disagree as not only wrong but immoral and dangerous, and believe that it would be fundamentally inconsistent with their perspective on "liberty" to compromise. A state resident who believes that life begins at conception and that abortion is murder is inclined to view a constitution protecting abortion access as illegitimate. A state resident who believes that abortion restrictions are a severe liberty infringement that unjustly burdens women will similarly be inclined to see a constitution prohibiting abortion or allowing abortion bans as illegitimate.

Disagreements over abortion have now influenced attitudes toward popular sovereignty. After residents in several states used a citizen-initiated referendum process to establish a constitutional right to abortion, abortion ban proponents have questioned whether the people should be able to circumvent legislatures to make constitutional change. Others have suggested that we should raise the threshold necessary to ratify a constitutional amendment or change the process for putting citizen-sponsored amendments on the ballot. Still others have mounted court challenges to such initiatives. Meanwhile, those who have secured abortion access and want to do so in other states have a stake in allowing citizen-sponsored initiatives and keeping ballot access rules and ratification requirements where they are instead of seeing them tightened. Both sides to the abortion debate, then, are also raising deep questions about what popular sovereignty means in the twenty-first century even if that is not their intent.[17]

While we disagree on who "the people" are and how much power they have, we also disagree on how to ascertain what the people want. That is the goal of elections and gerrymandering undermines it. No one openly says that partisan gerrymandering is a good thing, but plenty of legislators are happy to benefit from it and plenty of partisans are happy when a gerrymandered legislature delivers on their policy priorities. Since the US Supreme Court has foreclosed federal courts from stepping in, the question becomes what states will do. Should state courts invalidate districts a legislature has drawn? Can legislatures respond by impeaching and removing judges merely for ruling on a gerrymandering dispute in a way those legislatures dislike? What if those judges in good faith believe that a constitution's text does not permit removal under these circumstances and refuse to leave the bench? And if a court's ruling that a legislature was gerrymandered when it proposed constitutional amendments stands, are they null and void even if a majority of voters ratified?[18]

Finally, signs indicate that Americans are increasingly willing to resort to violence to accomplish their constitutional visions. During the COVID-19 pandemic, many Americans sincerely believed that government restrictions designed to combat the virus infringed on their liberty. We would not have been as surprised by January 6, 2021, if we had paid more attention to Oregon in December 2020. At that time, some Oregon residents aggrieved by the state's response to COVID-19 forced their way into the legislature and used chemicals and bear spray on officers. Later that day, protesters armed with guns swarmed the area and tried to break glass doors to get inside.[19] I fear we will see many other such incidents in the near future.

All of this may be discouraging. So let me close with an encouraging thought. We may have fifty-one chances at constitutional crisis. But our state constitutions could also give us fifty pillars to hold up our constitutional order. As we write the next draft of our constitutional story, may we pay special attention to the health of our state constitutions.

ACKNOWLEDGMENTS

I would like to thank Robert Williams, William Nelson, Judge Jeffrey Sutton, Erik Chaput, Nicole Etcheson, Rod Andrew, E. Gregory Wallace, K. L. Zipf, Anjanette Porter, Miriam Seifter, and my wonderful editor Clara Platter for helpful comments on this book at different stages. I would also like to thank Lucy Campbell, Andrea Renegar, Margaret Ireland, Anna Goldsmith, Taylor Norton, Andrew Milton, and Aurora May for excellent research assistance.

Finally, I would like to thank Valerie Zaborski and Annie Boisvert for their help in finalizing the manuscript.

NOTES

INTRODUCTION

1 "Transcript of Trump's Speech at Rally Before U.S. Capitol Riot," *Associated Press*, January 13, 2021, https://apnews.com.

2 David Andone and Jeremey Herd, "How the Assassination Attempt on Trump Unfolded," *CNN*, July 14, 2024, https://www.cnn.com; Brian Bushard, "What is the 25th Amendment? Why It's Under Discussion as Biden's Fate Remains Unclear," *Forbes*, July 9, 2024, https://www.forbes.com.

PART 1 OVERVIEW

1 *Merriam-Webster Dictionary*, s.v., "constitute (*v.*)," accessed March 23, 2024, www.merriam-webster.com; Farah Peterson, "Our Constitutionalism of Force," *Columbia Law Review* 122, no. 6 (2022): 1551n39.

2 William Blackstone, *Commentaries on the Laws of England* (Oxford: Clarendon Press, 1768), 91.

3 Akhil Amar, *The Words That Made US* (New York: Basic Books, 2021), 48, 60–61, 72–73.

4 Gordon Wood, *Power and Liberty: Constitutionalism in the American Revolution* (New York: Oxford University Press, 2021), 34–35.

5 Steven Calabresi and Sofia Vickery, "On Liberty and the Fourteenth Amendment: The Original Understanding of the Lockean Natural Rights Guarantees," *Texas Law Review* 93 (2015): 1319. See generally Pauline Maier, *American Scripture: Making the Declaration of Independence* (Vintage Books: New York, 1997), 97–105.

6 "Declaration of Independence: A Transcription," America's Founding Documents, US National Archives and Records Administration, accessed November 21, 2023, www.archives.gov; Barry Bell, "Reading and 'Misreading' the Declaration of Independence," *Early American Literature* 18, no. 1 (1983): 79.

7 1776 Va. Declaration of Rights sec. 2. It's worth noting disagreement over whether "the people" are all those in society or just the ones who exercise political rights. Compare Roger Hoar, *Constitutional Conventions: Their Nature, Power, and Limitations* (Boston: Little, Brown, and Company, 1917), 17, and John Jameson, *A Treatise on Constitutional Conventions: Their History, Powers and Modes of Proceeding* (Chicago: Callaghan and Company, 1887), 197.

8 Robert Steinfeld, "Property and Suffrage in the Early Republic," *Stanford Law Review* 41 (1989): 339–40; 1776 Va. Declaration of Rights, sec. 6; 1776 N.J. Constitution art. IV; 1777 N.Y. Constitution, sec. 7.

9 1777 Ga. Constitution art. IX.

10 Amar, *Words That Made US*, 161.

11 W. F. Dodd, "The First State Constitutional Conventions, 1776–1783," *American Political Science Review* 2, no. 4 (1908): 547–51; Hoar, *Constitutional Conventions*, 3–9.

12 Jonathan Marshfield, "Forgotten Limits on the Power to Amend State Constitutions," *Northwestern Law Review* 114, no. 1 (2019): 89–103.

13 As an example, consider 1776 Va. Declaration of Rights, sec. 3.

14 Dodd, "First State Constitutional Conventions, 1776–1783," 559.

15 Alexander Hamilton, James Madison, and John Jay, *The Federalist Papers*, ed. Ian Shapiro (New Haven: Yale University Press, 2009), 257–58; Thomas Jefferson to James Madison, September 6, 1789, Library of Congress, Washington, DC, www.loc.gov.

16 1776 De. Constitution art. XXX; 1776 Md. Constitution art. LIX; 1778 S.C. Constitution art. XLIV; 1776 Pa. Constitution Plan or Frame of Government, sec. 47; 1777 Vt. Constitution chap. 2, sec. 44; 1777 Ga. Constitution art. LXIII; 1780 Ma. Constitution art. X.

17 1776 Va. Constitution; 1776 Pa. Constitution Plan of Frame of Government, secs. 19 and 23 (giving judges fixed terms); Gordon Wood, *The Creation of the American Republic* (Chapel Hill: University of North Carolina Press, 1969), 138, 160–61, 434–36.

18 1776 Pa. Constitution Plan or Frame of Government, sec. 32; 1776 De. Constitution art. XXVIII; 1776 N.J. Constitution art. III (requiring annual elections); Wood, *Creation of the American Republic*, 170.

19 David Fischer, *Albion's Seed: Four British Folkways in America* (New York: Oxford University Press, 1989), 196, 461, 669, 874–79.

20 Abraham Lincoln, "Address at Sanitary Fair, Baltimore, Maryland," in *Collected Works of Abraham Lincoln Volume 7*, eds. Roy Basler, Marion Pratt, and Lloyd Dunlap (New Brunswick: Rutgers University Press, [1864] 1953), 301–2.

21 Calabresi and Vickery, "On Liberty and the Fourteenth Amendment," 1315–16; 1776 N.C. Constitution.

22 1777 Vt. Constitution chap. 2, sec. 1.

23 Thomas Jefferson, *Notes on the State of Virginia* (Boston: Lilly and Wait, 1832), 144, 169–70.

24 Michael Klarman, *The Framers' Coup: The Making of the United States Constitution* (New York: Oxford University Press, 2016), 89–92.

25 Klarman, *Framers' Coup*, 89–92; James Madison to George Muter, January 7, 1787, https://founders.archives.gov.

26 1777 N.Y. Constitution sec. 17; 1780 Ma. Constitution chap. 2, sec. 1.

27 U.S. Constitution art. I, sec. 2. For information about women's suffrage in New Jersey, see Judith Klinghoffer and Lois Elkins, "'The Petticoat Electors': Women's Suffrage in New Jersey, 1776-1807," *Journal of the Early Republic* 12, no. 2 (1992).

28 James Madison, *The Debates in the Federal Convention of 1787 Which Framed the Constitution of the United States of America*, eds. Gaillard Hunt and James Scott (New York: Oxford University Press, 1920), 117, 360, 444.

29 U.S. Constitution art. I, secs. 2, 9, art. IV, sec. 2.

30 Amar, *Words that Made US*, 225–26.

31 1790 S.C. Constitution, art 3, sec. 1; 1790 Pa. Constitution art. II, sec. 1; Wood, *Creation of the American Republic*, 615n3.

1. THE BUCKSHOT WAR

1 Neil York, "Freemasons and the American Revolution," *The Historian* 55, no. 2 (1993): 315; Milton Hamilton, "Anti-Masonic Newspapers, 1826–1834," *University of Chicago Press* 32 (1938): 71; John Reed, "Battleground: Pennsylvania Antimasons and the Emergence of the National Nominating Convention, 1835–1839," *Pennsylvania Magazine of History and Biography* 122, no. 1/2 (1998): 84–85.

2 Reed, "Battleground," 84–85.

3 Hans Trefousse, *Thaddeus Stevens: Nineteenth Century Egalitarian* (Chapel Hill: University of North Carolina Press, 1997), 2, 29, 42; "Death of Thaddeus Stevens," *Weekly Patriot*, August 20, 1868.

4 *American Sentinel*, December 25, 1835.

5 "Murder Will Out," *Pennsylvania Reporter*, reprinted in *The Globe*, November 27, 1838.

6 Robert E. Ross, "Federalism and the Electoral College: The Development of the General Ticket Method for Selecting Presidential Electors," *Publius* 46, no. 2 (2016): 152; *American Sentinel*, reprinted in *The Examiner*, May 7, 1836; "The Defeated Conspiracy," *The Pennsylvanian*, July 13, 1836.

7 Sean Patrick Adams, "Hard Times, Loco-Focos, and Buckshot Wars: The Panic of 1837 in Pennsylvania," *Pennsylvania Legacies* 11, no. 1 (2011): 13–15.

8 Roy Akagi, "The Pennsylvania Constitution of 1838," *Pennsylvania Magazine of History and Biography* 48, no. 4 (1924): 308–11; U.S. Constitution art. V.

9 *National Gazette and Literary Register*, May 6, 1837; "The Conventions," *Columbia Democrat*, May 13, 1837.

10 *Proceedings and Debates of the Convention of Pennsylvania, To Propose Amendments to the Constitution* (hereinafter *1838 Pennsylvania Constitutional Convention Debates*), Part II (Harrisburg: Packer, Barrett, and Parke, 1837–38), 527.

11 Eric Smith, "The End of Black Voting Rights in Pennsylvania: African Americans and the Pennsylvania Constitutional Convention of 1837–1838," *Pennsylvania History: A Journal of Mid-Atlantic Studies* 65, no. 3 (1998): 279.

12 Akagi, "Pennsylvania Constitution of 1838," 318–19; "The New Constitution," *Montrose Spectator*, reprinted in *Philadelphia National Enquirer*, April 12, 1838.

13 *1838 Pennsylvania Constitutional Convention Debates*, Part III, 83–91, 692–94, and Part X, 58; Robert Purvis, *Appeal of Forty Thousand Citizens Threatened with Disenfranchisement* (Philadelphia: Merrihew and Gunn, 1838), 16; Akagi, "Pennsylvania Constitution of 1838," 318–19.

14 1838 Pa. Constitution art. X.

15 Compare 1790 Pa. Constitution art. II with 1838 Pa. Constitution art. II.

16 *1838 Pennsylvania Constitutional Convention Debates*, Part IV, 300–10, 335.

17 *1838 Pennsylvania Constitutional Convention Debates*, Part VI, 83–85.

18 1838 Pa. Constitution art. I, sec. 25.

19 *1838 Pennsylvania Constitutional Convention Debates*, Part V, 414.

20 "David R. Porter," *American Sentinel*, reprinted in *Columbia Democrat*, June 16, 1838; "The Late David R. Porter," *Harrisburg Patriot*, August 24, 1867.

21 "The Dodger," *Pennsylvania Telegraph*, May 9, 1838; "The Certifier's vs. Porter's Profanity," *Pennsylvania Telegraph*, August 15, 1838.

22 "Undeniable Proof," *Pennsylvania Telegraph*, August 15, 1838; "John Stone-braker—A Base Perjurer," *Columbia Democrat*, September 1, 1838; "Much Ado About Nothing," *Carlisle Herald and Expositor*, reprinted in the *Pennsylvania Telegraph*, July 4, 1838 (discussing murder allegation); "The Abolition of Hobby-Porter and Amalgamation," *Pennsylvania Telegraph*, June 20, 1838. After the allegation of murder had been made, the *Carlisle Herald and Expositor* in "Much Ado About Nothing" wrote that it "disclaim[ed] ever intending to say or insinuate that David R. Porter presided over the lodge *where* Morgan was murdered."

23 "$500," *Pennsylvania Telegraph*, August 15, 1838.

24 "Estimate of the Result of the Election of 1838—Its Majorities," *Pennsylvania Telegraph*, August 15, 1838; "The Prospects," *Mifflintown Spirit of the Times*, reprinted in the *American Sentinel*, June 12, 1838.

25 "The Amendments and the Old Constitution," *Philadelphia Inquirer*, October 20, 1838.

26 *National Gazette and Literary Register*, October 15, 1838; "Vote for Governor," *Pennsylvania Telegraph*, December 13, 1838.

27 1790 Pa. Constitution art. II, sec. 2; 1838 Pa. Constitution art. II, sec. 2.

28 "The Origin of the Difficulty—Philadelphia County," *Pennsylvania Telegraph*, December 18, 1838; Edward Foley, *Ballot Battles* (New York: Oxford University Press, 2016), 84–86.

29 "Address of the Democratic State Committee," *National Gazette and Literary Register*, October 19, 1838. In fairness, Burrowes did also say that Whigs should "let [the investigation into the election] be commenced with an honest resolution to submit to the result whether it be favorable or unfavorable to our wishes." "Address of the Democratic State Committee," *National Gazette and Literary Register*, October 19, 1838.

30 "Stupendous Scheme," *Gettysburgh Compiler*, reprinted in the *Albany Argus*, November 28, 1838.

31 Akagi, "Pennsylvania Constitution of 1838," 331.

32 "New Constitution Adopted," *Philadelphia National Enquirer*, November 1, 1838.

33 William Egle, "The Buckshot War," *Pennsylvania Magazine of History and Biography* 23, no. 2 (1899): 144.

34 *National Gazette and Literary Register*, December 6, 1838; Egle, "Buckshot War," 152; "About the Buckshot War," *New York Times*, December 17, 1887; *Pennsylvania Telegraph*, April 10, 1839.

35 "The Progress of Outrage and Treason," *Pennsylvania Telegraph*, December 5, 1838; *National Gazette and Literary Register*, December 6, 1838; "Porter's Arrival Explained," *Pennsylvania Telegraph*, December 13, 1838; "About the Buckshot War."

36 "Documents," *National Gazette and Literary Register*, December 25, 1838.

37 U.S. Constitution art. IV, sec. 4, art. I, sec. 8, art. II, sec. 2, art. III, sec. 2.

38 "Documents."

39 *National Gazette and Literary Register*, December 8, 1838.

40 Egle, "Buckshot War," 150–52

41 "About the Buckshot War."

42 "Obituary," *Pittsburgh Commercial*, February 28, 1871; "Death of Ex-Governor Ritner," *Bedford Gazette*, October 28, 1869.

43 Trefousse, *Thaddeus Stevens*, xii, 149 (describing role in drafting the Reconstruction amendments); *Cambria Freeman*, August 20, 1868; Eric Foner, "Thaddeus Stevens and the Imperfect Republic," *Pennsylvania History: A Journal of Mid-Atlantic Studies* 60, no. 2 (1993): 152 (discussing Stevens's epitaph).

2. HOW A TRAITOR TO HIS CLASS BROUGHT RHODE ISLAND TO THE BRINK OF CIVIL WAR

1 Erik Chaput, *The People's Martyr: Thomas Wilson Dorr and His 1842 Rhode Island Rebellion* (Lawrence: University Press of Kansas, 2013), 14–22, 28, 32–34.

2 "The General Assembly," *Rhode-Island Republican*, June 29, 1836; *Newport Mercury*, November 5, 1836.

3 "The General Assembly"; Thomas Dorr (hereinafter "T. D.") to Lydia Dorr (hereinafter "L. D."), November 1, 1844, in *Dorr Letters Project*, http://pc-library-xtf.us.reclaim.cloud; American Anti-Slavery Society, *Fifth Annual Report of the Executive Committee in 1838* (New York: William Dorr, 1838), 17.

4 Royal Charter of Rhode Island (1663); U.S. Congress, House, *Report of the Select Committee to Investigate Interference of the Executive in the Affairs of Rhode Island* (hereinafter *Burke Report*), 28th Cong., 1st sess., 1844, H. Rep. 546, 9–11; Chaput, *People's Martyr*, 2–3.

5 "Rhode-Island Convention," *Newport Mercury*, September 13, 1834; Thomas Dorr, Joseph Angell, David Daniels, William Smith, and Christopher Robinson, *An Address to the People of Rhode Island; From the Convention Assembled at Providence on the 22d day of February* (Providence: Cranston & Hammond, 1834), 8, 13.

6 *Rhode-Island Republican*, July 19, 1837; *Republican Herald*, August 10, 1839.

7 "Things We Have Known," *New Age and Constitutional Advocate*, September 10, 1841.

8 Chaput, *People's Martyr*, 50–53.

9 Chaput, *People's Martyr*, 2, 50–54; People's Constitution, art. I, secs. 2 and 17, art. II, sec. 1, arts. V and VI; Alison Olson, "Eighteenth-Century Colonial Legislatures

and Their Constituents," *Journal of American History* 79, no. 2 (1992): 554; Clement Eaton, "Southern Senators and the Right of Instruction, 1789–1860," *Journal of Southern History* 18, no. 3 (1952): 303; Richard C. Rohrs, "Exercising Their Right: African American Voter Turnout in Antebellum Newport, Rhode Island," *New England Quarterly* 84, no. 3 (2011): 402; "Suffrage Convention," *New Age and Constitutional Advocate*, October 22, 1841. However, the People's Constitution provided that anyone who didn't own at least $150 of taxable property wasn't "entitled to vote on any question of taxation, or the expenditure of public moneys in such town, city, or district." In addition, the People's Constitution prevented "paupers" and criminals convicted of certain offenses from voting. People's Constitution art. II.

10 Eric Smith, "The End of Black Voting Rights in Pennsylvania: African Americans and the Pennsylvania Constitutional Convention of 1837–1838," *Pennsylvania History: A Journal of Mid-Atlantic Studies* 65, no. 3 (1998): 279; Linda K. Kerber, "Abolitionists and Amalgamators: The New York City Race Riots of 1834," *New York History* 48, no. 1 (1967); Roberts v. City of Boston, 59 Mass. 198 (1849).

11 Proposed Landholders' Constitution art. II, sec. 2, arts. I, V, and VI.

12 Robert Steinfeld, "Property and Suffrage in the Early Republic," *Stanford Law Review* 41 (1989): 339–41.

13 Christian Fritz, *American Sovereigns: The People and America's Constitutional Tradition Before the Civil War* (New York: Cambridge University Press, 2007), 248–51; Roger Hoar, *Constitutional Conventions*, (Boston: Little, Brown, and Company, 1917), 20.

14 Thomas Dorr, *The Right of the People of Rhode Island to Form a Constitution: The Nine Lawyers' Opinion* (Providence, 1842), 66–89.

15 Jonathan Elliot, *The Debates in the Several State Conventions of the Adoption of the Federal Constitution, as Recommended by the General Convention at Philadelphia in 1787, Volume II* (Philadelphia: J. B. Lippincott Company, 1836), 432 (italics in original).

16 Paul Thompson, "Is There Anything 'Legal' About Extralegal Action? The Debate Over Dorr's Rebellion," *New England Law Review* 36 (2002): 389–95; People's Constitution art I, sec. 3.

17 As an example, consider 1776 N.C. Constitution Declaration of Rights, sec. 1.

18 Samuel Adams to Noah Webster, April 30, 1784, in *The Writings of Samuel Adams*, ed. Harry Cushing (New York: G. P. Putnam's Sons, 1908), 303.

19 *New Age and Constitutional Citizen*, December 10, 1841; Thomas Jefferson, "Speech of Mr. Jefferson at His Inauguration," speech given in Washington, DC, on March 4, 1801, Library of Congress, Washington, DC, accessed November 22, 2023, www.loc.gov.

20 Francis Wayland, *The Affairs of Rhode Island: A Discourse* (Providence: B. Cranston, 1842), 7; "Proceedings of the General Assembly," *New Age and Constitutional Citizen*, January 28, 1842; Alexander Hamilton, James Madison, and John Jay, *The Federalist Papers*, ed. Ian Shapiro (New Haven: Yale University Press, 2009), 265; James Madison, *The Debates in the Federal Convention of 1787 Which Framed the*

Constitution of the United States of America, eds. Gaillard Hunt and James Scott (New York: Oxford University Press, 1920), 117.

21 *Proceedings and Debates of the Virginia State Convention of 1829–30, to Which Are Subjoined, the New Constitution of Virginia and the Votes of the People* (Richmond: Samuel Shepherd, 1830), 364; Dorr et al., *Address to the People of Rhode Island*, 26 (italics in original).

22 Frederick Douglass, *Narrative of the Life of Frederick Douglass, An American Slave* (Boston: Antislavery Office, 1845), 33–42, 68–73, 107.

23 Merle Curti, "Reformers Consider the Constitution," *American Journal of Sociology* 43, no. 6 (1938): 878.

24 "A Constitutional Republican," *New Age and Constitutional Advocate*, December 10, 1841 (criticism from Douglass); "Thomas W. Dorr," *Liberator*, August 26, 1842 (criticism from Garrison).

25 *Burke Report*, 203–5 (describing support for the People's Constitution); Michael Klarman, *The Framers' Coup: The Making of the United States Constitution* (New York: Oxford University Press, 2016), 11, 119; Chaput, *People's Martyr*, 84 (describing opposition to the Landholders' Constitution).

26 "A Judge in Politics," *New Age and Constitutional Advocate*, January 28, 1842; "Opinion of the Judges of the Supreme Judicial Court Upon the *Legality of the So Called 'People's Constitution*,'" *Providence Journal*, reprinted in the *Newport Mercury*, March 5, 1842. To this day, state courts sometimes issue advisory opinions without waiting for a party to initiate a case, unlike their federal counterparts.

27 "AN ACT in Relation to Offenses Against the Sovereign Power of this State," *Newport Mercury*, April 9, 1842.

28 William Goodell, *The Rights and Wrongs of Rhode Island* (Whitesboro, NY: Oneida Institute, 1842), 36; Chaput, *People's Martyr*, 85; Sullivan Dorr and L. D. to T. D., April 8, 1842, in *Dorr Letters Project*; Jeffrey Beneker, "The Crossing of the Rubicon and the Outbreak of Civil War in Cicero, Lucan, Plutarch, and Suetonius," *Phoenix* 65, no. 1/2 (2011).

29 Samuel Ward King (hereinafter "S. W. K.") to John Tyler (hereinafter "J. T."), April 4, 1842, in *A Compilation of the Messages and Papers of the Presidents Volume 4, Part 2: John Tyler* (hereinafter *Tyler Papers*), ed. James Richardson (N.p.: Project Gutenberg, 2004), 360; U.S. Constitution art. IV, sec. 4.

30 Hamilton, Madison, and Jay, *Federalist Papers*, 225; "Reasons for Voting Against the Landholders' Constitution," *New Age and Constitutional Advocate*, March 8, 1842.

31 Edward Crapol, *John Tyler, The Accidental President* (Chapel Hill: University of North Carolina Press, 2012), 2, 15–18; J. T. to S. W. K., April 11, 1842, in *Tyler Papers*, 367.

32 "Late from Rhode Island—No Bloodshed!" *American Sentinel*, May 5, 1842; T. D. to L. D., May 6, 1842, in *Dorr Letters Project*.

33 T. D. to Aaron White (hereinafter "A. W."), May 12, 1842, in *Dorr Letters Project*; T. D. to Walter Burges (hereinafter "W. B."), May 12, 1842, in *Dorr Letters Project*;

Judith Schafer, "The Immediate Impact of Nat Turner's Insurrection in New Orleans," *Louisiana History: The Journal of the Louisiana Historical Association* 21, no. 4 (1980): 361; Crapol, *John Tyler*, 61.

34 "In Senate," *National Daily Intelligencer*, May 18, 1842.

35 T. D. to A. W., May 12, 1842, in *Dorr Letters Project*.

36 J. T. to S. W. K., May 9, 1842, in *Tyler Papers*, 373 (italics in original); T. D. to A. W., May 12, 1842, in *Dorr Letters Project*; T. D. to W. B., May 12, 1842, in *Dorr Letters Project*.

37 "Rhode Island," *North American Daily Advertiser*, May 16, 1842; *New York Evening Post*, May 28, 1842.

38 *Florida Herald and Southern Democrat*, June 10, 1842; *Peoria Democratic Press*, June 15, 1842; *Augusta Chronicle*, May 9, 1842; *North American Daily Advertiser*, May 16, 1842.

39 *Evening Post*, May 16, 1842; Alex Ming Jr. and Alexander Craston to T. D., May 13, 1842, in *Dorr Letters Project*.

40 *Newport Mercury*, May 21, 1842. Dorr would later claim that opponents wrongly imputed the line about the sword "dyed in blood" to him. T. D. to William Simons (hereinafter "W. S."), August 7, 1842, in *Dorr Letters Project*.

41 Charles Jewett, *The Close of the Late Rebellion in Rhode-Island* (Providence: B. Cranston, 1842), 7, 15.

42 Ian Harrison, "Catiline, Clodius, and Popular Politics at Rome During the 60s and 50s BCE," *Bulletin of the Institute of Classical Studies* 51, no. 1 (2008); David Jordan, "Robespierre," *Journal of Modern History* 49, no. 2 (1977).

43 Jewett, *Close of the Late Rebellion in Rhode-Island*, 8–11.

44 *New York Evening Post*, May 28, 1842; T. D. to unknown newspaper, June 1842, in *Dorr Letters Project*; "State of Affairs," *Herald of the Times*, May 19, 1842.

45 *Report of the Trial of Thomas Wilson Dorr for Treason* (hereinafter *Dorr Treason Trial*) (Providence: B. F. Moore, 1844), 32.

46 J. T. to Elisha Potter, May 20, 1842, in *Tyler Papers*, 376.

47 T. D. to unknown newspaper, June 1842, in *Dorr Letters Project*; William Sprague to John Brown Francis, June 12, 1842, in *Dorr Letters Project*; A. W. to T. D., June 3, 1842, in *Dorr Letters Project*.

48 William Miller to T. D., June 15, 1842, in *Dorr Letters Project*; S. W. K. to J. T., June 23, 1842, in *Tyler Papers*, 389; unknown to Daniel Webster, June 3, 1842, in *Tyler Papers*, 385; J. A. S. Bankhead to J. C. Spencer, June 22, 1842, in *Tyler Papers*, 387; "Notice," *Herald of the Times*, June 30, 1842.

49 "An Act," *Newport Mercury*, June 25, 1842; "State of Affairs," *Providence Journal*, reprinted in *Herald of the Times*, June 30, 1842.

50 T. D. to W. S., August 7, 1842, in *Dorr Letters Project*.

51 "State of Affairs"; "General Orders," *Herald of the Times*, June 30, 1842; "From Chepachet," *Herald of the Times*, June 30, 1842.

52 *Burke Report*, 756 (describing forces available to Dorr); T. D. to W. S., August 7, 1842, in *Dorr Letters Project*; William J. Brown, *The Life of William J. Brown*

(Providence: Angell, 1883), 162–63; *Herald of the Times*, June 30, 1842 (italics in original).

53 T. D. to W. S., August 7, 1842, in *Dorr Letters Project*; Chaput, *People's Martyr*, 162–63.

54 Chaput, *People's Martyr*, 167; 1842 R.I. Constitution art. II, secs. 1–2; "Rhode Island and Connecticut," *Cincinnati Daily Enquirer*, April 13, 1872.

55 *Dorr Treason Trial*, 27.

56 *Dorr Treason Trial*, 38, 112; "More Judges in the Field," *New Age and Constitutional Advocate*, March 4, 1842 (italics in original); Chaput, *People's Martyr*, 183.

57 T. D. to L. D., October 11, 1844, in *Dorr Letters Project*; T. D. to L. D., January 17, 1845, in *Dorr Letters Project*; T. D. to L. D., November 1, 1844, in *Dorr Letters Project*.

58 Chaput, *People's Martyr*, 188–91.

59 *Daily Transcript and Chronicle*, March 21, 1845; "Dorrism Not Dead," *Daily Transcript and Chronicle*, November 17, 1846.

60 Fritz, *American Sovereigns*, 267–71; Luther v. Borden, 48 U.S. 1, 38–47 (1849).

61 *Boston Atlas*, December 28, 1854; "Death of Governor Dorr," *Pittsfield Sun*, January 4, 1855.

62 "The Dorr Rebellion," *Oakland Daily News*, May 20, 1874; "The Dorr Rebellion," *Maine Farmer*, October 17, 1874; "Arkansas," *Jackson Citizen*, April 28, 1874; "Rhode Island Erects Monument to Vindicate Leader of Dorr's Rebellion: Unveiled Today," *San Jose Evening News*, July 18, 1912.

63 Crapol, *John Tyler*, 264–68.

3. BLEEDING KANSAS AND A PARADE OF CONSTITUTIONS

1 "Remarks of the Hon. Stephen A. Douglas, on Kansas, Utah, and the *Dred Scott* Decision," speech at the Gilder Lehrman Institute of American History, Springfield, Illinois, delivered June 12, 1857, accessed November 21, 2023, www.gilderlehrman.org.

2 "Death of David R. Atchison, of Missouri Ex-President of the United States," *Butler Weekly Times*, February 3, 1886; "Letter from Hon. D.B. Atchison," *Edgefield Advertiser*, November 14, 1855; "The Southern Side," *Herald of Freedom*, March 24, 1855 (italics in original).

3 Abraham Lincoln, "Speech on the Kansas-Nebraska Act," in *Lincoln Political Writings and Speeches*, ed. Terence Ball (New York: Cambridge University Press, [1854] 2013), 22–35.

4 Nicole Etcheson, *Bleeding Kansas: Contested Liberty in the Civil War Era* (Lawrence: University of Kansas Press, 2004), 29; Michael Conlin, *The Constitutional Origins of the American Civil War* (New York: Cambridge University Press, 2019), 292 appendix C.

5 Horace Andrews Jr., "Kansas Crusade: Eli Thayer and the New England Emigrant Aid Company," *New England Quarterly* 35, no. 4 (1962): 497–500.

6 *Alta California*, November 30, 1850; "A Kansas Patriot," *Squatter Sovereign*, April 1, 1856; Charles Robinson, *The Kansas Conflict* (Lawrence: Journal Publishing Company, 1892), xiii, xiii–xviii, 64, 135.

7 "Address to the People of the United States," *Squatter Sovereign*, October 16, 1855; "Declaration of Independence: A Transcription," America's Founding Documents, U.S. National Archives and Records Administration, accessed November 21, 2023, www.archives.gov; Etcheson, *Bleeding Kansas*, 43.

8 Etcheson, *Bleeding Kansas*, 50.

9 1776 Pa. Constitution Declaration of Rights, sec. 7; 1857 Iowa Constitution art. II, sec. 1; "Kansas Election!," *Kansas Weekly Herald*, March 30, 1855.

10 "To the Friends of the South," *Squatter Sovereign*, March 27, 1855; U.S. Congress, House, *Committee of Elections Investigation into Kansas Affairs Report* (hereinafter *Kansas Affairs*) 34th Cong., 1st sess., 1856, H.R. Rep. No. 34–200, 849.

11 "Election in the Tecumseh District," *Kansas Herald of Freedom*, March 31, 1855; "Missouri and Kansas," *Kansas Herald of Freedom*, March 31, 1855; Etcheson, *Bleeding Kansas*, 56.

12 "Death of Ex-Governor Reeder," *North American and United States Gazette*, July 6, 1864; "Will Reeder be Removed?" *Kansas Weekly Herald*, July 28, 1855; "Squire Reeder's Veto Message" *Kansas Weekly Herald*, July 28, 1855; "Proclamation!" *Kansas Weekly Herald*, May 4, 1855; "By the Morning Mail," *Daily American Organ*, May 1, 1855 (covering Reeder's remarks about the election).

13 "The Outrage on Gov. Reeder of Kansas," *Journal of Commerce*, reprinted in *Evening Post*, July 7, 1855; *Squatter Sovereign*, June 26, 1855 (covering expulsion proceedings). Later, an investigating congressional committee—with a majority of Republicans—concluded that the Free-Staters had really won. *Kansas Affairs*, 30. Potential bias notwithstanding, there is plenty of evidence to substantiate their conclusions.

14 "Gov. Reeder's Veto Message," *Kansas Herald of Freedom*, July 14, 1855 (discussing moving capital); Robinson, *Kansas Conflict*, 157 (discussing slave code); James Malin, "The Proslavery Background of the Kansas Struggle," *Mississippi Valley Historical Review* 10, no. 3 (1923): 298 (quoting the *Leavenworth Herald*).

15 "Legislative News," *Kansas Weekly Herald*, July 28, 1855.

16 "Kanzas Election," *Boston Semi-Weekly Advertiser*, October 20, 1855. In fact, Chief Justice Samuel LeCompte refused to admit Jim Lane to the Kansas Bar because Lane refused to swear loyalty to the territorial legislature. "Hon. James H. Lane Disbarred," *Indiana American*, October 12, 1855.

17 *Boston Semi-Weekly Advertiser*, October 20, 1855; "Next Tuesday—State Constitution," *Herald of Freedom*, October 6, 1855.

18 "Autobiography of James H. Lane," *Freemen's Champion*, March 25, 1858; *Indiana Sentinel*, August 6, 1846; Edward Bridgman and Luke Parsons, *With John Brown in Kansas: The Battle of Osawatomie* (Madison: J. N. Davidson, 1915), 14–15; "Editorial Summary," *Plymouth Pilot*, June 11, 1851; Robinson, *Kansas Conflict*, 176–77; *Glasgow Weekly Times*, December 27, 1855.

19 Robinson, *Kansas Conflict*, 176–77.

20 Topeka Constitution art. I, sec. 6, art. II, sec. 2, art. X, sec. 1; Robinson, *Kansas Conflict*, 176–77, 217 (describing attitudes towards Black voting and alleging that

Lane attempted to purchase a slave); "Public Meeting at Pawnee," *Kansas Herald of Freedom*, March 24, 1855 (claiming that keeping slavery out of Kansas would benefit white people); "Constitutional Proclamation," *Kansas Herald of Freedom*, January 12, 1856 (describing referendum keeping free Black people out of Kansas).

21 "Kansas Affairs," *The Leader*, October 27, 1855; "Kansas Pro-Slavery Convention," *New York Herald*, November 30, 1855 (covering John Calhoun's remarks).

22 Etcheson, *Bleeding Kansas*, 79–81; *Kansas Affairs*, 1066; "The Kansas War," *Kansas Weekly Herald*, December 15, 1855; "A Full and Accurate Account of the Invasion of Kansas Ter.," *Kansas Herald of Freedom*, December 15, 1855.

23 "The Kansas War"; "A Full and Accurate Account of the Invasion of Kansas Ter."

24 "A Full and Accurate Account of the Invasion of Kansas Ter."; "The Burial of Mr. Barber," *Kansas Herald of Freedom*, December 22, 1855.

25 Oswald Garrison Villard, *John Brown: A Biography 50 Years After* (Boston, MA: The Riverside Press, 1910), 20; James Hamilton, "John Brown," *Quarterly Journal of the New York State Historical Association* 5, no. 2 (1924): 148 (documenting Brown's attitudes towards slavery); "A Full and Accurate Account of the Invasion of Kansas Ter."

26 *Kansas Affairs*, 1070–71; "The Treaty of Peace," *Kansas Herald of Freedom*, January 12, 1856; Robinson, *Kansas Conflict*, 207.

27 Etcheson, *Bleeding Kansas*, 75; "The War Renewed," *Kansas Herald of Freedom*, January 19, 1856.

28 "January 24, 1856, Message Regarding Disturbances in Kansas," in *A Compilation of the Messages and Papers of the Presidents Volume 5, Part 3: Franklin Pierce*, ed. James Richardson (Project Gutenberg, 2004), 212, 261.

29 Etcheson, *Bleeding Kansas*, 97–99.

30 "The Crime Against Kansas," *Speech of Hon. Charles Sumner in the Senate of the United States, 19th and 20th May, 1856* (Boston: John P. Jewett, 1856), 9, 79 (italics in original).

31 "An Authentic Account of the Fracas," *New York Herald*, May 23, 1856.

32 Thomas Gladstone, *The Englishman in Kansas: Or, Squatter Life and Border Warfare* (New York: Miller, 1857), 29, 31; David Atchison's speech to proslavery forces, delivered May 21, 1856, Kansas Historical Society, accessed March 25, 2024, www.kansasmemory.org; *Kansas Affairs*, 1177–79. In her thorough treatment of the era, Etcheson argued that Atchison never actually delivered this speech. Etcheson, *Bleeding Kansas*, 105.

33 Gladstone, *Englishman in Kansas*, 32–37.

34 *Kansas Affairs*, 1177–79; Etcheson, *Bleeding Kansas*, 111.

35 James DeNormandie, "May Meeting, 1908. The Centenary of Lincoln and Darwin; The Early History of Kansas Modernism," *Proceedings of the Massachusetts Historical Society* 41, no. 3 (1908): 493.

36 Robinson, *Kansas Conflict*, 273.

37 Bridgman and Parsons, *With John Brown in Kansas*, 16–18; "Titus's Camp Taken—Another Battle," *New York Daily Tribune*, August 29, 1856.

38 Bridgman and Parsons, *With John Brown in Kansas*, 6, 18, 21; Villard, *John Brown*, 243–49; Louis Lord, "The Historical Value of Tradition," *Classical Journal* 19, no. 5 (1924).

39 Etcheson, *Bleeding Kansas*, 135; "Civil War in Kansas—The Cause, the Danger and the Remedy," *New York Weekly Herald*, August 30, 1856.

40 John Gihon, *Geary and Kansas* (Philadelphia: King & Baird, 1857), 46.

41 At the trial, Robinson's attorney also argued that Robinson could not usurp the position of "Governor of the *State* of Kansas" because, since Kansas was a territory, there was no such office. "Trial of Gov. Robinson," *New York Daily Tribune*, August 27, 1857.

42 "The Topeka Convention," *Freemen's Champion*, July 16, 1857; Etcheson, *Bleeding Kansas*, 149.

43 "Free State Delegate Convention at Topeka," *Kansas Herald of Freedom*, March 14, 1857; Robert Johannsen, "The Lecompton Constitutional Convention: An Analysis of Its Membership," *Kansas Historical Quarterly* 23, no. 3 (1957): 225–43.

44 "Pen and Ink Etchings of The Traitors' Convention," *Kanzas News*, November 21, 1857.

45 Robinson, *Kansas Conflict*, 369–70; Johannsen, "Lecompton Constitutional Convention," 229.

46 Johannsen, "Lecompton Constitutional Convention," 229; "The Election," *Kanzas News*, October 24, 1857; "Much Ado About Nothing," *White Cloud Kansas Chief*, November 5, 1857; "Strange Sights," *Herald of Freedom*, November 7, 1857.

47 Lecompton Constitution Bill of Rights secs. 1, 23, art. VII, secs. 1–2, art. VIII, sec. 1, Schedule, secs. 7 and 14; "The Crowning Act," *Kanzas News*, November 7, 1857; Dred Scott v. Sandford, 60 U.S. 393, 488–90 (1856).

48 "The People Moving," *Kansas Herald of Freedom*, November 21, 1857 (comparing Lecompton Constitution supporters to Catiline); "Bogus Constitution," *Kansas Leader*, November 11, 1857.

49 Hoar, *Constitutional Conventions*, 193.

50 "President's Message," *Kansas Weekly Herald*, December 19, 1857; "First Annual Message to Congress on the State of the Union," in *A Compilation of the Messages and Papers of the Presidents Volume 5, Part 4: James Buchanan*, ed. James Richardson (Project Gutenberg, 2004), 42; "What the South Says Concerning Governor Walker," *White Cloud Kansas Chief*, September 10, 1857 (italics in original).

51 "Another Invasion," *Kanzas News*, December 19, 1857; Robinson, *Kansas Conflict*, 387 (italics in original).

52 Lecompton Constitution Schedule, sec. 8; Etcheson, *Bleeding Kansas*, 157.

53 Etcheson, *Bleeding Kansas*, 161; "Vote on the Lecompton Constitution," *Kansas Herald of Freedom*, January 9, 1858.

54 Etcheson, *Bleeding Kansas*, 166; "Gov. Stanton Veto," *Kansas Herald of Freedom*, January 23, 1858; Robinson, *Kansas Conflict*, 379.

55 *Kansas Tribune*, April 10, 1858.

56 Robinson, *Kansas Conflict*, 381–82.

57 *Kanzas News*, May 1, 1858; Leavenworth Constitution art. I, secs. 1 and 6, art. VII, sec. 6, art. XVIII, sec. 4, Schedule, sec. 12; Clark v. Board of School Directors, 24 Iowa 266 (1868); "The Suffrage Question," *Kanzas News*, May 1, 1858; Thomas Jefferson to James Madison, September 6, 1789; "The Election," *White Cloud Kansas Chief*, May 27, 1858.

58 *Alexandria Gazette*, February 20, 1858.

59 *Herald of Freedom*, March 20, 1858.

60 Etcheson, *Bleeding Kansas*, 179–84.

61 Edwin Sparks, ed., *The Lincoln Douglas Debates of 1858* (Springfield: Illinois State Historical Library, 1908), 305, 337.

62 "The Acquittal of Lane," *Kansas Herald of Freedom*, July 24, 1858; *A Reprint of the Proceedings and Debates of the Convention Which Framed the Constitution of Kansas at Wyandotte, in July 1857* (Topeka: Kansas State Printer, 1920), 9, 122, 300; 1859 Ks. Constitution art. II, sec. 1, art. IX, sec. 2; Richard C. Rohrs, "Exercising Their Right: African American Voter Turnout in Antebellum Newport, Rhode Island," *New England Quarterly* 84, no. 3 (2011): 402; "Fifth Day—Morning Session," *White Cloud Kansas Chief*, July 21, 1859.

63 "Constitutional Convention," *Leavenworth Times*, reprinted in *White Cloud Kansas Chief*, August 4, 1859; "The Election," *Kansas Herald of Freedom*, October 8, 1859.

64 Etcheson, *Bleeding Kansas*, 206–18.

65 "Senator James H. Lane Commits Suicide by Shooting Himself!" *Weekly Free Press*, July 7, 1866; "Gov. Robinson Dead," *Topeka State Journal*, August 17, 1894.

PART 2 OVERVIEW

1 See generally Michael Conlin, *The Constitutional Origins of the American Civil War* (New York: Cambridge University Press, 2019); Arthur Bestor, "The American Civil War as a Constitutional Crisis," *American Historical Review* 69, no. 2 (1964).

2 *Alexander Stephens, in Public and Private: with Letters and Speeches, Before, During, and Since the War*, ed. Henry Cleveland (Philadelphia: National Publishing Company, 1866), 721; Confederate Constitution art. I, sec. 7(2).

3 *Journal of the State Convention and Ordinances and Resolutions of Mississippi* (Jackson: E. Barksdale, 1861), 86–87; *Declaration of the Immediate Causes Which Induce and Justify the Secession of South Carolina from the Federal Union* (hereinafter *South Carolina Secession Ordinance*) (Charleston: Evans & Cogswell, 1860), 9, 4, 10; *A Declaration of the Causes Which Impelled the State of Texas to Secede from the Federal Union* (Austin: Austin Printing Company, 1912), 3–4; Declaration of Independence.

4 Richard C. Rohrs, "Exercising Their Right: African American Voter Turnout in Antebellum Newport, Rhode Island," *New England Quarterly* 84, no. 3 (2011): 402.

5 Drew Faust, "The Dread of Uncertainty: Naming the Dead in the American Civil War," *University of North Carolina Press* 11, no. 2 (2005): 7.

6 Thomas Jefferson, *Notes on the State of Virginia* (Boston: Lilly and Wait, 1832), 144; *Journal of the Reconstruction Convention of Texas* (Austin: Tracy, Siemering, 1870), 195.

7 Hans Trefousse, *Thaddeus Stevens: Nineteenth Century Egalitarian* (Chapel Hill: University of North Carolina Press, 1997), 205–9; John Harrison, "The Lawfulness of the Reconstruction Amendments," *University of Chicago Law Review* 68, no. 2 (2001): 405–7, 433–34; Ryan Williams, "The 'Guarantee Clause,'" *Harvard Law Review* 132, no. 2 (2018): 604. Originally, ratification required a majority of all registered voters and not just a majority of those who participated in the ratification vote. Congress changed that rule in March 1868.

4. THE BROOKS-BAXTER WAR

1 1864 Ark. Constitution art. II, sec. 21, art. IV, sec. 2; Paige Mulhollan, "Arkansas General Assembly of 1866 and Its Effect on Reconstruction," *Arkansas Historical Quarterly* 20, no. 4 (1961): 340–41.

2 Ted Worley and Elisha Baxter, "Elisha Baxter's Autobiography," *Arkansas Historical Quarterly* 14, no. 2 (1955): 172–74 (italics in original); John Hallum, *Biographical and Pictorial History of Arkansas* (Albany, NY: Weed, Parsons, 1887), 413, 416.

3 "Matters at Home," *True Democrat*, May 6, 1863; "Distinguished Arrivals," *True Democrat*, May 13, 1863; "Modern Catechism," *Hot Springs Courier*, reprinted in the *Little Rock Daily Republican*, August 2, 1873.

4 Bobby Lovett, "African Americans, Civil War, and Aftermath in Arkansas," *Arkansas Historical Quarterly* 54, no. 3 (1995): 333; Eugene Feistman, "Radical Disfranchisement in Arkansas," *Arkansas Historical Quarterly* 12, no. 2 (1953): 137–39; Carl Ledbetter, "Constitution of 1868: Conqueror's Constitution or Constitutional Continuity?" *Arkansas Historical Quarterly* 44, no. 1 (1985): 24.

5 *Daily Missouri Democrat*, July 2, 1861; "Hon. Joseph Brooks," *Arkansas Gazette*, May 2, 1877; Jimmy Hefley, "The Brooks-Baxter War," *Arkansas Historical Quarterly* 14, no. 2 (1955): 189; "Constitutional Convention," *Tri-Weekly Missouri Republican*, January 27, 1865; *Arkansas Biography: A Collection of Notable Lives*, ed. Nancy Williams (Fayetteville: University of Arkansas Press, 2000), 42; *Debates and Proceedings of the Convention Which Assembled at Little Rock, January 7, 1868* (hereinafter *1868 Arkansas Constitutional Convention Debates*) (Little Rock: J. G. Price 1868), 89.

6 "Judge M'Clure Called by Death," *Arkansas Gazette*, July 8, 1915; Logan Stafford, "Judicial Coup D'etat: Mandamus, Quo Warranto and the Original Jurisdiction of the Supreme Court of Arkansas," *University of Arkansas at Little Rock Law Review* 20 (1998): 909; "The Arkansas Impeachment Cases," *Cincinnati Daily Enquirer*, February 23, 1871; Orval Driggs Jr., "The Issues of the Powell Clayton Regime, 1868–1871," *Arkansas Historical Quarterly* 8, no. 1 (1949): 5.

7 Joseph St. Hilaire, "The Negro Delegates in the Arkansas Constitutional Convention of 1868: A Group Profile," *Arkansas Historical Quarterly* 33, no. 1 (1974): 39.

8 1836 Ark. Constitution art. I, sec. 1; 1868 Ark. Constitution art. I, secs. 3 and 14, art. VIII, secs. 2–4, art. IX; *1868 Arkansas Constitutional Convention Debates*, 96, 363, 365, 370, 372–73, 379–82, 452, 495, 515, 672, 706.

9   1868 Ark. Constitution art. XIII.

10 "To the People of the State of Arkansas," *Arkansas Gazette*, February 18, 1868.

11 "The Result," *Morning Republican*, April 3, 1868.

12 "Another Variety of Fraud," *Arkansas Gazette*, April 7, 1868; "A Pre-Concerted System of Frauds," *Arkansas Gazette*, April 7, 1868.

13 *1868 Arkansas Constitutional Convention Debates*, 807–9; Feistman, "Radical Disfranchisement in Arkansas," 153–55.

14 Feistman, "Radical Disfranchisement in Arkansas," 137. A subsequent registration raised the number of voters by a few thousand but doesn't contain a racial breakdown.

15 *Morning Republican*, January 16, 1868; "Confirmation," *Chicago Daily Tribune*, February 25, 1865; "General Powell Clayton is Dead," *Arkansas Gazette*, August 26, 1914; "Democratic Territorial Convention," *Herald of Freedom*, August 27, 1859; "The Battle of Pine Bluff," *Wood Country Reporter*, November 26, 1863; Driggs, "Issues of the Powell Clayton Regime," 5.

16 Driggs, "Issues of the Powell Clayton Regime," 9.

17 Chris Brantham, "'The Africans Have Taken Arkansas': Political Activities of African Americans in the Reconstruction Legislature," *Arkansas Historical Quarterly* 73, no. 3 (2014): 237–39.

18 "Governor's Message," *Arkansas Gazette*, November 26, 1868; "Treason Against the State," *Morning Republican*, April 22, 1869.

19 "Our Domestic Troubles," *Morning Republican*, December 24, 1868; "Four Militia Men Shot," *Morning Republican*, January 27, 1869.

20 "Nepotism," *Arkansas Gazette*, July 28, 1868.

21 "Political Apostasy," *Morning Republican*, May 21, 1869.

22 *Arkansas Gazette*, August 1, 1869; 1868 Ark. Constitution art. VI, sec. 10; *Arkansas Gazette*, August 14, 1869; Powell Clayton, *The Aftermath of the Civil War, in Arkansas* (New York: Neale Publishing Company, 1915), 269.

23 Clayton, *Aftermath of the Civil War, in Arkansas*, 312–17.

24 *Arkansas Gazette*, August 10, 1870; "A Short History of the Rev. Joseph Brooks," *Morning Republican*, October 6, 1870.

25 Clayton, *Aftermath of the Civil War, in Arkansas*, 329; "Farewell Bro. Brooks," *Morning Republican*, May 23, 1871; "Fred Douglass on Parson Joe Brooks," *Morning Republican*, March 15, 1872.

26 Clayton, *Aftermath of the Civil War, in Arkansas*, 316.

27 "Always on Extremes," *Morning Republican*, May 18, 1872; "Going to Force the Democracy," *Morning Republican*, June 17, 1872; "Political Parties in Arkansas," *Morning Republican*, March 28, 1872; "Joseph Brooks," *Arkansas Gazette*, September 28, 1871.

28 "Politics in Arkansas," *New York Times*, reprinted in the *Morning Republican*, May 29, 1873.

29 "Politics in Arkansas"; "Judge Elisha Baxter," *Arkansas Statesman*, reprinted in the *Morning Republican*, August 31, 1872; "For Baxter," *Morning Republican*, October 7, 1872.

30 "Judge Baxter Vindicated," *Morning Republican*, October 5, 1872; "A Little Nastiness," *Morning Republican*, September 30, 1872.

31 "It is a Poor Rule That Will Not Work Both Ways," *Morning Republican*, September 26, 1871; "Our Ticket," *Morning Republican*, September 6, 1872.

32 "Fort Smith," *Morning Republican*, September 14, 1872.

33 U.S. Congress, House, Select Committee on Arkansas Affairs (hereinafter "Poland Investigation Part 2"), 43d Cong., 2d sess., 1874, H.R. Rep. No. 43–2, 126, 129, 131, 200–01; U.S. Congress, House, Select Committee on Arkansas Affairs (hereinafter "Poland Report"), 43d Cong., 2d sess., 1874, H.R. Rep. No. 43–127, 2; Stafford, "Judicial Coup D'etat," 928.

34 "Our Victory," *Morning Republican*, November 9, 1872; "Politics in Arkansas"; "The Arkansas Situation," *Arkansas Gazette*, December 17, 1872.

35 Poland Report, 2; Stafford, "Judicial Coup D'etat," 931–32; Poland Investigation Part 2, 213.

36 *Morning Republican*, January 7, 1873.

37 Brantham, "'The Africans Have Taken Arkansas,'" 259 (discussing civil rights measures); Worley and Baxter, "Elisha Baxter's Autobiography," 173; Stafford, "Judicial Coup D'etat," 934 (discussing railroad controversy); "A Little Chain-Lightning," *Morning Republican*, May 21, 1873 (criticizing Baxter's railroad policy).

38 "Par Nobile Fratrum," *Arkansas Gazette*, April 10, 1873; "Little Chain-Lightning"; U.S. Congress, House, Select Committee on Arkansas Affairs, 43d Cong., 3d. sess., 1873, S. Rep. No. 42–512 (1873), 345; U.S. Congress, House, Select Committee on Arkansas Affairs (hereinafter "Poland Investigation Part 1"), 43d. Cong., 1st sess., 1874, H.R. Rep. No. 43–771, 18.

39 Stafford, "Judicial Coup D'etat," 933; "Elisha Baxter," *Arkansas Gazette*, April 29, 1873.

40 "A Little Chain-Lightning"; Poland Investigation Part 2, 427.

41 "The Brooks Contest," *Morning Republican*, April 21, 1873; "Elisha Baxter."

42 "More in Sorrow Than in Anger," *Morning Republican*, May 9, 1873; "What Does it Mean?" *Arkansas Gazette*, May 11, 1873; Poland Investigation Part 2, 271, 339, 408, 410, 426–27; Poland Investigation Part 1, 37; "The Quo Warranto," *Fort Smith New Era*, June 9, 1873; "Affairs in Arkansas," *Morning Republican*, May 29, 1873; Stafford, "Judicial Coup D'etat," 929; 1868 Ark. Constitution art. VI, sec. 19, art. VII, sec. 4; Joshua Douglas, "Procedural Fairness in Election Contests," *Indiana Law Journal* 88 (2013): 9–11; "The Judgment of the People," *Morning Republican*, August 1, 1873; "Notice to the Kuklux," *Morning Republican*, September 8, 1873; "Doxology," *Morning Republican*, September 30, 1873; "State Central Committee," *Morning Republican*, October 8, 1873; "The Quo Warranto," *Arkansas Gazette*, June 4, 1873; "Politics in Arkansas"; Clayton, *Aftermath of the Civil War, in Arkansas*, 347.

43 Poland Investigation Part 2, 223–27, 426, 431; 1868 Ark. Constitution amend. 1; Poland Investigation Part 1, 90–103.

44 Poland Investigation Part 2, 468; Poland Investigation Part 1, 97.

45 "Coup D'etat," *Morning Republican*, April 16, 1874; "A Coup D'etat," *Arkansas Gazette*, June 18, 1893.

46 "The Situation," *Morning Republican*, April 18, 1874.

47 Stafford, "Judicial Coup D'etat," 955; U.S. Constitution art. IV, sec. 4; "The Dorr Rebellion," *New York Herald*, May 10, 1874; "Arkansas," *Jackson Daily Citizen*, April 28, 1874; "And Now Arkansas," *Rutland Daily Globe*, April 17, 1874.

48 Stafford, "Judicial Coup D'etat," 955–57; Poland Report, 5–6.

49 Stafford, "Judicial Coup D'etat," 959; Poland Investigation Part 2, 463–64, 476.

50 Poland Investigation Part 2, 258–60; "The Rebellion," *Arkansas Gazette*, May 6, 1874; "A Desperate Cause," *Morning Republican*, May 7, 1874.

51 Poland Investigation Part 2, 261; "Supreme Court," *Morning Republican*, May 8, 1874; Stafford, "Judicial Coup D'etat," 965.

52 It is worth noting that some of men who supported Baxter, even though he was by now siding with conservative whites, were Black men. "The First Blood," *Morning Republican*, April 22, 1874. However, this doesn't detract from the overall point, made later, that the results of the Brooks-Baxter War later led to Black disenfranchisement.

53 "The First Blood"; "Desperate Cause"; "More Bloodshed," *Memphis Daily Appeal*, May 9, 1874; Stafford, "Judicial Coup D'etat," 972.

54 Stafford, "Judicial Coup D'etat," 967–74; Poland Investigation Part 2, 565.

55 U.S. Congress, *Journal of the Senate*, 43d Cong. 1st. sess., Doc. No. 1, May 12, 1874, 552; U.S. Congress, Senate, Message from the President of the United States (hereinafter "Grant Response to Senate Resolution"), 43d. Cong., 2d. sess., 1875, Ex. Doc. No. 25, 1.

56 1868 Ark. Constitution art. I, sec. 1, art. XIII, sec. 1; Poland Investigation Part 2, 544; *Arkansas Gazette*, July 3, 1874.

57 1874 Ark. Constitution art. VI, art. XVI; Chris Branam, "Another Look at Disfranchisement in Arkansas, 1888–94," *Arkansas Historical Quarterly* 60, no. 3 (2010): 245; Stafford, "Judicial Coup D'etat," 976–77; Poland Report, 12.

58 *Arkansas Gazette*, November 15, 1874; "Personal," *Troy Daily Times*, November 27, 1874; Poland Report, 3; Stafford, "Judicial Coup D'etat," 978–79.

59 Grant Response to Senate Resolution, 1; Stafford, "Judicial Coup D'etat," 981.

60 Willard Gatewood Jr., "Theodore Roosevelt and Arkansas, 1901–1912," *Arkansas Historical Quarterly* 32, no. 1 (1973): 9–10; "General Powell Clayton is Dead."

61 "Judge M'Clure Called by Death."

62 "Hon. Joseph Brooks"; *Russellville Democrat*, May 23, 1878; "An Exciting Time," *Arkansas Gazette*, June 11, 1899; Hallum, *Biographical and Pictorial History of Arkansas*, 413.

63 Branam, "Another Look at Disfranchisement in Arkansas, 1888–94," 245–46; John Graves, "Negro Disfranchisement in Arkansas," *Arkansas Historical Quarterly* 26, no. 3 (1967): 220–23; 1874 Ark. Constitution art. I, secs. 2–3.

5. A WHITE SUPREMACIST REVOLUTION

1 Rod Andrew, *Confederate Warrior to Southern Redeemer* (Chapel Hill: University of North Carolina Press, 2008), 24–25, 39, 49, 69, 79, 243, 267, 306; "The Ideal Carolinian," *Charleston News and Courier*, April 12, 1902.

2 Tim White, "Robert Smalls: From Slave to War Hero, Entrepreneur, and Congressman," *Objective Standard* 15, no. 2 (2020): 33–41.

3 Richard Zuczek, *State of Rebellion: Reconstruction in South Carolina* (Columbia: University of South Carolina Press, 1996), 13–14; 1776 S.C. Constitution; 1778 S.C. Constitution art. XLI; 1790 S.C. Constitution art. IX secs. 1–2, art. I, sec. 4; U.S. Constitution Preamble; *South Carolina Secession Ordinance*, 7–10.

4 *Journal of the Convention of the People of South Carolina, Held in Columbia, S.C., September 1865* (Columbia: J. A. Selby, 1865), 14; *Acts of the General Assembly of the State of South Carolina* (Columbia: J. A. Selby, 1865), 275, 291–304; Phoebe Faucette, *Slave Narratives: A Folk History of Slavery in the United States From Interviews with Former Slaves Vol. 14, South Carolina, Part 1, Abrams-Durant* (Washington, DC: Federal Writers' Project of the Works Progress Administration for the State of South Carolina, 1941), 157–58.

5 Zuczek, *State of Rebellion*, 31; 1865 S.C. Constitution arts. IV and XII.

6 Erik Chaput, "Proslavery and Antislavery Politics in Rhode Island's 1842 Dorr Rebellion," *New England Quarterly* 85, no. 4 (2012): 675.

7 "Convention or No Convention," *Abbeville Press*, November 1, 1867; "Proceedings of the Conservative White Convention," *Keowee Courier*, November 16, 1867; "The Ideal Carolinian."

8 "The Convention—How Shall We Vote?" *Anderson Intelligencer*, October 30, 1867; "The Crisis and Our Duty," *Anderson Intelligencer*, October 2, 1867.

9 *Charleston Daily News*, November 20, 1867.

10 Edward Sweat, "Some Notes on the Role of Negroes in the Establishment of Public Schools in South Carolina," *Phylon* 22, no. 2 (1961): 161; "The Convention," *Charleston Daily News*, January 31, 1868.

11 *Proceedings of the Constitutional Convention of South Carolina, Held at Charleston, S.C., Beginning January 14th and Ending March 17, 1868* (hereinafter *1868 South Carolina Constitutional Convention Debates*) (Charleston: Denny & Perry, 1868), 205, 268, 309, 707, 838; 1868 S.C. Constitution art. VIII, secs. 2 and 8, art. I, secs. 31–33, art. IX, sec. 2, art. X, sec. 5.

12 1868 S.C. Constitution art. V, sec. 3, art. XI, secs. 1 and 5; *1868 South Carolina Constitutional Convention Debates*, 100; 1851 Ind. Constitution art. I, sec. 18; 1784 N.H. Constitution art. I, sec. 18.

13 1868 S.C. Constitution art. X, secs. 4 and 10; Joe Richardson, "Francis L. Cardozo: Black Educator During Reconstruction," *Journal of Legal Education* 48, no. 1 (1979): 73; Roberts v. City of Boston, 59 Mass. 204 (1849); Brown v. Board of Education, 347 U.S. 483, 494 (1954). There was language in South Carolina's 1868 constitution suggesting that segregation was unconstitutional: "All the public schools, colleges, and universities of this State supported in whole or in part by the public funds, shall be free and open to all the children and youths of the State, without regard to race or color." 1868 S.C. Constitution art. X, sec. 10. However, in practice, South Carolina's public schools (except the University of South Carolina) weren't integrated during Reconstruction. William Vaughn, *Schools for All: Blacks*

& *Public Education in the South, 1865–1877* (Lexington: University of Kentucky Press, 1974), 67–70.

14 *The Respectful Remonstrance on Behalf of the White People of South Carolina, Against the Constitution of the Late Convention of That State, Now Submitted to Congress for Ratification* (Columbia: Phoenix Book and Job Power Press, 1868), 7–8, 12.

15 *Evidence Taken by the Committee of Investigation of the Third Congressional District Under Authority of the General Assembly of the State of South Carolina, 1869–70* (hereinafter *Third Congressional District Investigation*) (Columbia: J. W. Denny, 1869–70), 334–36; "The Murder of Randolph," *Charleston Daily News*, February 24, 1869; "The Ku Klux Klan," *Edgefield Advertiser*, reprinted in the *Anderson Intelligencer*, April 1, 1868.

16 *Third Congressional District Investigation*, 339–40, 364.

17 "Murder of Randolph"; Herbert Shapiro, "The Ku Klux Klan During Reconstruction: The South Carolina Episode," *Journal of Negro History* 49, no. 1 (1964): 38.

18 *1868 South Carolina Constitutional Convention Debates*, 100–101, 539; "Murder of B.F. Randolph, Negro Senator from Orangeburg," *Charleston Daily News*, October 19, 1868; "Murder of Randolph"; "Release of Col. Aiken," *Daily Phoenix*, November 13, 1868; *Third Congressional District Investigation*, 389–91, 566.

19 "To the People of South Carolina," *Anderson Intelligencer*, October 28, 1868.

20 U.S. Congress, Senate, Joint Select Committee to Enquire into the Condition of Affairs in the Late Insurrectionary States, Hearings before the *Joint Select Committee to Enquire into the Condition of Affairs in the Late Insurrectionary States* (hereinafter *1871 Congressional Investigation into South Carolina*), 41st Cong., 2d. sess. 1871, Doc. No. 41, 25–28.

21 Zuczek, *State of Rebellion*, 73–75; "Further from Edgefield Court House," *Charleston Daily Courier*, July 28, 1869.

22 Reginald Hildebrand, *The Times Were Strange and Stirring: Methodist Preachers and the Crisis of Emancipation* (Durham, NC: Duke University Press, 1995), 47–48; Zuczek, *State of Rebellion*, 88; "The Difficulty in Laurens," *Daily Phoenix*, October 25, 1870; "The Laurens Murders," *South Carolina Republican*, October 29, 1870 (italics in original); *New York Herald*, October 23, 1870.

23 Zuczek, *State of Rebellion*, 88–91.

24 See Zuczek, *State of Rebellion*, 94–101, 106; Shapiro, "Ku Klux Klan During Reconstruction," 46.

25 Francis Simkins, *South Carolina During Reconstruction* (Chapel Hill: University of North Carolina Press, 1932), 441.

26 Eric Foner, "South Carolina's Forgotten Black Political Revolution," *Slate*, January 31, 2018, https://slate.com; "Death of Judge Wright," *Charleston News and Courier*, February 20, 1885

27 "The New Regime," *Charleston Daily News*, March 17, 1870.

28 "The Election of United States Senator," *Abbeville Press and Banner*, December 18, 1872; "Honest John Patterson," *Charleston Daily News*, March 6, 1873; "The Legislative Proceedings," *Yorkville Enquirer*, December 21, 1871; "The Legislature,"

Beaufort County Republican, December 28, 1871; "A Strong Letter from Representative W.J. Whipper," *Beaufort County Republican*, December 28, 1871.

29 "Strong Letter from Representative W.J. Whipper"; "Is it Republicanism?," *Anderson Intelligencer*, September 22, 1870; "The Situation," *Camden Journal*, October 27, 1870.

30 *1871 Congressional Investigation into South Carolina*, 52.

31 Andrew, *Confederate Warrior to Southern Redeemer*, 221; Simkins, *South Carolina During Reconstruction*, 564–68 (italics in original).

32 Wilton Fowler, "A Carpetbagger's Conversion to White Supremacy" *North Carolina Historical Review* 43, no. 3 (1966): 286–87.

33 U.S. Congress, Senate, Special Committee Investigating Denial of the Elective Franchise in South Carolina, Hearings before *Special Committee Investigating Denial of the Elective Franchise in South Carolina*, 44th Cong. 2d. sess. 1877, Mis. Doc. No. 48, 40, 43–47; "The Hamburg Collision," *Anderson Intelligencer*, July 20, 1876; "The Hamburg Verdict," *New York Herald*, August 2, 1876.

34 "The Ellenton Riot," *Yorkville Enquirer*, October 26, 1876; "Democracy in South Carolina," *New York Times*, reprinted in the *Salem Register*, October 19, 1876; Ulysses Grant, "Law and Order in the State of South Carolina, October 17, 1876," in *Public Papers of the Presidents of the United States: Ulysses Grant, Volume 23-January 1 to October 31, 1876* (Carbondale: Southern Illinois University Press, 2005), 329–30.

35 "Official Report of the United States Marshall on the Cainhoy Riot," *New York Herald*, October 21, 1876; "The Cainhoy Massacre," *Winnsboro News and Herald*, October 26, 1876; "Further Accounts from the Scene of the Attack," *News and Courier*, reprinted in the *Anderson Intelligencer*, October 26, 1876; Simkins, *South Carolina During Reconstruction*, 508–9.

36 "Hampton's Day in Charleston," *Anderson Intelligencer*, November 2, 1876; U.S. Congress, Senate, Special Committee Investigating Denial of the Elective Franchise in South Carolina, Hearings before *Special Committee Investigating Denial of the Elective Franchise in South Carolina* (hereinafter *1876 South Carolina Election Congressional Testimony*), 44th Cong. 2d. sess. 1877, Mis. Doc. 31 Part 1, 310–11; Zuczek, *State of Rebellion*, 100; Andrew, *Confederate Warrior to Southern Redeemer*, 409.

37 "More Radical Infamy," *Anderson Intelligencer*, November 2, 1876; "How We Lost Darlington," *News and Courier*, November 10, 1876.

38 *Journal of the Constitutional Convention of the State of South Carolina* (hereinafter *1895 South Carolina Constitutional Convention Debates*) (Columbia: Charles A. Calvo Jr., 1895), 463; Simkins, *South Carolina During Reconstruction*, 515.

39 "The Banner County," *Port Royal Standard and Commercial*, November 9, 1876; "The Elections," *Pickens Sentinel*, November 9, 1876.

40 Zuczek, *State of Rebellion*, 193; 1868 S.C. Constitution art. II, sec. 14, art. I, secs. 31–33.

41 *1876 South Carolina Election Congressional Testimony*, 53–62, 237.

42 "Latest from Columbia," *Anderson Intelligencer*, November 30, 1876; Simkins, *South Carolina During Reconstruction*, 518–23.

43 "Congressman Mackey Dead," *Anderson Intelligencer*, January 31, 1884; "Latest from Columbia"; "Judge W.H. Wallace Dead," *Lancaster Ledger*, March 23, 1901.

44 1868 S.C. Constitution art. II, sec. 4; "The Combat Deepens," *News and Courier*, December 4, 1876; "The Legislative Lock," *News and Courier*, December 1, 1876; "The Events of Yesterday as Seen Last Night," *News and Courier*, December 5, 1876; "The Conspiracy to Culminate Today—A Desperate Game," *News and Courier*, December 4, 1876.

45 "The Dismal Ceremony," *News and Courier*, December 8, 1876.

46 State ex rel. Wallace v. Hayne, 8 S.C. 367, 371, 381 (1876).

47 Simkins, *South Carolina During Reconstruction*, 534–35; *Winnsboro News and Herald*, December 14, 1876.

48 Zuczek, *State of Rebellion*, 196; "Details of the Inauguration," *News and Courier*, December 15, 1876; "Pressing Our Rights," *News and Courier*, December 19, 1876.

49 Simkins, *South Carolina During Reconstruction*, 535.

50 1868 S.C. Constitution art. III, sec. 4; Ex Parte Norris, 8 S.C. 408, 463–69 (1877); "Death of Judge Wright."

51 Jerry Goldfeder, "Election Law and the Presidency: An Introduction and Overview," *Fordham Law Review* 85 (2016): 978–82; Robert Delahunty and John Yoo, "Who Counts? The Twelfth Amendment, the Vice President, and the Electoral Count Act," *Case Western Law Review* 73 (2022): 135.

52 Zuczek, *State of Rebellion*, 199, 201; "Chamberlain Abdicates," *Anderson Intelligencer*, April 12, 1877.

53 Andrew, *Confederate Warrior to Southern Redeemer*, 423; "Death of Judge Wright"; "Editorial Notes," *Abbeville Messenger*, February 25, 1885; Neil Kinghan, "A Brief Moment in the Sun: Francis Cardozo and Reconstruction in South Carolina," PhD diss., (University College London, 2019), 3, 268–72.

54 George B. Tindall, "The Question of Race in the South Carolina Constitutional Convention of 1895," *Journal of Negro History* 37, no. 3 (1952): 277–79; "The Proceedings in Detail," *Charleston News and Courier*, October 27, 1895; *1895 South Carolina Constitutional Convention Debates*, 464.

55 D. D. Wallace, "The South Carolina Convention of 1895," *Sewanee Review* 4, no. 3 (1896): 355; 1895 S.C. Constitution art. II, secs. 4(a), 4(c), 4(d), 6.

56 "The Work of the Convention," *News and Courier*, October 27, 1895.

57 "Congressman Mackey Dead"; "Tributes to Judge Wallace," *Evening Post*, March 22, 1901.

58 Daniel Henry Chamberlain, "Reconstruction in South Carolina," *The Atlantic*, April 1901; "Daniel H. Chamberlain," *News and Courier*, April 16, 1907.

59 "General Wade Hampton," *News and Courier*, April 15, 1902; "The Burial of Hampton," *People's Journal*, April 24, 1902.

60 White, "Robert Smalls," 42.

61 S.C. Constitution art. II, sec. 6.

6. THE SPIRIT OF 1868 RESURRECTED?

1 Karin Zipf, "'The Whites Shall Rule the Land or Die': Gender, Race, and Class in North Carolina Reconstruction Politics," *Journal of Southern History* 65, no. 3 (1999): 505.

2 1868 N.C. Constitution art. I, sec. 1; "Thoughts for the People," *Wilmington Daily Journal*, March 27, 1868.

3 1868 N.C. Constitution art. I, secs. 13, 22, art. VI, sec. 1, art. VII, art. IX, sec. 6; 1776 N.C. Constitution Declaration of Rights, sec. 9; *Journal of the Constitutional Convention of the State of North-Carolina, at Its Session 1868* (hereinafter *1868 North Carolina Constitutional Convention Journal*) (Raleigh: Joseph Holden, 1868), 487.

4 "Thoughts for the People," March 27, 1868; *1868 North Carolina Constitutional Convention Journal*, 236.

5 "Thoughts for the People," March 27, 1868; "Thoughts for the People," *Wilmington Daily Journal*, March 25, 1868; *1868 North Carolina Constitutional Convention Journal*, 473; Elizabeth Balanoff, "Negro Legislators in the North Carolina General Assembly, July, 1868–February, 1872," *North Carolina Historical Review* 49, no. 1 (1972): 55; "Ratification and Its Advocates," *Wilmington Daily Journal*, March 25, 1868.

6 "Ratification and Its Advocates" (italics in original).

7 "State Political News," *Wilmington Daily Journal*, April 3, 1868; *Tarboro's Southerner*, April 30, 1868; "Table 1: Population of the United States, 1790–1870," US Census Bureau, accessed November 21, 2023, www.census.gov.

8 *Wilmington Daily Journal*, April 22, 1870.

9 Jim Brisson, "'Civil Government Was Crumbling Around Me': The Kirk-Holden War of 1870," *North Carolina Historical Review* 88, no. 2 (2011): 123; "Free Speech Threatened in Warren County," *Weekly North Carolina Standard*, April 22, 1868.

10 Brisson, "'Civil Government Was Crumbling Around Me,'" 129–30, 133–34; "Alamance County," *Wilmington Daily Journal*, March 25, 1870.

11 "Life in North Carolina," *Albany Evening Journal*, February 27, 1873; Brisson, "'Civil Government Was Crumbling Around Me,'" 133.

12 U.S. Congress, Senate, Joint Select Committee to Inquire into the State of Affairs in the Late Insurrectionary States, *Hearings Before the Joint Select Committee to Inquire into the State of Affairs in the Late Insurrectionary States*, 42d Cong., 2d sess., Report no. 41, pt. 2, 1872, 29.

13 1868 N.C. Constitution art. I, sec. 21; "The Reign of Terror in North Carolina!," *Tarboro's Southerner*, August 25, 1870; Brisson, "'Civil Government Was Crumbling Around Me,'" 161.

14 Brisson, "'Civil Government Was Crumbling Around Me,'" 155.

15 1868 N.C. Constitution art. I, sec. 10, art. VI, sec. 1; People of N.C. ex rel. Van Bokkelen v. Canaday, 73 N.C. 198, 221–25 (1875).

16 N.C. Constitution art. VI, sec. 2(3); "Constitutional Convention," *Wilmington Morning Star*, October 8, 1875; 1875 N.C. Constitution art. IV, sec. 10.

17 Helen Edmonds, *The Negro in Fusion Politics in North Carolina 1894–1901* (Chapel Hill: University of North Carolina Press, 1951), 68–69; 1875 N.C. Constitution art. IV, sec. 21.

18 William Mabry, "Negro Suffrage and Fusion in North Carolina," *North Carolina Review* 12, no. 2 (1935): 81.

19 Edmonds, *Negro in Fusion Politics in North Carolina*, 23–37.

20 "Has it Come to This?" *Goldsboro Weekly Argus*, January 17, 1895.

21 "Adjourned in Honor of Douglass," *Henderson Gold Leaf*, February 28, 1895; "George Washington and Robert E. Lee," *Durham Recorder*, February 27, 1895; "Thoughts for the People," March 25, 1868.

22 "Hon. F.M. Simmons," *State Chronicle*, November 16, 1888; "The Black District," *State Chronicle*, October 7, 1886; "Hon. F.M. Simmons Withdraws," *Daily Chronicle*, July 29, 1890.

23 David S. Cecelski and Timothy B. Tyson, eds., *Democracy Betrayed: The Wilmington Race Riot of 1898 and its Legacy* (Chapel Hill: University of North Carolina Press, 1998), 20.

24 "Object Lessons in Government," *Wilmington Semi-Weekly Messenger*, August 23, 1898; "A Plot to Turn North Carolina Into a Negro State Forever," *Wilmington Semi-Weekly Messenger*, October 25, 1898; *Watauga Democrat*, August 18, 1898; "Sizzling Talk," *Wilmington Semi-Weekly Messenger*, October 28, 1898.

25 "Another Negro Outrage," *Elizabeth City Fisherman*, September 16, 1898.

26 "Woman's Place on the Farm," *Savanna Morning News*, August 12, 1897.

27 "Besmirchers of the Characters of Our Best People," *Wilmington Semi-Weekly Messenger*, September 9, 1898.

28 Harriet Jacobs, *Incidents in the Life of a Slave Girl* (Boston, 1861), 79–80; Martha Hodes, *White Women, Black Men* (New Haven: Yale University Press, 1997).

29 Alfred Waddell, *Some Memories of My Life* (Raleigh: Edwards & Broughton, 1908), 51–55, 112.

30 "Sizzling Talk."

31 "Glorious Day in Cumberland," *Wilmington Semi-Weekly Messenger*, October 25, 1898.

32 H. Leon Prather, "The Red Shirt Movement in North Carolina 1898–1900," *Journal of Negro History* 62, no. 2 (1977): 178; "A Proclamation by the Governor," *Progressive Farmer*, November 1, 1898; "Compliment and Insult," *Henderson Gold Leaf*, November 3, 1898.

33 "Two Correspondents," *Wilmington Semi-Weekly Messenger*, November 4, 1898.

34 Prather, "Red Shirt Movement in North Carolina," 179; *Contested Election of Oliver H. Dockery v. John D. Bellamy, from the Sixth Congressional District of the State of North Carolina* (Washington, DC: Government Printing Office, 1899), 28–30, 104; "Whites Under Arms in North Carolina," *New York Evening Journal*, November 8, 1898; David Zucchino, *Wilmington's Lie: The Murderous Coup of 1898 and the Rise of White Supremacy* (New York: Atlantic Monthly Press, 2020), 211–14.

35 Harry Hayden, *The Wilmington Rebellion* (North Carolina: 1936), 8; Mabry, "Negro Suffrage and Fusion in North Carolina," 99.

36 1875 N.C. Constitution art. IV, secs. 2–4.

37 Jeffrey Sutton, *Who Decides?* (New York: Oxford, 2021), 308.

38 1875 N.C. Constitution art. VII, sec. 14; North Carolina General Assembly, *Chapter CXLIII: An Act to Establish a Board of Audit and Finance for the City of Wilmington*, North Carolina Public Sessions Laws, 1876–77, 230–33.

39 LaRae Umfleet, *1898 Wilmington Race Riot Report*, with the 1898 Wilmington Race Riot Commission (N.p.: Research Branch, Office of Archives and History, NC Department of Cultural Resources, 2006), 39–49, https://digital.ncdcr.gov; Hayden, *Wilmington Rebellion*, 3.

40 Umfleet, *1898 Wilmington Race Riot Report*, 44; "Pretty Kettle of Fish," *Wilmington Semi-Weekly Messenger*, March 30, 1897; Harriss v. Wright, 121 N.C. 172 (1897).

41 Zucchino, *Wilmington's Lie*, 136; Hayden, *Wilmington Rebellion*, 8.

42 Zucchino, *Wilmington's Lie*, 136; *Wilmington Semi-Weekly Messenger*, October 14, 1898.

43 Hayden, *Wilmington Rebellion*, 9.

44 "Remarkable Meeting," *Wilmington Semi-Weekly Messenger*, November 11, 1898.

45 Zucchino, *Wilmington's Lie*, 223–25; "Awful Calamity," *Wilmington Semi-Weekly Messenger*, November 11, 1898.

46 "Awful Calamity"; Alfred Waddell, "The Story of the Wilmington, NC Race Riots," *Collier's Weekly*, November 26, 1898.

47 "Awful Calamity"; "Bloody Day at Wilmington," *Daily Picayune*, November 11, 1898; Hayden, *Wilmington Rebellion*, 21; Umfleet, *1898 Wilmington Race Riot Report*, 176.

48 *Contested Election of Oliver H. Dockery v. John D. Bellamy*, 364; 1875 N.C. Constitution art. I, sec. 1, art. IV, sec. 5; Waddell, "The Story of the Wilmington, NC Race Riots."

49 Ceceleski and Tyson, *Democracy Betrayed*, 36; Zucchino, *Wilmington's Lie*, 380; Umfleet, *1898 Wilmington Race Riot Report*, 155; "Why They Left Wilmington," *Savanna Morning News*, November 15, 1898.

50 "Driving Out the Negroes," *New York Tribune*, November 12, 1898.

51 1875 N.C. Constitution art. I, sec. 10, art. VI, sec. 1; "Dead to Rise No More," *Wilmington Semi-Weekly Messenger*, November 22, 1898.

52 "A Lie Out of the Whole Cloth," *Wilmington Semi-Weekly Messenger*, September 30, 1898; "In North Carolina," *Indianapolis Freeman*, November 5, 1898.

53 William Mabry, "'White Supremacy' and the North Carolina Suffrage Amendment," *North Carolina Historical Review* 13, no. 1 (1936): 3; Umfleet, *1898 Wilmington Race Riot Report*, 209.

54 "The Law and the Facts," *The Caucasian*, July 5, 1900.

55 "Some Arguments for the Amendment," *Progressive Farmer*, July 31, 1900.

56 Plessy v. Ferguson, 163 U.S. 537, 564 (1896); "Add a Section to the Amendment," *Watauga Democrat*, February 15, 1900; Mabry, "'White Supremacy,'" 20.

57 Mabry, "'White Supremacy,'" 17; "Slanders of White Men," *Orange County Observer*, March 22, 1900.

58 "A Magnificent Demonstration," *Wilmington Semi-Weekly Messenger*, May 4, 1900.

59 "The Danger to Registrars for Refusing to Register Qualified Voters," *The Caucasian*, July 12, 1900; "Letters from Every Section of the State," *The Caucasian*, August 9, 1900; Zucchino, *Wilmington's Lie*, 382.

60 Stephen Weeks, "The History of Negro Suffrage in the South," *Political Science Quarterly* 9, no. 4 (1894): 675–76; 1875 N.C. Constitution art. I, sec. 1.

61 Harold Wilson, "The Role of Carter Glass in the Disfranchisement of the Virginia Negro," *The Historian* 32, no. 1 (1969): 81; Darlene Hiney, "The Elusive Battle: The Black Struggle Against the Texas Democratic White Primary, 1932–1945," *Southwestern Historical Quarterly* 81, no. 4 (1978): 372–74; Dewey Grantham Jr., "Georgia Politics and the Disfranchisement of the Negro," *Georgia Historical Quarterly* 32, no. 1 (1948): 19–20; James Akenson and Harvey Neufeldt, "Alabama's Illiteracy Campaign for Black Adults, 1915–1930: An Analysis," *Journal of Negro Education* 54, no. 2 (1985): 190.

62 *Atlanta Journal*, June 29, 1906; Timothy Tyson, "The Ghosts of 1898: Wilmington's Race Riot and the Rise of White Supremacy," *Raleigh News and Observer*, November 17, 2006.

63 "Alfred Moore Waddell," *Charlotte Chronicle*, reprinted in the *Winston Salem Journal*, March 22, 1912; "Simmons Rites Are Conducted," *Greensboro Record*, May 1, 1940; N.C. Constitution art. VI, sec. 4.

CONCLUSION

1 *An American Dictionary of the English Language* (Springfield, MA: George and Charles Merriam, 1860), 613, 916, 1000, 1171.

2 "Table 1: Population of the United States, 1790–1870," US Census Bureau, accessed November 21, 2023, www.census.gov.

3 U.S. Constitution art. III, sec. 3.

4 1818 Ct. Constitution art. XI; 1819 Ala. Constitution Mode of Amending and Revising the Constitution; John Dinan, *The American State Constitutional Tradition* (Lawrence: University of Kansas Press, 2006), 30–32, 43–45.

5 *Proceedings of the New Jersey Constitutional Convention of 1844* (N.p.: New Jersey Writers' Project, 1942), 57–58; 1844 N.J. Constitution art. IX; *Official Proceedings of the Proceedings and Debates of the Kentucky Constitutional Convention of 1890 Volume II* (Frankfort: E. Polk Johnson, 1890), 1659.

6 U.S. Constitution art. IV, sec. 4; James Klotter, *William Goebel: The Politics of Wrath* (Lexington: University of Kentucky Press, 1977), 86–112; Taylor v. Beckham, 178 U.S. 548, 578–79 (1900).

7 Baker v. Carr, 369 U.S. 186, 242 (1962) (Douglas, J., concurring); Rucho v. Common Cause, 139 S. Ct. 2484, 2506 (2019).

8 Kelsey Dallas, "Many Americans Say God Inspired the Constitution . . . Except that Part About Guns," *Deseret News*, April 23, 2022, www.deseret.com; Jeffrey Sutton, "Why Teach—and Study—State Constitutional Law," *Oklahoma City University Law Review* 34, no. 2 (2009): 169; Michael Conlin, *The Constitutional*

Origins of the American Civil War (New York: Cambridge University Press, 2019), 33–34.

9   Frederick Douglass, *Oration, Delivered in Corinthian Hall, Rochester*, pamphlet of speech given by Frederick Douglass, July 5th, 1852 (Rochester: Lee, Mann, American Building, 1852), 36 (italics in original); *Journal of the Public and Secret Proceedings of the Convention of the People of Georgia* (Milledgeville: Boughton, Nisbet & Barnes, 1861), 104–5.

10 Ken Gormley, ed., *The Presidents and the Constitution: A Living History* (New York: New York University Press, 2016), 77.

11 Francis Simkins, *South Carolina During Reconstruction* (Chapel Hill: University of North Carolina Press, 1932), 544.

12 Jeffrey Sutton, *51 Imperfect Solutions: States and the Making of American Constitutional Law* (New York: Oxford University Press, 2018), 7–19.

13 "The Federal Pillars," ca. 1788, illustration, in *The Massachusetts Centinel*, Library of Congress, Washington, DC, accessed March 16, 2024, www.loc.gov.

14 "Fact Check: Re-Examining How and Why Voter Fraud is Exceedingly Rare in the U.S. Ahead of the 2022 Midterms," *Reuters*, June 2, 2022, www.reuters.com; "Four People Plead Guilty in North Carolina Ballot Probe of 2016 and 2018 Elections," *NBC News*, September 26, 2022, www.nbcnews.com.

15 "Here Are the Results of All Races for Secretary of State in 2022," *NPR*, November 8, 2022, www.npr.org.

16 "Can People Convicted of a Felony Vote? Felony Voting Laws by State," *Brennan Center*, July 5, 2023, www.brennancenter.org; Rusty Jacobs, "Voting Rights for North Carolinians with Felony Convictions Now up to the State Supreme Court," *WUNC*, February 2, 2023, www.wunc.org.

17 Jordan Boyd, "Abortion Radicals Will Expand Their Schemes from Ohio to Your State. Here's How to be Ready," *The Federalist*, November 7, 2023, https://thefederalist.com; Brendan Pierson, "Florida Top Court Weighs Letting Voters Decide Abortion Rights Amendment," *Reuters*, February 7, 2024, www.reuters.com.

18 Kyle Sammin, "Why Republicans Are Right to Impeach Pennsylvania's Rogue Supreme Court Justices Over Gerrymandering," *The Federalist*, March 22, 2018, https://thefederalist.com; NC NAACP v. Moore, 876 S.E.2d 513 (N.C. 2022).

19 Sara Cline, "Tensions Rise Inside and Outside Oregon's Capitol," *Detroit News*, December 21, 2020, https://apnews.com.

INDEX

abortion, 203, 211, 214, 215

Adams, D. L., 155–56

Adams, John, 7, 17

Adams, Samuel, 44

Aiken, Wyatt D., 147–48

Allen, William, 51

American Civil War: Arkansas politics impacted by, 110, 114; beginning in South Carolina, 137; casualties, 95; as constitutional crisis, 93; liberty defined by North and South before, 96; North Carolina politics impacted by, 185; "the people" defined before, 94, 95; slavery as cause of, 93–95; South Carolina elections after, 143

American Revolution, 42, 46, 51, 54, 75, 142, 162; German mercenaries used by Britain in, 68; leadership during, 66; one-hundred-year anniversary, 153; People's Convention as successor to, 43; state constitutions drafted during, 2, 9, 84; state constitutions not drafted during, 38

Arkansas: Civil War impact on politics in, 110, 114; Clayton as governor of, 109–13; 1872 elections disputed in, 115–17; Ku Klux Klan in, 109; popular sovereignty understanding in, 100; Republican Party in, during Reconstruction, 111

Arkansas Constitution: 1864, 100; 1868, on resolving election disputes, 121; 1868, ratification, 106; 1868 constitutional convention, 101–5; 1874, 132–33; racism and, 103, 106

Articles of Confederation, 15, 47, 209

Atchison, David, 66–67, 78

battles and massacres: Battle of Osawatomie, 79; Ellenton Massacre, 156–57; Hamburg Massacre, 155–56; Pottawatomie Massacre, 78–79; Shays's Rebellion, 14, 15

Baxter, Elisha, 114–15; biographical details of, 101, 135; Brooks-Baxter War participation of, 123–31; Republican Party deteriorating relationship with, 117–23

Bennett, John, 129, 130, 131

Biden, Joseph, 4

Black Codes, 139

Black community: North Carolina politics involvement of, after Reconstruction, 176; race war in North Carolina and, 189, 192

Blackstone, William, 6

Black voters: in North Carolina eliminated from political process, 194–98; in North Carolina suppressed after Reconstruction, 176–78; in South Carolina 1868 elections, 146–47; in South Carolina and racism, 154

Britain, 6–7, 68

Brooks, Joseph, 108, 123–32; biographical details of, 102, 135; 1872 gubernatorial campaign, 113–17; on race, 105; Republican Party deteriorating relationship with, 111–12

Brooks, Preston, 77

Brooks-Baxter War, 123–34

ABOUT THE AUTHOR

Marcus Alexander Gadson is Assistant Professor of Law at Campbell University and one of the leading national authorities on state constitutions. He has written several articles in top law journals about state constitutional law and has won multiple awards for his work teaching the subject.

———